EDUCATION/TECHNOLOGY/POWER

SUNY Series
FRONTIERS IN EDUCATION
Philip G. Altbach, Editor

The Frontiers in Education Series draws upon a range of disciplines and approaches in the analysis of contemporary educational issues and concerns. Books in the series help to reinterpret established fields of scholarship in education by encouraging the latest synthesis and research. A special focus highlights educational policy issues from a multidisciplinary perspective. The series is published in cooperation with the School of Education, Boston College. A complete listing of books in the series can be found at the end of this volume.

EDUCATION/TECHNOLOGY/POWER

Educational Computing as a Social Practice

EDITED BY

Hank Bromley

and

Michael W. Apple

STATE UNIVERSITY OF NEW YORK PRESS

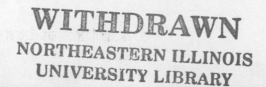

Published by
State University of New York Press, Albany

© 1998 State University of New York

For information, address State University of New York Press,
State University Plaza, Albany, N.Y. 12246

Production by M. R. Mulholland
Marketing by Anne M. Valentine

Library of Congress Cataloging-in-Publication Data

Education, technology, power : educational computing as a social
   practice / edited by Hank Bromley and Michael W. Apple.
       p.   cm. — (SUNY series, frontiers in education)
    Includes bibliographical references and index.
    ISBN 0-7914-3797-3 (hc : alk. paper). — ISBN 0-7914-3798-1 (pbk.
  : alk. paper)
    1. Education—Data processing—Social aspects. 2. Computer
  -assisted instruction—Social aspects. 3. Computer managed
  instruction—Social aspects. 4. Critical pedagogy. I. Bromley,
  Hank. II. Apple, Michael W. III. Series.
  LB1028.43.F372 1998
  371.33′4—dc21   97-35887
                                                                        CIP

10 9 8 7 6 5 4 3 2 1

Contents

Figures

Introduction: Data-Driven Democracy? Social Assessment of Educational Computing[1]

HANK BROMLEY

Interest in educational computing has grown explosively in recent years, with many school districts rushing to invest in new technologies. Hundreds of millions of dollars are being spent on hardware and software in hopes of "equipping" students with skills that are said to be needed in today's world of intense economic competition. At a time when shrinking resources at all levels of government have made it extremely difficult for many school districts to keep up with overdue building maintenance, buy up-to-date textbooks, or even, in some cities, keep schools open for the requisite number of days each year, is this enormous investment in computing technology a good idea?

The question is, of course, one without a simple "yes" or "no" answer. There is little doubt that some instances of educational computing have been extraordinarily valuable, some others have been downright foolhardy, and still others have been simultaneously beneficial for some students and harmful to others. Reaching a useful answer will require a more finely grained question: investment in what kind of educational computing? a good idea for whom? under what conditions? We need to know who is affected, how, and by what specific practices, but that sort of analysis is generally not available. And without it, the tremendous pressure schools are under to "keep up" technologically is likely to push them down unwise paths. In this introductory essay, I would like to suggest what might be entailed in performing such an analysis, which the book as a whole is an initial attempt to provide.

The Computer as a Symbol

One feature that distinguishes the work collected here from most other efforts to evaluate the computing presence in schools is an abiding concern with how the computer functions as a *symbol* of the quality of education children are receiving. As with any symbol, this one has an indeterminate meaning, enabling various social actors to attach distinct meanings to it. Because it can be read in very different—and even contradictory—ways, the computer serves as an umbrella under which disparate groups can cooperate on a seemingly common agenda. Although all may agree on the importance of enhancing the technological resources of schools, and support that goal via similar rhetoric, what unites them is the deployment of a shared symbol more than shared interests or a shared vision of the future.

The power of this symbol depends on an unstated yet powerful set of assumptions about the nature of technology. Among those assumptions are that computing technology benefits all students equally, as a neutral instrument with no connection to the unequal distribution of power along lines of gender, race, class, religion, and ethnicity; that access to such technology is a guarantee of upward social mobility; and that wider facility with high technology will alleviate the problems of the United States economy. It is assumed that anything involving new technologies must be an improvement; that it can, and indeed will, make life much easier for educators who now suffer in undertechnologized situations.

One of the most significant assumptions is the belief that we can deal with the new technologies in a purely instrumental way. The issues are seen simply as only technical questions of how best to apply the technology toward goals around which a consensus is assumed to exist. A supposedly neutral instrument like the computer can then be considered in the narrow terms of, say, cost-benefit analysis. If it meets "our" goals—elevated test scores, improved competitiveness, a more highly skilled workforce, and so on—it is "good," and we need think only of how to use it most efficiently in pursuit of those goals.

Despite their popularity, these assumptions are of dubious validity. Far from being neutral instruments, computers, like other technologies, are involved in many ways in the construction and use of power: in the way they are designed and built, in how they are sold and to whom, and in how they are used. They partake in an epistemology that promotes certain visions of knowledge and notions of who counts as a knowing subject. We need to ask what characteristics of the technology interact with the social context of its use to benefit some people at the expense of others and to reinforce existing power relations; and what possibilities exist for constructing alternative contexts of use favoring more progressive outcomes, for breaking down existing power relations. The relevant issues are demonstrably not technical ones; this is what I mean in advocating the view that technology is a social practice.

If the computer is a symbol, and the kind of education (and society) it represents is the object of strong desires, but with just what it does represent being a disputed matter, then this book is an intervention in the dispute over what to read in the-computer-as-symbol. The way we describe any phenomenon, the stories we tell about it, shape what we do and don't see in it (see the chapter by Mary Bryson and Suzanne de Castell in this volume), and multiple stories can be told about technology. The "technological determinism" story, for instance, presents the emergence of a new technology in a way that highlights its impact on the way we live; the "technology as a social practice" story, on the other hand, highlights the actions of those individuals and institutions responsible for introducing the technology. Which story one tells is a political matter of grave importance.

What follows is the sketch of a story that develops a social assessment of educational computing by challenging the assumptions behind common readings of the computer.

Thinking about Technology

Most writing about computers and schools has a narrow, internalistic orientation. It implicitly assumes that technology is beneficent, sure to bring us a better tomorrow if we simply attend to a little fine-tuning now and then. Thus the myopic focus on the technology itself and on how to do things with it. Some critics of technology make the opposite assumption that technology is inherently evil and is properly dealt with only through complete avoidance. Both positions are ahistorical in the sense that they assume that the impact, or meaning, of a given technological artifact is constant at all times and in all places. They fail to see that the impact can vary with the context, according to the purposes of the humans involved in the particular situation. They attribute too much to the technology itself, treating it as an implacable external force that autonomously drives the rest of society in one direction or another, and not enough to the social context of its use. Such technological determinism ascribes agency to technology rather than to people; it naturalizes technological change, implying inevitability and cloaking the social processes actually accountable for the path taken. The result can be a public sense of resigned acceptance, and a (learned) helplessness in the face of technological change, unless we shift our focus from the technology per se to the surrounding culture.

But overemphasizing the social context can lead to another problem: the technology may come to be seen as a "neutral tool" whose impact depends wholly on the intent of its users. This line of thought is extremely common; references to computers as intellectual tools, flexibly applied to whatever problem one wishes, have proliferated wildly. The "tool" metaphor is appealing but misleading: tools can be flexible but only within certain limits, because their design inevitably favors some applications and prohibits others. The claim that a hammer can be used to build anything overlooks the fact that hammers don't work particularly well with screws. Calling computers "neutral tools" amenable to any application utilizes the same logic as the slogan "guns don't kill people, people kill people." It is true that guns can murder only through the agency of human murderousness, but guns as a technology lend themselves to certain uses. They have a built-in propensity to be used in certain ways toward certain ends. They may depend on human action to consummate those ends, but the predisposition exists in the design of the artifact before it ever gets used.[2]

What I have said thus far may suggest an opposition between a technology's predispositions and its context of use, with one located "in the technology" and the other "in society." But that apparent opposition exists only if we limit our view to the present. Where did the built-in propensities, now located "in the technology," come from? They originated in the social context that was in effect when the technology was designed; they reflect the goals and assumptions of the people who created the technology. There is no inherent opposition between built-in factors and social factors, for what is now built-in is simply a petrified form of past social factors.[3] Recognizing both considerations as rooted in the social is important, for it reminds us that both result from human action, rather than from some immutable fact of nature. Of course, what is past is past, and a given technology's propensities, being the sediment of the past, cannot be changed. Once a piece of technology has been designed, its predispositions are locked in. But if we keep in mind that what is now fixed need not have turned out as it did, that it might have been different, we will prepare ourselves for actively shaping the technologies of the future, instead of passively adjusting to whatever happens to come along.

What, then, would constitute an adequate analysis of the likely impact of a technological artifact (the computer, for instance)? On the one hand, we need to look at the site where that artifact is put to use. We need to consider who is using it and why, what goals those people have, and how they're likely to utilize the technology in pursuit of their goals. Otherwise we risk assuming that the artifact will have the same impact everywhere, under all circumstances. At the same time, we need to examine what the technology carries with it into any context. We must ask what predispositions constrain how it may be used, keeping in mind that however stuck we are now with those predispositions, they were not inevitable but resulted from someone's pursuit of their goals, lest we fall into thinking of the artifact as a neutral tool equally applicable to any purpose.

In other words, we need to remain attentive to the way technologies both *reflect* and *affect* the surrounding social conditions.[4] But one further element needs to be present: both halves of the analysis must be attuned to the operation of power. In classrooms, as elsewhere, some groups and individuals have more power than others and are consequently in a position to parlay the presence of a new technology into even greater advantage than they previously possessed. Understanding the effect of adding a potent artifact like the computer to the classroom hence requires perceiving whatever aspects of the social structure involve power differentials. Controlling the effects of new technologies may well necessitate altering social relationships rooted in unequal power.

The rest of this essay reflects the twin concerns outlined above. The next section considers the context of use, the conflicts now ongoing in educational settings, and how computers are utilized by the parties to those conflicts. The following section focuses on the propensities built into computing technology, the baggage it carries as a result of its cultural heritage and the institutional setting of its development. The last portion provides an overview of the remainder of the book.

The Context of Use: Computers and Existing Agendas

Pressure to ensure that students acquire computer-related skills has arisen from several directions. Business groups, anticipating the demands that may be placed on the next generation of workers, are one source, even though most new jobs actually will be in the low-skill (and low-pay) service sector. Professional educators also have been urging schools to furnish students with knowledge associated with the new technologies; the recent National Council of Teachers of Mathematics proposal for a restructured curriculum in mathematics has urged "technology-rich classrooms" where students will be "freed" from text-based curricula and teachers will be able to present their subjects in greater depth and sophistication.[5] Pressures also issue from middle-class parents with jobs centered on manipulating information (in paper or electronic form), whose own upward mobility appears to have depended on values and skills connected to technical knowledge, and who consequently place the inculcation of such a sensibility at the forefront of what they expect schools to do for their children, particularly at a time when stable employment is increasingly scarce. For such parents, a computer-based curriculum appears to guarantee that these particular students will be ready for the demands of the best universities and the increasingly competitive paid labor market later on.

Each of these groups (and multiple factions within each group) has a distinct agenda, more general than and prior to their engagement with educational computing. The arrival of the technology offers an opportunity to advance these agendas, and, not surprisingly, each actor's stance regarding proper goals and methods for computer use is consistent with their own interests, with the eventual outcome depending largely on the course of contention among them.

Spanning the various agendas as an underlying condition, and suffusing their rivalry, is the rationalization of public life. Among other civic institutions formerly governed by alternative standards, schools are becoming ever more subject to economic reasoning. Under pressure from many quarters to improve their "productivity," to maximize some measurable output (frequently standardized test scores) while containing their costs, educational institutions are increasingly being run as businesses. That practice is, of course, not entirely new. A previous generation of reformers explicitly modeled schools after factories, and outspoken involvement of the business community in various bodies making public recommendations on educational policy is a time-honored, well-established practice. Business leaders were prominent among Progressive Era reformers, for example, and the rhetoric of that movement emphasized the adoption of impersonal, businesslike methods by local government (including schools) as a remedy to the wasteful corruption of fief-like big-city machine politics. But some recent applications of business methods to education are actually quite novel.

The various proposals for some sort of voucher system would directly convert schools to businesses in a literal sense. Meanwhile several cities have hired private firms to operate individual schools or entire districts on their behalf. Of course, such arrangements have not spread unopposed. Consider the rapid rise, and even more rapid fall, of Education Alternatives, Inc., with the recent cancellations of its sole remaining contracts (with Baltimore and Hartford), due in part to community opposition. Clearly many parents and professional educators continue to resist the extension of the profit motive into public education, and at times quite effectively. Such responses, however, face an uphill battle in an environment that is increasingly characterized by an apparent "naturalization" of economic logic. The business presence in oversight of public schools was dramatized when the governor of California nominated a specialist in turning around failing corporations, with no background in education, to be the state Superintendent of Public Instruction: "The 62-year-old Mr. Sigoloff is known in the corporate community for his cost-cutting tactics in making troubled companies profitable. His nomination . . . is the strongest indication yet that public education is turning to the private sector for help in turning around the financial and managerial problems of school systems. . . . Mr. Sigoloff said in his statement that he intended 'to insure that whatever resources are available for education will be spent efficiently and appropriately'" (Celis 1993). There is no mention in the article of the role of the private sector in *creating* the financial problems of school systems they now offer to solve, and ensuring that few resources will be available to be spent (efficiently or otherwise), through insisting on low tax rates and demanding exemptions from local taxes in return for locating their operations in given communities.

Administrators in higher education have embraced the business mindset as thoroughly as have some of their K–12 counterparts. A *Wall Street Journal* article describes cost-cutting measures at Salem College in North Carolina: "Salem's president, Julianne Still Thrift,[6] explains such measures with the business-world language that has become common among college administrators. 'It's the same here as at IBM or AT&T,' she says. 'I've got to have a slimmer staff, I've got to produce more with what I have, and I've got to market aggressively'" (Horwitz 1994). Such pressure to "produce" more efficiently, to yield a higher level of measurable student performance with little or no increase in funding, is one reason for the influx of computers. Just as their use in the business world enables firms to produce more with fewer employees, it is hoped that computerizing the operations of the educational world will enable more learning to happen without hiring more teachers. "Roger C. Schank, director of the Institute for the Learning Sciences at Northwestern University, figures that classroom versions of the interactive training systems he is designing for industry could be a big factor in fixing America's schools. How so? 'We need a way to economically provide individualized instruction,' says Schank. 'Computers provide that economy'" (*Business Week* 1994, p. 82). While Schank's statement stands out for its directness, its substance has long been expressed. As early as 1967, Patrick Suppes was promoting computer-assisted instruction on the same basis. It would free teachers from the bulk of routine whole-class instruction, he wrote, so they could concentrate on working individually with students without the need to hire additional staff, thus offering "perhaps the most practical hope for a program of individualized instruction under the supervision of a single teacher" (Suppes 1980 [1967], p. 234).

Unfortunately for this line of argument, far from saving money, adding computers to the classroom commits the school to *additional* spending in the future (for software, equipment upgrades, maintenance, staff training, etc.) and actually *increases* teacher workload rather than reducing it (see Ragsdale 1988, p. 207, for citations to studies demonstrating the added burden on teachers). With teachers already pushed to the limit as schools "streamline" their operations, adding new responsibilities is practicable only if something else is dropped. Reducing class sizes would be a healthy solution, but that would mean spending more on teacher salaries, just the opposite of the economies computer advocates are promising. Some even suggest computer purchases should be funded by increasing class sizes further to save on salaries.

The argument from economic efficiency just doesn't hold, even in terms of a narrow cost-benefit analysis. Other pedagogical innovations, like peer tutoring programs, produce better results more cheaply (studies cited in Tucker 1985, p. 15) without consuming resources from all sides as computers do. But given that the computers are there, and the teachers are increasingly short on time due in part to the computers' effect on school budgets, the computers do get used. The chapter by Michael Apple and Susan Jungck in this volume shows how the day-to-day realities of teachers' lives lead conscientious professionals to employ an utterly routinized and vapid computer curriculum, simply because it was already prepared (freeing them from having to write one) and it kept the students busy (freeing the teacher to complete other tasks). Perversely, the least intellectually engaging instructional software (such as drill-and-practice programs) can become the most attractive to teachers—for keeping students wholly occupied in a known activity with few surprises to require the teacher's attention, for a predictable amount of time—because of work conditions brought about partly by the very reforms touted as freeing teachers to spend more time working with students individually.

Thus far I have stressed how running schools as though they were businesses provides one impetus for purchasing computers. A different way of applying economic logic to schools is to treat them as a potential market or a customer base, which in fact they are. With several million microcomputers already in U.S. schools alone, educational institutions are a significant source of sales for both hardware and software manufacturers.

A variation on treating schools as a market for new products is the practice of packaging access to their inhabitants as a product to sell to someone else. Channel One, the satellite-delivered news program carrying paid advertisements, is transmitted to more than 10,000 schools. This enterprise (owned by K3 Communications since the collapse of Chris Whittle's financial empire) is notable for converting students themselves into a commodity, as the program's sponsors purchase access to the captive audience. Moreover, a report in *Media Culture Review* (cited in Aufderheide 1994) found that schools in poor districts sign up disproportionately for Channel One. Schools that have the least to spend on texts are the most likely to depend on Whittle's (now K3's) version of public affairs, a situation hardly likely to diminish the gap between the kinds of education available in poor and wealthy districts.

Another way to generate profits via the schools is to enlist them in training students to be consumers of one's products, creating a future customer base.[7] It is no coincidence that regional telephone companies are generously underwriting school purchases of computers at the very same time they are busily seeking regulatory changes or merging with cable television operators in preparation for offering new information services piped into homes. For the new products to be profitable, someone has to buy them. In addition to funding general educational computing, the phone companies are also more directly promoting school use of new telecommunications services. The following announcement, headlined "Classroom of the future," was enclosed with one of my phone bills:

> At Ameritech, we want to see our innovations help prepare today's children for the changing world of tomorrow. We're creating a traveling exhibit, called *SuperSchool®*, to show schools how communications technology can improve the quality and efficiency of education. The SuperSchool classroom demonstrations include distance learning—where students attend classes in distant locations via interactive video and teleconferencing, and home learning—where people can study on their own schedules and busy parents can get more involved in their children's education.

This one paragraph manages to use all the symbolic terms prevalent in futurist rhetoric: 'change,' the 'world of tomorrow,' 'quality,' 'efficiency.' One might wonder, though, if the purpose is to show *schools* how beneficial communications technology is, why is the exhibit being advertised to the general public? Wouldn't it be more "efficient" to demonstrate the benefits directly for school officials? Or does the exhibit have more to do with cultivating broad-based public pressure on schools to "recognize" the evident benefits? Perhaps this is grassroots politics as an instrument of corporate interests.

Another way economic rationality is applied to schools is by stressing their supposed responsibility to prepare students for the workplace. Equating schooling with the production of a labor force is, of course, not new. An earlier generation of reformers rallied to the banner of "manpower" planning (a label whose gender politics are replicated in slightly more subtle form by today's reformers). But the prominence of information technology lends some distinguishing features to the current version of this outlook.

Many claims about how schools "need" to change begin with discussions of how the workplace has changed recently. There is much talk about the "post-Fordist" mode of production, and "flexible manufacturing systems." In the new economy, the story goes, rigid, centralized organizations that do one thing with machinelike efficiency are out. Firms must be adaptable, opportunistic, quick to respond to constantly changing circumstances, "lean and mean," all of which implies considerable dependence on information technologies to track both external conditions and the firm's operations. Labor-management trench warfare is no longer affordable; it must be replaced by a more collaborative teamwork model. And the new firm needs a new worker: rather than being a cog in the machine, s/he must exercise responsibility, recognize what needs to be done and do it, solve problems creatively.

Accordingly a new education is called for: to thrive in a work environment involving continual shifting to new tasks, students will need to become self-motivated learners who are prepared to keep acquiring new skills their whole lives and are adept at "critical thinking" (which has come to mean simply applying their skills to whatever unfamiliar situations may be presented to them, rather than questioning and challenging the premises of those situations). Most of all they'll need proficiency with the high-tech equipment that will typify their work environment. Tales of this sort often refer forebodingly to the supposed advantage other nations enjoy over the U.S. in these matters, with the admonition that we can save our standard of living from plummeting only if we make whatever sacrifices are necessary to retool our schools and companies along these lines.

So what's wrong with this story? (See Robins and Webster 1989, chapters 4 and 6, for a fuller development of the following points.) For one thing, it blames schools for problems they can't solve. It is simply not the case that the failure of the schools to provide enough of this new kind of worker is what's constraining the economy. Jobs are in short supply, especially full-time, permanent ones. Even if every graduate matched the profile of the post-Fordist worker perfectly, there still wouldn't be post-Fordist jobs for them. Although the occupations with the greatest *rate* of growth are in prime, high-tech fields, the actual *number* of such jobs being created is quite modest, as the high-percentage increases are from a small initial base (discussed in Apple 1996, pp. 68–90). The vast majority of new jobs being created are in relatively menial service occupations. The Bureau of Labor Statistics projects that the occupation in which the most new jobs will be created over the next decade is salesclerk, followed by nurse, cashier, general office clerk, truck driver, waiter/waitress, nursing aide, janitor, and food preparation worker (*The New York Times* 1994). Even though nurses are relatively well paid, the median wage across all these occupations is approximately $14,500 *if* one were employed full-time, and new entrants are likely to start well below the median.

Clearly, what the post-Fordist labor market presents is not a ravenous demand for as many self-motivated, multiply skilled, critically thinking young people as can be supplied, but a split demand for a few such fortunates and a much larger population shunted into marginal and temporary work, at best. The "flexibility" in flexible manufacturing includes payroll flexibility, wherein the employer adds and drops workers immediately as they're needed. For increasing numbers of workers, that means temporary employment. (In fact, the temp agency Manpower is now the largest employer in the U.S.) Moreover, even for those working consistently and in highly technologized environments, high-tech schooling is largely irrelevant. Productivity on the job is essentially unrelated to what happens in school, and the skills needed are overwhelmingly acquired in the workplace (see Collins 1979, chapters 1 and 2).

The impending Information Age is nonetheless a convincing *pretext* for initiating major educational change. Despite the irrelevance of curricular content to job performance, the rhetoric of high-tech schooling for a high-tech economy has lent effective support to various reforms, including the installation of computers in schools. One reason the rhetoric has been so effective is that parents are legitimately worried about the job prospects of their children. No matter what the data say, common opinion has it that computer skills will be an increasingly necessary job qualification, and no one wants to be left behind. Groups whose participation in the mainstream economy is already marginal fear being totally closed out if their schools don't keep up. And groups which historically had no trouble securing more lucrative positions are finding it more difficult. What was once virtually automatic upon receiving a college degree, for instance, is now not so easy to obtain. With wider distribution of educational credentials and shrinking opportunities for employment, the same credentials no longer "buy" what they once did.

If such an effort by the historically privileged to redifferentiate themselves is, in fact, a significant element of computer adoption by schools, one would expect parental pressure to be a visible factor in computer purchases. That's exactly what Marc Tucker of the Carnegie Forum reports. In his experience, the push for computers in schools came not from educators but from upper-middle-class parents. The pressure was also backed up with money: in one year during the major build-up, funds raised by suburban parents paid for fully 27 percent of all computers bought for U.S. schools (Tucker 1985, p. 14).

These actions can be seen (borrowing from Collins 1979 again) as a response to credentials inflation. Although curricular changes have little to do with on-the-job performance, new technologies of production do enable the creation of new forms of cultural currency. The older credentials have become badly inflated; everyone has them and they no longer guarantee a cushy sinecure. The formerly privileged react by creating a new credential. Initially, of course, no one has it, so the first few to acquire it are now distinguished from the crowd that has inflated the old credentials, and stand to benefit substantially. Once the computer credential catches on, a mad rush for it is likely to follow, yielding exponential growth in school computers—precisely what ensued throughout the 1980s. But not everyone is in a strong enough position to obtain access to the new credential. The computer-intensive classroom is a very expensive innovation that is out of reach for the many communities that cannot afford it (or lack the clout to force their school officials to find a way to afford it).

Meanwhile, efforts to promote educational computing encounter in schools an institutional history of reluctance to adopt new technologies. Larry Cuban has written of the high hopes that have been frustrated throughout this century, as every twenty years or so a fresh wave of instructional technology has arrived, promising to "revolutionize" education, with ultimately little effect: film, radio, broadcast TV, VCRs, and finally computers (Cuban 1986). What tends to be adopted are those aspects of the new technologies that can be fitted into existing practice; the rest somehow never get assimilated. The rejection of the more transforming possibilities isn't necessarily due to any hostility toward innovation on teachers' part. The exigencies of everyday life in school simply render infeasible those reforms that add to the already barely tolerable burden.

David Cohen emphasizes the need to keep this history in mind when predicting the reception given computers. He believes they will be widely adopted *and used* if, and only if, they "can be used flexibly, like books . . . because they could be accommodated within extant patterns of practice" (Cohen 1987, p. 155).

Given the frequently extra-educational reasons for computer purchases (the aforementioned pressure from parents and from business groups, plus the occasional teachers or administrators who champion computer use to enhance their own standing), many computers enter the schools amid no clear agenda for how they are to accomplish educational objectives. Among the teachers interviewed for an Australian study,

> there was a general belief that computers were an inevitable part of everyday life and hence that it was "good" for students to learn about them. The statements of teachers did not go beyond this level of analysis, so no clear indication was given on exactly what students should know about computers and how the knowledge learnt at school would help the students in that school to understand the "new age" or to secure a job after leaving school. (Firkin et al 1985, p. 11)

Buying computers does address the needs of school officials. Under pressure to do something, *anything*, about the economy, the supposed threat posed by international competitors, students' job prospects, and the impending information age, installing computers enables them to appear to be responding to all these assorted crises. The problem of then rendering the machines educationally useful is something else:

The responsibility of the administration is often limited to ensuring that the equipment is there, a room found, and the timetable running well. The introduction of the computers and the development of a program around them are left to those enthusiasts amongst teachers who have initiated the innovation or who have come forward once it was proposed. (Firkin et al 1985, p. 29)

As Cohen argues, the computers are likely to be used only where they readily fit into existing practice. Given the degree of institutional inertia and the absence of a clear mission for them, it shouldn't be surprising that once purchased, a considerable number of computers sit largely unused. And disturbingly many of those in use are doing little more than automating the least adventurous kinds of instruction.

None of this, though, should be taken to mean the computers have no impact. Although for the reasons discussed they don't appear likely to trigger the transformation in schooling envisioned by their proponents, their presence and usage can still have all sorts of consequences. In one sense, if the school context shapes computer use so as largely to reinforce existing practice, that can be seen as denoting no change at all. But the reinforcement of existing practice is itself a development with very serious consequences, especially for those students already benefiting the least from their schooling. Moreover, the computer is a potent artifact, and as the next section will illustrate, even when from an administrative perspective it appears domesticated into serving pre-existing objectives, it still carries a lot of baggage with it.

The Shaping of a Technology: Computers and their Inheritance

The previous section has argued that the impact of a given technology depends significantly on the context in which it is used, that the attributes built into the technology do not fully determine how it may be used and to whose benefit. Without losing sight of the variation due to context of use, I would like to argue in this section that the environment in which a technology is developed—especially the power relations prevailing there—does nonetheless instill in the technology traits that favor some uses (and beneficiaries) rather than others.[8]

The Myth of the Information Age

The ubiquitous talk of an impending Information Age suggests that benefits will accrue automatically. In an example of what I called "technological determinism" above, most of the Information Age rhetoric invokes an image of vast improvements in civic participation and access to resources, brought about by the mere presence of new technologies. Langdon Winner lists some of the key fallacies underlying these claims in his essay "Mythinformation": (1) people are bereft of information; (2) information is knowledge; (3) knowledge is power; and (4) increasing access to information enhances democracy and equalizes social power (1986, p. 108).

To suggest that participation in public life is currently limited by inadequate amounts of information is misleading. While some specific kinds of potentially helpful information are not well distributed, on the whole people are drenched in information. The problem isn't getting enough, but making sense of what we already have; providing everyone with an on-ramp to the "Information Superhighway" won't help with that problem. Information—raw data and facts—does not amount to knowledge until it is organized somehow, shaped by an intelligence, gathered toward some end. And knowledge does not constitute ideas, let alone wisdom, until it is further digested and pondered. Ideas may in some sense be power, but knowledge is not, much less information. Ideas are what help people make sense of public events. There is plenty of raw data about, so much in fact that it inhibits our ability to perceive and grapple with the operant ideas:

> When we blur the distinction between ideas and information and teach children that information processing is the basis of thought . . . we bury even deeper the substructures of ideas on which information stands, placing them further from critical reflection. For example, we begin to pay more attention to "economic indicators"—which are always convenient, simple-looking numbers—than to the assumptions about work, wealth, and well-being which underlie economic policy. Indeed, our orthodox economic science is awash in a flood of statistical figments that serve mainly to obfuscate basic questions of value, purpose, and justice. What contribution has the computer made to this situation? It has raised the flood level, pouring out misleading and distracting information from every government agency and corporate boardroom. (Roszak 1986, pp. 106–07)

While the computer has intensified the problem, it certainly did not create it. The power of low-level facts to sway public opinion derives from a worldview of which the computer is simply the latest incarnation. "Behind the style stands the mystique of scientific expertise that lends authority to those who marshal facts in a cool, objective manner. The computer is simply a mechanical embodiment of that mystique" (Roszak 1986, p. 164).

Information is no substitute for the ideas that enable understanding of the social world. Nor does it suffice to enable affecting the world; that capacity depends more on organized action than on information. "The formula information = knowledge = power = democracy lacks any real substance. At each point the mistake comes in the conviction that computerization will inevitably move society toward the good life. And no one will have to raise a finger" (Winner 1986, p. 113).

If information glut is useless for democratic action, it is far from useless for other forces.

> The bureaucratic managers, the corporate elite, the military, the security and surveillance agencies are able to make good use of computerized data to obfuscate, mystify, intimidate, and control. . . . These social elements have deeply rooted, long-standing interests to which information can be assimilated and from which programs can be deduced. In military affairs, they work to preserve the nation-state system; in economics, they work in response to the entrepreneurial ethic; in politics, they work to further Utilitarian managerialism. (Roszak 1986, p. 208)

It really should come as no surprise if information technologies turn out to benefit primarily the most powerful actors in society. After all, they are the ones most able to influence the development of the technology.[9]

But if the myth of the Information Age is indeed a myth, then what exactly is the cultural inheritance of computers? The network of influences on computing technology form a complex web which is explored below, clustered around issues of control and domination. Among the elements are: the separation of mind from body and conception from execution; militarism; the treatment of people as machines; the growth of a formalized mode of social organization based on structural position, not individual relationships; and a discourse of fully specifiable "closed worlds."

Technologies of Control

In principle, computing technologies could support independent action and variety as easily as centralization and standardization, but in practice the latter tendencies predominate. Typical is the story Arthur Cordell tells of a local branch manager for a bank. A new computer system gave the regional vice president immediate access to all information about the branch's operations with a few keystrokes: up-to-the-second data on deposits, withdrawals, loan payments, defaults, etc. When asked what his role was now, with all this information being delivered directly to the central office, the branch manager answered "I'll be damned if I know" (cited in Mosco 1988, p. 9).

Why should computerization so often lead to more centralized control? The key may lie in formalized symbolic representation of events in the world. Although formalized systems discard much of the texture of everyday life in their stylized representations of it, that very attribute allows them to be applied identically across many sets of circumstances. Once any process (computerized or not) is constrained to heed symbolic directives, it can be controlled from a distance. Indefinitely many such processes can then be controlled simultaneously, be they physical (say, petroleum refineries whose operations are regulated automatically), psychological (missile launch officers instructed precisely how to respond to encoded commands), or social (government agencies following a standardized planning and budgeting system). This capacity to control operations at diverse, scattered sites with one design strongly favors centralization, with a great deal of power residing with the designers at the center—or whoever directs the designers.

This concentration of power is essentially the same as the one that accompanies a shift from oral to written literacy. The written form of a directive is amenable to being reproduced and transported, enabling exactly the sort of centralized remote control I am describing. This capacity is independent of the mechanical automatization of the computer, though certainly amplified by it. The increasing separation in the workplace of conception from execution is one clear example. The practice has been well understood at least since F. W. Taylor (see Braverman 1974 and Edwards 1979 for influential histories of this topic), but with computerized operations, ever more skill can be embedded in machinery directed by programs written elsewhere, rather than by human operators. And for production which remains labor-intensive, computing technology also makes possible the exportation of the actual labor to sites arbitrarily far from the design work, so that "a predominantly young, nonwhite and female workforce executes production which is conceptualized thousands of miles away" (Burris 1989, p. 449). This theme of an affinity for control will recur in various guises below.

Militarism and the Discourse of Closed Worlds

Computing technology in particular, and engineering in general, have long had a symbiotic relationship with the military. In one direction, many new technologies have come into existence solely because of military sponsorship, and many more have had their ultimate contours shaped by military interest; in turn, the sponsored technologies have made possible the "command-and-control" style of modern military operations (more recently, "command, control, communications, and intelligence" or C^3I). This section will discuss the influences in both directions.

Contemporary engineering education has its roots in military institutions of the eighteenth century and in reform movements prompted by World War I.[10] The development of the computer, in particular, has been driven almost entirely by military applications throughout its history (see Hanson

1982 for a full account), from the gigantic masses of wire and vacuum tubes constituting the first digital computers, brought into being by World War II, through the invention of the solid-state transistor and of the integrated circuit (silicon microchip) down to the present. As of the late 1980s, the top tier of university computer science departments—MIT, Stanford, Carnegie-Mellon, and Berkeley—drew 90 percent of their research funding from the Department of Defense (Thomborson 1987), rendering them essentially a private preserve of DoD, with tremendous sway over the research agenda of the entire field. In return, the military has gained use of a technology which is a perfect embodiment of military philosophy and facilitates its furtherance. If the computer carries an innate bias toward centralized control, as I suggested earlier, a convergence between computing and the military, which relies on rigid centralized control of dispersed components, is only to be expected (see Robins and Webster 1989, chapter 8, for a fuller discussion of this convergence).

Another outgrowth of this symbiosis is the treatment of people as machines. Since World War II, in order to cope with increasingly complex weaponry and accelerated battle conditions, military training has been based on the concept of the "man-machine system,"[11] viewing the human operator and the automated equipment as a single functioning unit. In "man-machine" thought, people are seen simply as components of some larger system, typically computer-based, and all the components (both human and mechanical) are reduced to their information processing functions. The person thus becomes an "information transmitter and processing device interposed between his machine's displays and . . . controls" (cited in Noble 1989, p. 18).

Lewis Mumford similarly credits the military with creating "complex human machines composed of specialized, standardized, replaceable, interdependent parts" (that is, armies). As this mode of organization spread through society, the entire social structure has become a megamachine "composed of living, but rigid, human parts" and devoted to control above all else (cited in Levidow and Robins 1989, p. 160).

What has thus long been true for the control of human bodies is now being extended, via more elaborate technologies, to the human mind as well. And it should be expected that computing technology, sponsored by institutions which depend internally on exactly such modes of control, would tend to function both directly and ideologically so as to propagate these rigid and standardized modes throughout society. One way this baggage is transmitted ideologically is via the practice of artificial intelligence. Since actually replicating human intelligence on a machine is such a formidable task, what happens instead is the redefinition of 'mind' down to a lower level that *can* be imitated by machines. Roszak argues that it is typical with social applications of computer power for "a complex social phenomenon [to be] reduced to something brutally simple that falls within the province of the machine. Politics is revised to become opinion mongering; war is revised to become the calculation of velocities and trajectories" (1986, p. 208). And mind is reduced to information processing.

As a result, when computers are introduced to the classroom, they bring along a hidden curriculum of "deep assumptions about the nature of mentality":

> No other teaching tool has ever brought intellectual luggage of so consequential a kind with it. A conception of mind—even if it is no better than a caricature—easily carries over into a prescription for character and value. . . . The subliminal lesson that is being taught whenever the computer is used (unless a careful effort is made to offset that effect) is the data processing model of the mind. . . . Powerful corporate interests are at work shaping a new social order. The government (especially the military) as a prime customer and user of information technology is allied to the corporations in building that order. Intertwined with both, a significant, well-financed segment of the technical and scientific community—the specialists in artificial intelligence and cognitive science—has lent the computer model of the mind the sanction of a deep metaphysical proposition. All these forces, aided by the persuasive skills of the advertisers, have fixed upon the computer as an educational instrument; the machine brings that formidable constellation of social interests to the classrooms and the campus. (Roszak 1986, pp. 217–18)

The contemporary treatment of humans as components of a megamachine, bred by military needs and facilitated by computing technology, overlaps and converges with another longstanding trend: a shift in the basis of social organization from individual relationships to structural positions. The sociologist Dorothy Smith sees this shift to a more formalized mode of organization as encompassing several parallel changes (Smith 1993). As individuals become separable from the offices they hold, social organization becomes expressed in the relations among the offices rather than among the people who happen to occupy them at any given time. And with this shift from the particularized to the formalized, organizations rather than individuals become the repositories of knowledge and the exercisers of judgment. These observations dovetail with a concern raised earlier that systems based on formalized symbolic representation tend to support concentration of power and centralized control-from-a-distance. Similarly, Smith believes the changes she lists promote a form of social organization based on extra-local rule via "out-of-body experiences," that is, through formalized interactions detached from the circumstances of the persons involved, as well as progressively excluding women while depending entirely on them to support the disavowed bodies of the men participating in this regime through, for instance, cleaning their offices and feeding them at home.

The original Luddites were primarily protesting an early manifestation of these changes (see Webster and Robins 1986, chapter 1). Their ultimate target was not so much the machinery they smashed (quite a bit more selectively than popular mythology suggests) as the ideological shift it expressed, from paternalistic employment to the impersonal, contract-oriented relations of liberal political philosophy. The changes they objected to did not originate in the technology, but they did see technology as "expressive of particular structures of social relations" (p. 5). As I have been arguing, technologies embody the conditions out of which they emerge and tend to reinforce those conditions wherever they are used. With reference to the specific social conditions both Smith and the Luddites decry, "technology has a general drift of denying the particularity of place, of group, or of person" (Goldhaber 1986, p. 47).

As an example of how computer use enforces this formalized, abstracted mode of social interaction, consider this experience I had a few years ago: I received a blank form from the publisher of a directory of households in my city of residence, with a request to fill in information pertaining to our household and return the form. The first line was marked "husband," the second was marked "wife," and the rest were designated for "other occupants over 18 years of age." My household at the time happened to consist of five unrelated adults. We had no husbands and no wives. I called the publisher to complain about their apparent assumption that all households contain a married couple. The person who answered the phone was pleasant but not particularly helpful. She suggested I cross out the labels "husband" and "wife," and fill in our names in any order. I asked how the information would then be entered into their database. She said that was no problem, whoever happened to be on the first line would be labeled head of the household, and we would be listed in the directory under their name. Which is to say I could cross out whatever I liked, but it would have no effect on what got into their database. I told her our household had no head, and we would not be returning the form.

Had their listings not been standardized into a fixed format with everything stuffed into an abstract set of categories, had their final product simply been a large sheaf of cards users could flip through, then I could have scribbled any sort of explanation on our card and it would remain there for users to see. But in formalizing the information in preparation for computerizing it, they conclusively imposed an ordering on it whose exclusions will not necessarily be obvious to users of the directory, who will just see a tidy list of households, organized "naturally" by name of household head.

In a similar experience during a recent job search, I received "affirmative action" forms from most of the universities I applied to work at, requesting that I volunteer information on my sex, race, veteran status, etc., so the university could gauge their success at reaching goals of diversifying their employee pool. One of the by-products of this particular method of pursuing those laudable goals is that applicants' identities are classified into arbitrary, fixed categories. For instance, one such form, under the "Racial/Ethnic Data" section, asked me to choose which of five groups I identify with [American Indian or Alaskan Native; White (not Hispanic); Black (not Hispanic); Asian or Pacific Islander; and Hispanic], noting that "we can record only one racial/ethnic choice; if more than one is chosen, it will be recorded as *unknown*." Now what if I had one Black and one White parent, or one Asian and one Black parent? Or parents who were themselves bi- or multi-racial? Or if I affiliated culturally with more than one group for other reasons? In response to the imperative to count the members of various categories and abstract the entire applicant pool into a single set of numbers, this university (like many others) formalized racial identity in a manner that excluded many possibilities and rendered the exclusions invisible to users of their data, just as with the city directory example. But what's worse, in this case an initiative specifically intended to welcome a broader range of people into an institution effectively tells many of them they don't even exist.

What is the social import of this tendency to formalize and quantify, expressed in and bolstered by the computer but not originating in it?

> Something very big, new, and threatening is permeating our political life. It makes use of the computer as its vehicle, but more important than the means is the mentality that uses the machine. . . . No ambiguities, no subtleties, no complexities. The information that data banks hold is life stripped down to the bare necessities required for a quick commercial or legal decision. *Do or don't give the loan. Do or don't rent the property. Do or don't hire. Do or don't arrest.* This is human existence neatly adapted to the level of binary numbers: off/on, yes/no. What we confront in the burgeoning surveillance machinery of our society is not a value-neutral technological process; it is, rather, the social vision of the Utilitarian philosophers at last fully realized in the computer. (Roszak 1986, pp. 186–87)

The military concern with control, the treatment of people as machines, and the shift to a formalized, structural mode of social organization all fuse in what Paul Edwards calls "closed-world discourse," which views the world mechanistically, as composed of interlocking systems amenable to formal mathematical analysis (Edwards 1989, 1996). This application of systems sciences to social systems, exemplified in U.S. military thought since World War II, tends to assume the closure of the systems analyzed, that is, the systems are treated as composed of a finite number of elements, free of influence from beyond the boundaries of the system. If such conditions in fact hold, it becomes possible to calculate precisely all the possible interactions among the elements and predict the system's behavior. But of course such conditions don't hold in the real world, so the reliability of systems analysis turns on the question of how much of significance is lost when a complex reality is modeled as a closed system.

American geopolitical strategies throughout the Cold War period centered on such an approach. The convergence of the technical tools of systems sciences and the political practices of the time generated a model of the world as politically closed, as amenable to understanding and manipulation via the methods of systems engineering. This approach reached its disastrous zenith with the Vietnam War: through the application of techniques developed at the Rand Corporation to plan for nuclear war, "the Pentagon came to view Vietnam as a token in a political game played between the two superpowers, instead of seeing it for the much more complicated, local, historical situation it actually was" (Edwards 1989, p. 152). Relying on an overly abstracted model "had obscured the realities of the situation" (p. 154).

As systems science came to pervade geopolitical strategizing throughout the 1950s and 1960s, it was simultaneously absorbed into educational philosophy as well. In an analysis quite parallel to Edwards' of military strategists, Robins and Webster argue that learning theorists who treat the mind as an information processor employ a "cybernetic ontology" which is essentially about the control of closed worlds (1989, chapter 9).

Closed-world discourse, wherever it is applied, always has the computer at its core. The computer is central, not only as the perfect tool to execute the intricate models of systems analysis, but also as a "symbol of power and metaphor for scientific precision" (Edwards 1989, p. 140). When computers are introduced to schools, they bring with them the closed-world discourse whose history is inescapably intertwined with their own.

All the components of closed-world discourse—the command-and-control mindset, "man-machine" ideology, formalized modes of social organization, abstraction of human behavior into mathematical constructs—come together in integrated learning systems (ILS), a rapidly growing form of instructional computing. Increasingly resorted to by urban school districts under pressure to show measurable improvements in student performance and swayed by vendors' talk of assured consistency and all-in-one convenience, ILS combines presentation of material, testing, and tracking of student progress into one automated package. But it is a package with a deeply impoverished understanding of education. ILS "labs," equipped to process students by the roomful, are prime examples of the non-neutrality of technology. They do not foster all or even several types of learning but rather one particular, and particularly narrow, conception whose origin is not with teachers who work with children but with the technologists, industrialists, and military designers who develop "man-machine systems." They do not encourage or even permit many types of classroom organization but only one. They instantiate and enforce only one model of organization, of pedagogy, of relationship between people and machines. (Hodas 1993)

Fortunately, although it is the path of least resistance to allow these biases to prevail when using computers in schools, many teachers find ways to ensure that something else happens instead. In this discussion I have highlighted the negative case, the hidden assumptions and effects of the new technologies that are often overlooked. Yet these are by no means the only possible outcomes; it need not be this way. While my coeditor and I are deeply concerned with illuminating the most troubling implications of educational computing, we are equally concerned with documenting more progressive possibilities. A significant portion of this book therefore addresses programs and strategies now in place that evoke a different and more democratic future for computers in classrooms and beyond, challenging the relations of unequal authority over cultural, political, and economic capital that presently organize so many of the institutions of this society.

Although isolated success stories are sure to crop up even under current conditions, like weeds in the cracks of the status quo, by themselves they are unlikely to have much lasting effect. For these growths to flourish into a thriving patchwork of alternative practices, it will be necessary to modify the terrain. And what kinds of practices are likely to lead to fundamental alterations in present conditions? Clearly such educational experiences must be based on critical interrogation of what computers now do, and who benefits; they must equalize not only formal access but actual engagement with the technology in personally meaningful ways; they must support the making of *new* meanings; they must be based on a clear recognition of the present nature of our society and be well articulated to an inclusive vision of a more democratic education—specifically one not subservient to a corporate agenda.

But considerable numbers of administrators and teachers are indeed contesting (both overtly and covertly) the technocratic mindset and its influence in education—its presumptions about what schooling is for, how suitable "productivity" and "efficiency" measures are, and who should determine how education is conducted.[12] One example I find particularly inspiriting is that of students themselves organizing against Channel One (the advertising-laden news broadcasts discussed earlier). A group called Unplug offers those wanting to oppose Channel One training and resources, including a video they produced entitled "Commercial Free Zone." Unplug's literature states:

We believe that democracy requires a free exchange of ideas. We stand against all those who want to commercialize our classrooms to make a profit and for increased funding of education. Most of all, we stand for community controlled, free public education. . . . Channel One and major corporate backing of public schools raises many serious questions that are clearly linked to the underfunding of schools and teachers. What does it mean for government to abdicate its responsibility of properly funding public education and let private entities take over? Does it mean education is no longer public? Does it mean that anyone with ready cash can buy the minds of our young people? Will public education be sold to the highest bidder? (Unplug 1993)

These are questions with the potential to expose and erode the extensive network of power relations, institutional structures, and cultural norms that undergirds technocratic practices in schools as elsewhere. The possibility of educational computing ultimately doing more to bring about equality and social justice than to sustain the oppressive power relations that now exist depends on questions such as these.

Possibilities, however, will remain just that—only potentially effectual— if we ignore the social and epistemological determinations that already serve to structure the institutions from which the new technology emerges and into which it is placed.

Organization and Contents of the Volume

The overall structure of this book moves from conceptual discussions of how we think and speak about educational computing, through studies of specific classroom practices, to analysis of efforts to realize the democratic possibilities of the technology. The contributors all share a concern with how technological practices align with or subvert existing forms of dominance, but otherwise represent a broad range of perspectives. The collection deliberately encompasses a multiplicity of views, with contributors adopting disparate stances on such questions as the degree to which computing technology is inherently tainted by its institutional origins, the most promising locales and strategies for interrupting the status quo, and the utility of postmodern forms of social analysis.

In some ways, though, the scope is not as broad as might be hoped. Assembling this book has taken far longer than anticipated, primarily because it proved surprisingly difficult to locate contributors for certain topics (plus some authors who had planned to participate needed to withdraw). As editors, we would particularly have liked to offer a more consistently international perspective, more work specifically concerned with questions of race, and more analysis of the political economy of the computer industry. The difficulties we encountered seem themselves to convey a great deal about the construction of expertise in relation to technology, which simultaneously enforces the isolation of technological questions from social and political ones and positions nearly everyone as unentitled to speak on boundary-crossing topics such as those listed above.

In other areas, however, we were quite fortunate, as we hope the reader will agree. What follows is a brief summary of the book's contents.

Part I addresses the ways we think and speak about computing: who is positioned as authorized to speak, what kinds of language are available for them to use, what social interests does that language reflect, how does it regulate what possibilities we can envisage, and what alternative forms of language might we develop?

Zoë Sofia's chapter analyzes the discourse of computing culture, showing how particular definitions of rationality privilege masculine modes of interaction with the technology. Her discussion provides a valuable counterpart to my own introduction, in that it identifies many of the same themes in prevalent understandings of computers (technological determinism, the military origins of the technology, the persistence of "command-and-control" presumptions, the conflation of information with power) but approaches those themes from a psychoanalytic and semiotic perspective, unearthing the "irrational" and "erotic" dimensions of computing culture.

In his chapter, Anthony Scott uses an expansive notion of aesthetics, incorporating all aspects of the embodied experience of interacting with the technology, as a vehicle for exploring the social and cultural facets of computer-based education. He too, through yet another route, finds the military heritage of the technology and the accompanying command-and-control mindset a continuing influence on contemporary practice.

Mary Bryson and Suzanne de Castell focus on the discourse of educational *researchers*, comparing three different narrative strategies—modernist, critical, and postmodern—to be found in the tales researchers tell about educational computing. Each kind of tale (some more than others) functions so as to regulate the meaning we make of computing practices, thereby sustaining continued inequitable relations to educational technologies.

Matthew Weinstein's chapter analyzes advertising for PCs and software and traces how the representations (both textual and visual) of women and of men in these advertisements support the construction of particular gendered identities. As Weinstein notes, actual gender practices are complex performances in no way confined to stereotyped media images, yet those representations do nonetheless provide the background in relation to which actual practices unfold.

Part II concentrates on specific classroom settings, addressing issues similar to those discussed in Part I, but doing so via exploration of how those issues arise in given locations.

In their chapter, Brad Huber and Janet Schofield extend U.S.-based research on gender-linked differences in how students experience educational computing to an international setting. They examine the ways boys and girls think about and use computers at a primary school in Costa Rica, viewed in relation to a social context that involves pervasive gender stereotyping.

Michael Apple and Susan Jungck also highlight the role of the surrounding social conditions in shaping the ways computers end up being employed in a given setting. The everyday realities of working life in schools favor some uses of computers while inhibiting others, and the teachers included in this study felt impelled by their circumstances to utilize a routinized and stifling computer-based curriculum unit, in spite of their own professional judgment.

Part III, the final section of the book, turns to analysis of attempts to realize the constructive potential of the technology. Although we have tried to document a variety of factors that can favor the reinforcement of inequitable social relations when computers are in use, there is nothing inevitable about that outcome. Indeed, the best reason to outline such factors is precisely to help ensure that they may be foreseen and counteracted. The chapters in this section report on efforts to do just that.

Peter Kahn and Batya Friedman begin with a philosophical treatment of the concepts of control and power, and from that perspective offer a survey of ways to use computers in classrooms to foster greater ethical awareness, emphasizing the importance of attributing agency to people rather than machines.

Brigid Starkey's chapter discusses a well-developed and widely used curriculum that appears to have been highly beneficial. "Project ICONS" depends quite heavily on the long-distance, inexpensive, and rapid communication made possible by email, but—very significantly—the value of the curriculum does not derive from the technology itself. The computers serve as a *vehicle* for a curricular philosophy and an involved set of classroom (and building-wide) practices that promote international understanding and a collaborative, cross-disciplinary, self-organized form of learning.

Antonia Stone is the founder of Playing to Win, a nonprofit organization which has been operating neighborhood technology learning centers in low-income urban areas since 1983. In her chapter, she reviews the features of their program which have rendered it accessible and useful, and she identifies the changes in the larger political scene that would be needed for Playing to Win's successes to be replicated on a larger scale.

I

Discursive Practices:
Who Speaks of Computing, and How?

CHAPTER 1

The Mythic Machine:
Gendered Irrationalities
and Computer Culture

ZOË SOFIA

The computer is an educational technology that did not arise within the class-room, but was imported into it as a result of vigorous corporate and government efforts to commercialize and eventually domesticate a tool initially developed within military-industrial complexes. Well before it became a household or classroom item, the computer was a cultural artifact familiar from actual and fictional accounts of aerospace and military operations, and its consequent associations with images of extraterrestrialism and futurity, as well as appeals to consumer fears about being "left behind" by the impending digitalized future, were strong features of promotional campaigns for educational and personal computer technologies during the 1980s.[1] It is therefore a mistake to discuss computer pedagogy as though computers and their users were innocent of the myths and meanings circulating in a broader cultural context whose dominant current is described by cultural theorist Arthur Kroker as "the growth of cyberauthoritarianism, a stridently pro-technology movement, particularly in the mass media, typified by an obsession to the point of hysteria with emergent technologies and with a consistent and very deliberate attempt to shut down, silence, and exclude any perspectives critical of technotopia."[2]

Within a general climate of technological utopianism, "technophilia," an excessive and uncritical love of equipment, is not only taken for granted as normal but equated with technoscientific rationality, while a lack of enthusiasm for new computer technologies is readily diagnosed as its pathological opposite: "technophobia." A widely reported finding from classroom studies is that boys comprise the vast majority of those computer users who, in Sherry Turkle's words, "love the machine for itself,"[3] and who like to spend long hours tinkering and game-playing on computers, whereas girls are far more likely to reject emotional identification with the computer as a "second self"

29

and instead think of it in dispassionate and instrumental terms as "just a tool" for use in specific task-oriented contexts.[4] Despite the fact that girls exhibit the more mature kind of relationship to equipment in terms of intersubjective psychology (in so far as Winnicott has shown that the "use of an object" is a more advanced stage than simple identification with it),[5] so strong are the cultural biases towards technophilia, technotopianism, and identification with equipment as a second self, that even professional social psychologists may interpret girls' cooler and more rational approach to computer tool use as a sign of phobia, supposedly symptomatic of feminine discomfort with the cold and unemotional rationality expressed in machines. Turkle, for example, has diagnosed women's "computer reticence" and resistance to emotional engagement with the "intimate machine" as a "romantic reaction" aimed at preserving feminine self-definitions in terms of capacities for love and emotion that computers lack.[6] Turkle would like women to be more like men: to overcome their ambivalence about being intimate with computers and to treat virtual computational objects as real, tactile, and personal. In Turkle's later collaborative paper with Seymour Papert on "epistemological pluralism," the argument seems less masculinist and acknowledges that the style of "soft mastery" preferred by many girls and more artistically inclined boys (who build programs from the "bottom up" by bricolage of intimately known parts) can produce just as effective results as that of "hard mastery," the approach favored by many boys and teachers (who emphasize formal reasoning and a "top down" style of building programs by black-boxing subcomponents and knocking them into shape later).[7]

Gender differences in attitudes towards computers and styles of computer learning could be interpreted differently from a perspective that was critical of technotopianism, alert to masculinist bias, and more sensitive to the relations between individual and cultural imaginaries. As Sue Curry Jansen has argued, overly disciplined research paradigms (such as sociological or psychological education research) can produce knowledge of the *observable* or *reportable* differences in the field of gender and information technology, but lack access to semiotic and philosophical vocabularies and the deeper currents of *interpretive* and *critical* thinking needed to "grasp or treat" the subtle factors shaping meaning and action in ways not necessarily recognizable to more scientistic disciplines.[8] Interpretive approaches do not predict behaviors of individuals or groups but generate narratives aimed at clarifying tendencies, and perhaps encouraging interventions, within a discursive field. Thus from a framework of feminist critical cultural studies, which also avails itself of psychoanalytic insights, this chapter explores personal fantasies and cultural mythologies associated with some of the observed and reported gender differences in computer culture.[9]

My starting point here is the suspicion that it is not so much the excessive *rationality* or abstraction of computer logic that turns girls off computers—particularly not now they are networked and their interfaces so "friendly"—but that the masculine *irrationalities* surrounding, embedded in, and signified by this technology may cause girls and women to feel alienated from computer culture. The quality of their engagement with computers could be enhanced if computer educators directly addressed, rather than ignored as irrelevant to the classroom, the irrational excess of meaning—the hopes, the fears, the desires—associated with what J. David Bolter has called the "defining technology" of our epoch.[10] For psychologically and culturally, ambivalence towards computers is not a pathology to be overcome but a healthy response that can lead users to a more balanced perspective on both the powers and limitations of the computer, not to mention providing incentives to design computing tools that work better for a greater variety of people employing a diversity of expressive styles. Ambivalence can also inspire more creative uses of information media, as inventive and artistically inclined people push against the grain of the values encoded in currently available equipment.

(Ir)Rationality: The Dreams Of Reason

The rationality of "hard mastery" harbors its own irrationality in that "dream of Reason"[11] which seeks pleasure from possessive command and control of a programmable microworld, an ideal and idealized space where a disembodied consciousness might escape anxieties about lack of control over contingent and messy actualities of physical and social lives, and enjoy the sense of domination that comes from achieving total mastery of a partial, virtual system. The synecdochic substitution of the controllable part for the messy whole is a move that brings pleasure and power: the part can be mastered and the complexities of the whole ignored. In what Donna Haraway calls "the god trick," a partial perspective can be claimed as a total picture and other views repressed, and through this kind of synecdoche the disembodied, alienated objective rationality of a certain class, gender, ethnicity, and historical epoch can be proclaimed universal, while other styles and components of rationality, such as embodiment, situatedness, and affect, may be ignored or dismissed as nonrational.[12] A quote from psychoanalytic cultural theorist Norman O. Brown can remind us of an holistic standpoint from which computer-mediated knowledge and top-down rationality can be criticized:

> What is being probed, and found to be in some sense morbid, is not knowledge
> as such, but the unconscious schemata governing the pursuit of knowledge in

modern civilization—specifically the aim of possession or mastery over objects (Freud), and the principle of economizing in the means (Ferenczi) . . . possessive mastery over nature and rigorously economical thinking are partial impulses in the human being (the human body) which in modern civilization have become tyrant organizers of the whole of human life; abstraction from the reality of the whole body and substitution of the abstracted impulse for the whole reality are inherent in *Homo economicus*.[13]

Likewise, the philosopher Heidegger has critiqued modern instrumental rationality as a reduction of Aristotle's four mutually indebted causes (material, formal, efficient, final) to a subcomponent of the efficient cause—predictive calculation—which has been developed into a mode of knowledge-seeking where the world is "challenged forth" to efficiently report itself as mathematically processable bits of data.[14] As a machine for the most speedy and efficient forms of calculation and projection, a reporting technology whose very sustenance is digitized bits of data, the computer can exemplify this narrow but powerful way of knowing. Winograd and Flores, who respond to Heidegger's warnings about the way the digitized world could reduce humans to being merely the "orderers of the orderable," have pointed out that the metaphors of control and command embedded in the computer could be taken up as exemplars of communication in a dangerous synecdoche that ignores the way speech acts are requests and promises exchanged amongst members of a community.[15]

Nowhere is the seduction of synecdoche so alluring as in the fantasy of total control, mobility and reproduction promised by computer microworlds and virtual realities. Once the privilege of military and corporate elites, these illusions are now home delivered on personal computers. Paul North Edwards has drawn an analogy between the programmable computer microworld and the military institution, which "already has the character of a microworld" where every move and chain of command is regimented and clearly defined in advance from the top down.[16] This logic of domination is encoded into the programming languages of computers, and although it may be partly disguised in "user-friendly" interfaces, it is nevertheless experienced each time the computer obeys our "command," and when it prints out even the most disordered thoughts in neat typographical display. The microworld engages us in an "abstraction from the reality of the whole body," and the full range of senses (including olfactory and tactile) is subordinated to visual, and to a lesser extent aural, perception. The legendary hackers studied by Turkle and immortalized as the "console cowboys" of cyberpunk fiction, abandon the "meat" of their bodies while traveling data networks.[17] These (anti-) heroes are not only expressing and escaping their adolescent social ineptness but also acting out Reason's Frankensteinian dreams of achieving a form of male-only reproduction through knowledge and union with equipment. One particularly spermatic version of this idealist reproductive fantasy is expressed by hacker Mike Synergy in the documentary *Cyberpunk*: "For me a computer virus is a way of building a little AI [Artificial Intelligence] of me that can go out and copy itself millions of times and do whatever it has to do."[18]

The irrationalities of hard mastery and disembodied abstraction encoded into computers and computer culture do not necessarily appeal to women. The top-down control approach is thoroughly enshrined in popular computer and games magazines, with their screeds of columns quantitatively rating qualities like the "playability" of new products. These numerical ratings presuppose and construct a masterful self who judges from an omniscient perspective, confident it can measure any particular game against its authoritatively held (yet for all that unstated) hundred percent ideal. Despite the consistent finding since the early 1980s that it is boys, not girls, who are most passionate about computer game playing,[19] many subsequent developments of educational and entertainment software reproduce game-like formats. The problem is not that girls don't like playing games, but that they prefer games that are not readily programmable on computers. As Carol Gilligan has reported from earlier research into children's game playing, boys tend to put a legalistic emphasis on the rules of a game, quarreling intensively to clarify rules, then continuing play to a conclusion.[20] Girls, by contrast, tend to subordinate game playing to other goals, such as maintaining harmonious social relations, and play games where each gets a turn; if a quarrel develops, the game is abandoned. They are happy to negotiate to change the rules; indeed transforming the game is part of the enjoyment. Computer games and game-like programs which work by iterations of invariant rules seem inherently unsuitable for those people whose rationality emphasizes flexibility in social contexts over applying and obeying rules as absolute and conclusive laws.

Instead of assuming that the masculinist models are the best, we need to be sensitive to the emergence of other kinds of rationalities in computer culture. For example, the close relations between masculinist technophilia and hard mastery, as well as the strengths of the soft mastery style of computer learning, are suggested in this quote from computer artist Moira Corby, who in an interview with Virginia Barratt makes the following comment on gender differences in approaching new equipment:

> With the boy's thing it's always "Oh, here's the newest latest software. Let's do what we can do with it, then throw it out and get the newest, *latest* software." There's this big competition thing happening, whereas that doesn't happen amongst the women I know. We like to spend a bit more time on *one thing* and really explore it. You come up with things that so-called experts on the machine don't even know you could do. That's happened to me several times.[21]

Like a number (though not all) of the women artists in digital media interviewed by Barratt and myself, Corby prefers to learn by looking up things in
the manuals and help files, rather than by just hacking away at the equipment
or relying on patronizing "tech-heads" who often prefer to solve problems
themselves rather than bother explaining procedures to women. From a variety of comments we've gathered, it seems that women are less fearful than
ambivalent about computer culture: they appreciate the power of the smart
machine but reject much of the hype surrounding it; they suffer less from
technophobia than from "tech-head dysphoria," discomfort with the
approaches taken by most male technicians and teachers. And even where
women don't want to know the intricacies of programming, they want to
understand basic principles of how the hardware and software work, and feel
uncomfortable with the purely operational knowledge and minimal explanations given by many technicians and manuals.

Women who do get enthusiastic about computer culture may not do so for
the same reasons as men. It is salient to note that the current intensity of feminist (or "post-feminist") interest in the cyberworld and cybersex is not based
on eroticized relations with the equipment itself but excitement about the possibilities for communication and the exchange of knowledge and eroticism
made possible by the emergence of computer *networks,* the prototype of which
is that highly feminized technology, the telephone.[22] And whereas men's cyberfiction celebrates the idealist model of disembodied rationality achieved
through absorption into the virtual matrix, cyberfiction by women authors
tends to place more positive value on embodiment: in Marge Piercy's *He, She,
It* (Retitled *Body Of Glass* in Australia), the cyborg Yod has a fascinating sex
life, and the cybernetic workers of the Tikva collective manage to balance their
virtual life on-line with time spent in face-to-face communication and social-
izing with friends and families,[23] while in Pat Cadigan's *Synners*, as analyzed
by Anne Balsamo, the physical and physiological realities of the laboring body
provide counters to fantasies of total disembodiment.[24] The Sydney-based
geekgirl, a "cyberfeminist" magazine about developments in network culture,
always includes references to good local eating houses and web sites listing
foods, restaurants, and great recipes. In contrast to the computer nerds who
escape from reality into cyberspace, even the "grrrls" and "wired women" of
the 1990s see computer-mediated communications as a complement to, rather
than a substitute for, f2f (face-to-face) encounters: "Being online is an adjunct,
a backyard fence, a coffee shop, a favorite hangout, a weekly support group.
It's not my life, but it's a nice medium to have in one's life. It is not a social
revolution, but at times . . . it can be a revelation."[25]

In contrast to the hacker's individualistic politics of invasive mastery and
fantasies of destroying/taking over the corporate master by vandalizing/appro-

priating its data, "Feminist cyborg stories in the "cyborg politics" first articulated by Donna Haraway have the task of recoding communication and intelligence to subvert command and control."[26] Haraway was too much of a socialist-feminist to assume that play at the lower levels of the C³I (command-control-communications-intelligence/information) would *automatically* subvert the upper levels; this is only a *possibility* afforded through the longer processes involving alliance-building across irreducible differences, infiltration across leaky boundaries, and local and tactical resistance. Although she proposes the metaphor of the cyborg—a creature formed from the union of organism and cybernetic technology, with no single origin or fully programmed destiny—as potentially empowering for a feminist politics of technology, Haraway also acknowledges that cyborg myths are only as subversive as the theories and political actions they inspire: "Cyborg gender is a local possibility taking a global vengeance. . . . There is a myth system waiting to become a political language to ground one way of looking at science and technology and challenging the informatics of domination—in order to act potently."[27]

Like Haraway, I believe that the critique, transformation and invention of myths is an important part of any strategy to bring about technoscientific and epistemological change, and I suggest that overt pedagogical attention to the mythic meanings of computers might empower some students to overcome the (ir)rational obstacles they face when confronting these powerful and ambiguous machines. In the rest of this chapter, I continue to examine the myth system that surrounds computers in mainstream culture, as well as some of the countermyths—feminine and feminist challenges to dominant (ir)rationalities of the information age—looking first at images of computers and space, and at the bodies found there, and then at metaphors of discovery and heroism.

"Jupiter Space" and Cyberspace

The mythic dimensions of classroom computing, if they are not ignored, may be addressed from within inadequate interpretive frameworks. An example of the latter is a paper on cultural factors in computer participation by Australian researcher Glenn Russell, who discussed science fiction films, amusement arcades, and computer/video games and simulations.[28] Russell identified the 1968 film *2001: A Space Odyssey* as an important popular cultural text dealing with computers. One of innumerable versions of the Frankenstein myth, the film shows the computer HAL as a product of the most supposedly rational procedures and "highest" ideals of technoscience which also turns out to be the repository of the most sadistic and irrational destructiveness: it goes crazy and kills all of the spaceship *Discovery*'s crew except Dave. In Russell's reading, the main problem was that HAL and all the protagonists were male and that the film gave the message, "Women are not important where computers are concerned."[29] Comments on other films focused on the narrow "stereotypes" and lack of "role models" for girls in relation to computers.

It would perhaps be unfair to criticize an educational theorist for being unaware of nearly two decades of developments in feminist film theory, which have taken interpretation well beyond the behaviorist and psycho-sociological concerns with role models and stereotypes that characterized feminist film criticism of the early 1970s. These early approaches did not appreciate the phantasmic and semiotic character of signs like 'woman' in visual texts, and often naively assumed a direct correlation between "images of women" in advertising or film and "real women," which permitted reading fictional narratives as quasi-sociological statements.[30] But from a psychoanalytic and semiotic perspective, what is important is not simply the statistically measurable presence or absence of women role models on screen, but the qualities of the whole fantasy scenario: its origin, its trajectory, its motivating desires, and, importantly, its ambiguities. For example, *2001*'s computer HAL was not always a male, but was called Athena in earlier versions of the screenplay, after the goddess of wisdom, war, and numbers who was born from the head of Zeus (the Roman Jupiter) after the god had swallowed the pregnant Methis, goddess of wisdom. The computer voice is often female in subsequent science fiction film and television (for instance, the computer "Mother" in *Alien*), and the notion of the computer as a female friend, an "Amiga," is not unfamiliar to many computer users. HAL's barely suppressed femininity returns to the surface in a recent series of Australian television ads for KFC, set in a space ship in which the astronaut is addressed as "Dave" and served KFC chicken strips by a computer with the same intonations as HAL, but possessing a female voice. The myth of Athena, and more specifically the notion of the male head as a pregnant womb-like space, was invoked in *2001* by the term 'Jupiter Space,' used at a crucial moment to refer simultaneously to the outer space near Jupiter and to the accompanying image of the womby red interior of the computer HAL's brain, in which the space-suited astronaut floats like a fetus. The entire film can be read as a fantasy of reproductive techno-sex, featuring seminal emissions of radio waves and sperm-shaped space ships like the *Discovery*, which travel out to the moon and beyond, pass down various tunnels, fertilize diverse kinds of spaces, and ultimately generate a planet-sized embryo, the Star Child.

One has to agree with Russell that *2001: A Space Odyssey* is a central and influential myth for computer culture, and thus is relevant in the classroom computing context. The metaphorical connections between the fertile space of masculine intellect, computer space, outer space, and all other kinds of tech-nospaces (including grids of city streets, electronic circuits, video-game space, etc.) which were outlined in the film, and especially the psychedelic Star Gate sequence, were widely elaborated in science fiction and high-tech advertising during in the 1980s and continued at less intensity into the 1990s. The frequent image of a grid of lines going off to infinity is interpretable as a visual pun on the notion of the "matrix" as a mathematical and/or a maternal womblike space. Often shown floating or zooming above the grid are objects—computers, other high-tech components, various more mundane commodities (toothbrushes, coffee grinders, pizzas), or simply spheres repre-senting ideas or new worlds arising from the fertile matrix. Innumerable tele-vision advertisements have referred to the music and imagery of *2001*. Jupiter Space imagery was the house style in 1980s issues of the pop science and technology magazine *Omni* and found its definitive verbal articulation in William Gibson's much quoted descriptions of the data landscape in the mid-1980s novel *Neuromancer.*[31] Jupiter Space images are now largely superseded by the fractured, multiscreen style and McLuhanesque typography of cyber-culture magazines like *Wired*.

Jupiter Space imagery is thoroughly intricated with the historical trajec-tories of highness and futurism. The computer is represented as part of a high-tech domain of equipment and is thereby aligned with mathematical rational-ity (the grid), outer space, and such things as nuclear reactors and bombs, space rockets and probes, as well as robots and other imagined artificial life forms.[32] The iconography of the post-World War Two period makes it clear that the "high" is quite literally the extraterrestrial, and that the extraterrestrial is futuristic and vice versa. Notions of progress become aligned with a race into space and a rush towards a future which is not in centuries to come but something that happens today, or at the very latest, tomorrow, just as soon as you get the latest upgrade. As we get closer to the millennium and further away from the euphorics of extraterrestrialism elaborated in US science fic-tion films of the Reagan years (then partly deflated by the Challenger disas-ter), the horizon of futurity is shrinking to just a few years hence, or in the case of Max Headroom, a mere "20 seconds into the future," and there is some evi-dence of a disenchantment with outer space, together with an increased fasci-nation with the potentially more accessible domain of cyberspace, now hailed as the "electronic frontier." In recent popular computing magazines I have found advertisements juxtaposing outer space imagery with computers and the slogans: "SPACE. THE FINAL FRONTIER" and "YOU NEED YOUR SPACE." While extraterrestrial references are still present, and space is still portrayed as something the implicitly male addressee is entitled to invade, occupy, and possess, it is notable that like "the future," "space" has also shrunk to being a personal resource that is on hand, manageable, and as close as a desktop computer.

It would be very difficult to prove how these high-tech fantasies of commanding space, capturing the future, eliminating organic reproduction, and engineering artificial (and often female) selves directly determine reported gendered differences in classroom computing. But it seems reasonable to speculate that if the computer is represented as part of a broader mythic context that legitimates these masculinist fantasies as cultural ideals, then many boys and men will readily feel "at home" in computer culture. They don't need to question the contexts or higher purposes of computing because these are already defined by hegemonic masculine myths in which they are invested. They can uninhibitedly love for itself a machine that offers them one more port of entry into a world of command/control technology to which they already feel entitled. By contrast, while some women are seduced by the possibilities of command and control over microworlds offered by computers, they usually either cannot or do not want to bracket off their awareness of the computer's broader contextual framework, of which they may be explicitly critical, and from which they are emotionally distanced. To become meaningful to women's artistic and pedagogical projects, computers may have to be recontextualized, stripped of their mythic grandiosity, and redefined simply as tools for use in tasks that make sense to the women users.

Athena Figures and Cyberfeminists

High-tech masculine reproductive fantasies like *2001* do not offer women much with which to identify. However, increasing the number of anatomical women in the plots of such fantasies would not necessarily alter their male-centeredness. On the contrary, individual women characters can be perfectly well incorporated as Athena figures (such as daughters of scientists whose wives are dead; female robots, androids, or computers) in what is still basically a euro-masculine fantasy of circumventing maternal reproduction by incorporating it, equating it with mental powers, and superseding it via technological reproduction. As a brainchild of masculine invention, the computer is the inheritor of a well-established iconographic tradition in which various branches of knowledge and science are personified as female figures or ethereal muses, at least until the nineteenth century, when the emblem of "Science" became the figure of a solitary man in a white coat.[33] Athena figures at this point became exemplars of "Technology," especially in the form of clockwork, mechanical, and later robotic women (such as the robot Maria in Fritz

Lang's *Metropolis*). In a well-known essay, Andreas Huyssen has discussed how with the rise of a modern mechanistic view of nature, the figure of the mechanical "vamp" was attributed with powers previously associated with an unruly "Mother Nature": a dangerous or demonic sexuality and the ability to escape masculine control.[34] More recently, the connections between femininity and technology have been elaborated in the language and imagery of computer culture via the brain-womb metaphor and terms like the 'matrix,' 'mother boards,' 'consoles,' 'sexy' and 'user-friendly' interfaces, and images of fembots (feminine robots) and seductive "Amigas." In one computer advertisement, a larger photo shows a woman "senior executive" and her laptop computer at a meeting of men. The print narrative tells how she used her laptop to seduce the men into buying her advertising campaign for a girls' product: "After I played our new TV spot on my T4700 they wanted both my project and the computer." Not only are the "project" and the "computer" conflated here, for a smaller photo inset at the bottom shows the woman's face displayed on the computer; the erstwhile female user has been devoured and incorporated as a "user-friendly" component of the equipment itself.

A quasi-sociological reading of high-tech Athena figures cannot account for their ambiguous meanings. The gendering of computers as feminine may inhibit some women from learning to "master" a technology or "hack" into a space that is metaphorically equivalent to themselves (computers and women as the "to be used" rather than "the users," as occupiable spaces rather than space invaders). The computer's association with a lineage of technological brainchildren may facilitate men's narcissistic enjoyment of the computer as a "second self," while women are likely to be more cynical about the limitations of these quasi-others as substitutes for actual humans, and less likely to share the fantasy of technological reproduction (which does, after all, involve the cannibalization and elimination of organic maternal fertility and its replacement by the fecundity of male-dominated corporate bodies). But for other women, the feminization of computers can have a positive counter-effect, allowing cyberspace to be imagined as a helpful and familiar space in which to explore and act in ways not entirely governed by masculine/patriarchal logics. The idea of being aligned with a feminized technology can enable learning and discovery.

Some contemporary feminists (especially "cyberfeminists") hail mechanical women and feminine cyborgs as potentially empowering emblems of a femininity that is not natural but constructed, not fearful of technology but akin to it. The British cyberfeminist Sadie Plant argues for the positive feminist potential of women identifying with machines, those increasingly active agents that have never been fully controlled by their patriarchal makers.[35] Donna Haraway's "Cyborg Manifesto," with its vision of a cyborg politics that embraces "partiality, irony, intimacy and perversity" and is based on contingent affinities rather than immutable identities, is an important reference for many feminist theorists and artists interested in computer culture, including the Australian feminist art group VNS Matrix, whose *Cyberfeminist manifesto for the 21st century* is reproduced here (see Figure 1).[36] Developing Haraway's insights into the perverse and embodied character of cyborg technics, the artists articulate erotic and physical metaphors of a feminist technobody, and acknowledge possibilities for a creative woman-centered technophilia: "the clitoris is a direct line to the matrix." The feminized imagery of the brain-womb-mathematical grid may be entered from another starting point, with other ends and processes in view. Resonant with the viral metaphor, the female monster in this image appears as a phallic and penetrative force capable of moving in the cyberspace matrix, seeking pleasure and knowledge. The uncensored version of the billboard text proclaims "we are the modern cunt . . . we are the future cunt." The many references to feminine genitals and secretions, including what the artists call the "cybercunts" down the left hand edge of the image, are not about maternal reproduction or origins. The (censored) proclamation "we make art with our kunst" mobilizes the generative force of the vagina as a metaphor of cultural rather than biological production. In proclaiming themselves "mercenaries of slime" these cyberfeminist artists call attention to ways of lubricating exchange, friction, and traffic at the contested borders of categories, entities, and meaning systems. Viral and hacker themes are appropriated ironically and dominant imagery parodied in VNS Matrix's prototype video game *All New Gen*, set in the "Contested Zone" where the player receives help from the pervasive feminine intelligence All New Gen and increases their stores of "G-Slime" by bonding with the sublimely monstrous DNA Sluts, in order to do battle with the data banks of Big Daddy Mainframe and his ally Circuit Boy (a chrome-plated "dangerous techno-bimbo" imaged as a counter to the usual mechanical woman, and whose penis morphs into a mobile phone). In their various works, VNS Matrix are interested in counteracting the computer's own biases towards disembodiment and abstraction by using it to present visceral images and language.

Epistemophilia and the Metaphorics of Discovery

The narrative of discovery is not, as the French philosopher Lyotard has argued, a "mere epic" to replace the former "grand narratives" of truth, unity of knowledge, and humanity, but is itself a guiding metanarrative which has been continuously elaborated from early modern science into the postmodern

Figure 1.1. VNS Matrix *Cyberfeminist Manifesto for the 21st Century* (1992)
Offering women more visceral and sensuous pathways into computer-age technophilia. VNS Matrix.

present.[37] Discovery has been pictured as an obsessive Frankensteinian quest for an enlightenment achieved through the aggressive invasion and possessive mastery of an unknown created through various technologies that estrange the familiar and push ever outwards (or inwards) the horizons of the known—a quest "to boldly go where no man has gone before." Computers are very much caught up in the myth of discovery through their associations with scientific and technological progress, especially with extraterrestrial and futuristic trajectories in which they are represented as vital components of space exploration and a new form of space themselves, a virtual frontier to be invaded, explored, and possessed.

Discovery metaphors have their unconscious sources in the symbols and fantasies of epistemophilia (curiosity) that first arise in the pre-oedipal period of infantile development when the differences between self and (m)other, male and female, fantasy and reality, are not well understood, and oral, anal and bisexual fantasies are common. The child often presumes that the organs and powers of both sexes are possessed by itself and its mother, a powerful figure on whom it depends for sustenance, pleasure, discipline, and punishment. While even the youngest of infants exhibits curiosity towards new stimuli, the epistemophilic impulses, as described in particular by psychoanalyst Melanie Klein, arise when infants become curious about origins and sexual difference, ask lots of questions ("where do babies come from?") and in fantasy direct their "researches" at the maternal body, whose objects and organs are imaginatively appropriated out of greed and a desire to escape the disempowering position of "not knowing."[38] Fear over damaging the mother's body prompts the impulses to make reparation, for example by fashioning new whole bodies from appropriated resources to produce artworks, tools, or ritual objects.[39] Klein argues boys are disappointed by their research findings, which show they cannot have children.[40] Expressions of womb-envy and maternal identification are not often explicitly verbalized in hegemonic culture (though more recently, even he-men like Arnold Schwarzenegger are shown carrying pregnancies), but usually take metaphoric form (as in Jupiter Space imagery) or are played out in mythic narratives and real-life quests to discover or create new bodies of knowledge, land, resources, techniques—or, in cyberculture, undertake heroic hacks to plunder programs and information. These plunders, discoveries, brainchildren, and stolen data become symbolic replacements for the mother's body, just as Zeus produced his brainchild Athena in partial reparation for having cannibalized her mother Methis (who continued nevertheless to provide him with "gut wisdom").

In parallel with Turkle and Papert's *epistemological* pluralism there is an *epistemophilic* pluralism, and parallel arguments can be made about the need for computer pedagogy to acknowledge and support a diversity of metaphors of discovery, knowing, and creating. Speaking in general terms (for, of course, everyone has their own particular epistemophilic formation and fixations): whereas boys can fantasize improving their fertility by hacking into and appropriating organs from maternal bodies of knowledge, girls might fear the destruction of their fertility, and may be anxious that in raiding a maternal body, a body with some similarities to their own, they risk destruction or despoliation of their own body.[41] Thus girls tend to be more concerned with the reparative or restorative sides of knowledge-seeking, perhaps more needy of reassurance and, as many teachers have observed, more interested in producing neat and beautiful work—creating texts as restored bodies. Boys may be less concerned about causing damage to the equipment than girls, who seek knowledge of basic principles and the reassurance of manuals to avoid damaging systems.

The sadistic model of discovery, pictured as an aggressive penetration of an unknown body and heroic efforts to bring it under control, has been taken as *the* model of discovery in western popular culture, while the reparative approach emphasizing care, caution, and familiarity is dismissed as lacking the necessary "cutting edge" for making "real" discoveries, just as women are often dismissed as less than "incisive" researchers.[42] But as the earlier quote from artist Moira Corby suggests, the top-down method does not necessarily work best in practice, especially when it comes to computer programs, not all of whose capabilities are known even to their designers, and whose intricate possibilities may elude those who simply put new systems through their paces from a position of already assumed mastery. A pedagogical emphasis on hard mastery and the sadistic appropriation of a maternal space may enhance the self-esteem of masculine users, reassuring them of their powers to command and toy with the feminine or maternal objects of their desire. By contrast, exploring the computer's space and powers through a progressive enlargement of the circle of familiarity, starting with basic principles and with assistance from help screens and manuals, allows girls and women to bypass the sadistic model of discovery and give themselves permission to become competent users of the technology without arousing (pre-oedipal) fears of internal destruction as punishment for raiding a feminine body.

Hard Mastery and Cyber-Submission

Psychoanalytic interpretation of cultural or personal symptoms cannot rest content with identifying only their most obvious and one-sided meanings; its task is to investigate the shadowy sides of meaning, those paradoxical, ambiguous and excessive counter-meanings that allow the cultural or personal symptom to do its work of mediating between official or conscious rationalities and unofficial or unconscious irrationalities. The discussion so far has emphasized the culturally dominant fantasies of discovery and control associated with hard mastery and masculinist desires to command space. In this last section I turn to the other side of masculinist fantasies of controlling machines and spaces: those of masochistic submission to equipment.

Although young children grasp principles of gender difference in their oedipal phase, masculine identity is more problematic because it involves a transfer of identification from the mother to the father and may not be fully consolidated until adolescence, when the boy typically deals with his remaining attachments to the pre-oedipal mother. Many cultures and religions work this through in formal initiation rites, but in secular westernized cultures, this function is fulfilled in a range of informal practices and consumption of heroic quest myths. These heroic quests typically involve entry into another world, the encounter with and defeat of some monster (usually symbolic of the pre-oedipal mother), the rescue of a weapon, prize, a princess or Athena figure, and reentry to the mundane world as a mature male.[43] Sherry Turkle has discussed how hacker subculture of MIT in the early 1980s was one that involved special languages, identities, and initiation rituals including masochistic all-night feats of "sport death,"[44] and it has been widely noted that computer/video games are generally phrased as variations of typical adolescent hero fantasies in which protagonists enter bizarre virtual terrains, prove themselves doing mortal battle with fantastic enemies, rescue prizes, and take control over and/or save the world.[45]

In a 1949 article that drew much from Kleinian theories, the psychoanalyst Anton Ehrenzweig reflected on epistemophilia, heroism, and the tensions between intellectually and physically oriented masculinities, as expressed in the common narrative pattern of a pair of men: "one the manly, unintellectual hero, the other the unmanly clever villain who accompanies, helps or fights him" (such as Thor and Loki, or *Star Trek's* Kirk and Spock).[46] Ehrenzweig analyzed the complementary figures of the scientist and the hero in terms of relations to the pre-oedipal mother. Epistemophilic tendencies (which Ehrenzweig calls "Promethean" urges) are involved in both scientific and heroic quests: the scientist continues his investigative probings of the mother's body, while the hero decisively confronts the devouring maternal monster (for example, the dragon to be slain). Noting the frequency with which heroes are shown as wounded (that is, "castrated"), and scientists represented as "unmanly," Ehrenzweig interprets both figures in terms of their relations to the oral mother. The scientist attempts to master fear of the oral mother by identifying with her; his investigative eyes become in a sense the vagina dentata as he pursues an "oral voyeurism" in his quest to discover and devour secrets. The hero, by contrast, is not a guilty voyeur but a proud exhibitionist who puts himself—and implicitly his genitals—on display in acts that unconsciously invite his own castration or wounding by his opponent, the onlookers, or the monster. Although Ehrenzweig considers the scientist to have sublimated self-destructive feelings into the search for knowledge, I'd contend that even though the intellectual hero might not subject himself to the same kinds of physical injury as his muscular macho mate, masochism has been central to scientific heroism and the Frankensteinian metaphorics of discovery.

Masochism is not just about enjoying pain, it is also about the fantasy of letting go, of submitting to the controlling power of the stern father or the discipline of the potentially devouring mother.[47] Those who entertain sadistic fantasies of hard mastery and total top-down control of technologies are vulnerable to the return of repressed masochistic desires for submission to them, as expressed, for example, in expressions of passivity towards the supposedly inevitable "future" of technotopian vision, or of the willingness to "change for the machines."[48] In cyberfiction, to "jack into the matrix" via an electronic umbilicus can also mean submitting oneself to its control, losing oneself within the computer's oceanic maternal space, perhaps being devoured by it, becoming a body of fragments, or entering a psychotic state akin to "psychasthenia," where the distinctions between self and environment, inner world and outer world, break down.[49]

The complementarity of physical and mental forms of heroic masochism can be observed in computer culture imagery. While the great popularity of Schwarzenegger-style action adventure movies demonstrates that active physical heroism and sheer brute strength are still highly valued in western and nonwestern cultures, the information age also intensifies interest in the clever hero who uses his (or sometimes her) head, enhanced via consumable technologies like smart drugs, and succeeds through intelligence and trickery. For boys who don't make it on the sports field, heroic hacking offers an alternative mode of heroism, an opportunity to plunder the stores of data in the matrix, to trick the system into yielding up its resources, and to express reparative impulses by sharing the treasures with the hacker community. Many computer games mediate between physical and cerebral forms of heroic masochism, requiring cleverness, observational powers and rapid responses as users play out heroic action-adventure scenarios where they destroy foes—or are destroyed or injured by them—via a variety of weapons and with an increasing degree of gory (hyper)realism. One games magazine advertisement for a plug-in card, which allows various kinds of cheating, modifications, freezes, and saves, on computer games features an image of a heavily armored metallic cyborg on the run and contains two fine-print endorsements: one anthropomorphizes the product in terms emphasizing cleverness (". . . a sophisticated and multi-talented piece of equipment"), while the other praises its physical strength (". . . combining powerful code crunching with lethal game busting").[50] Another example of this combination of mental and physical power is an advertisement that puns on the caption "Providing tools for powerful thinkers," showing the powerfully muscular body of weightlifting champion Flex Wheeler posed as Rodin's *Thinker* before some Morse computer equipment (see Figure 1.2). Computer brain-power is here equated with black masculinity in a connection mediated by the well-entrenched racist typification of blackness as pure animal and sexual prowess.[51] The ad allows notions of "power," "thinking," and "thinkers" to flow between the equipment (a power-tool for thinking and a thinker itself) and its users, who can fantasize themselves and their tools in terms of powerful masculine physicality. Moreover, it's not just in fantasy that the opposition between physical and mental power can be bridged; anyone who buys a system is offered seven free visits to a gym, where they too can masochistically subject various parts of their body to pleasurably painful biomechanical rituals aimed at achieving a "shredded," "cut," or "ripped" musculature.

Tensions between sadistic fantasies of control and masochistic fantasies of loss of control are also observable in the images of different kinds of bodies within computer culture and electronic image making. Images of smooth whole bodies floating on or above the grid or zooming over a luminous virtual landscape suggest to me the sadistic and masterful side of control fantasies, where the body is held together as an impenetrable or seamless container. But recalling the schizoid (or splitting) processes of the pre-oedipal ego, as well as the embarrassingly out of control adolescent body, at the "grunge" end of the cyberarts spectrum we find bizarre images of a body pieced together, not unified by any top-down logic: a scrambled body whose zones and parts move around and meld into each other (see Figure 1.3).

Invoking these experiences is the protean and polymorphous creature associated with oral-devouring themes in a computer game *Super Putty*, described in the Australian games zine *Hyper* as a hamburger-munching male persona who is "small, gooey and burps a lot" as he defends fellow Puttians from an evil wizard who wants to turn them into bubble gum for human consumption. Apparently this creature

> . . . can elongate into what looks like a long drip of something unmentionable. . . . And when roused . . . he extends his hands into blue boxing gloves, and gives the opposition a solid smack in the chops. Putty can also stretch out on the floor and absorb enemies into his body, which is the best way to kill them . . . and most interestingly of all, [he can] polymorph into a character he has come in contact with. Very T2.[52]

Figure 1.2. Morse Computer Advertisement
Recent computer imagery bridging the opposition between intellectual and physical forms of masculine heroic prowess. *Australian Personal Computer* (June, 1994), 240.

Figure 1.3. *Hyper* **Games Magazine Promotion**
The adolescent "grunge" aesthetic representing a fragmented and unstable body-ego.
Hyper 7 (July, 1994), 20.

The body here, as in *Terminator 2*, is not so much fragmented as fluid; instead of existing in a Frankensteinian mode as a cobbled-together pastiche, its multiple and partial identities are manifested sequentially. But in either case, the body ego is quite different from that rationalist ideal of a perfectly proportioned, smoothly coordinated, and well controlled whole.

Another site where the interlinked and contradictory tendencies of control and submission are manifested is at the human-computer interface, where a demand for masochistic submission to machinic imperatives is frequently disguised as a "donation" of control to the user. It is perhaps affective distance from masculinist fantasies of control and submission that leads many women artists to express dissatisfactions with what they experience as the "false interactivity" of "point and click" style multimedia interfaces. Whereas the hype about interactive multimedia stresses the empowerment of users by giving them "control" over the narrative sequence, the actual experience is more like one of having to obey the program, making choices only when and where it lets you do so from a restricted range of pre-programmed options. Many of Virginia Barratt's and my interviewees express views similar to those of Florida-based artist Christine Tamblyn, who argues that most computer interactivity "is not much different from buying a soda from a vending machine" and that "the potential for computer interactivity is really quite limited and dictated by the programmer."[53] Media theorist Ken Wark has made a similar point: "Far from giving the user more 'choices,' multimedia can be seen as empowering the creator and restricting the users' choices."[54] Some women artists respond by exaggerating and making explicit the sadomasochistic dimensions of human-computer interactivity. Linda Dement, for example, revels in the way computers give her aesthetic control over "every single little change that happens in the work,"[55] and like most of VNS Matrix's installations and interactives, Dement's CD-ROMs *Typhoid Mary* and *Cyberflesh Girlmonster* include overtly sadomasochistic erotic content, as well as explicit reminders to the user/player that they are not in complete control. A number of women artists (such as Nola Farman, Sarah Waterson, Joan Brassil) prefer to employ computers in the "background" of installations whose interfaces rely on various kinds of sensors, physical actions by visitors, and randomizing computer programs in an effort to produce more genuinely interactive works and experiences that arise from the unique and unpredictable interactions of the visitors with objects, spaces, and each other.[56]

There may be a lesson here for computer educators: if you want to get girls or women interested in programming or learning more about cybernetic technologies generally, encourage them to use computers in art projects—not only virtual but physical.

Conclusion

The myth of the computer as a second self—whether a sexy companion, a smart opponent, or a lethal code-cruncher—is likely to have greater appeal to boys than to girls. The kind of epistemophilia encouraged in computer culture is associated, on the one hand, with a general masculinist and technoscientific trajectory of discovery and, on the other hand, with specifically masculine fantasies of sadistic control over and masochistic submission to the machine.

It is not that girls and women don't have sadomasochistic fantasies but that the styles of learning and play promoted in the mainstream of computer culture represent normalized versions of certain masculine heroic fantasies, while women's more careful, dispassionate, and thorough approaches to new systems are devalued or ignored. Girls and women seem more able to both playfully acknowledge and ironically distance themselves from the affective and mythic dimensions of computing and can distinguish their own approaches from those exhibited by technophilic technicians and nerdy boys. These latter can avoid being emotionally self-reflexive, deny the influence of the passions that inspire them, and dismiss any alternative attitudes as emotional, phobic, or stupid because they are supported by a culture that legitimates their own irrational fantasies as part of a supposedly universal rationality, and so by definition in the province of efficiency, logic, and reason, not desire. From years of giving lectures and papers on these themes, I can say that while some men find it embarrassing, many women find it empowering when discursive space is created to acknowledge and critically discuss the irrational and perverse dimensions of dominant technotopian rationalities. In pedagogical contexts, this kind of discussion could help dis-embed computers from hegemonic mythologies and allow them to be translated into other systems of myth and meaning. Explicitly addressing the fantasies associated with computing may help learners identify creative alternatives to sado-masochistic schemata of discovery and the deceptive kinds of interactivity promoted in mainstream/malestream culture.

Certain patterns of gender difference in computer learning have already been well documented; others are emerging as the technology and its applications change (for example, towards more networked and interactive computer-based media). Instead of wishing that girls (or other nondominant peoples) behave more like technophilic (especially western) boys in their approaches to computer learning and human-computer interactions, or dismissing gender differences on either pre- or post-feminist grounds, would it not be better to pay attention to these subtle, aesthetic, emotional, and political factors? And better still to redesign interfaces, rewrite manuals, reorient pedagogical approaches, and broaden computer applications to suit the aesthetics, expressive styles, and epistemophilic modalities of those many computer users who are uninterested in or alienated from western rationality and its narcissistic, "technotopian" fantasies of reproducing, controlling, and submitting to a digital second self? By acknowledging ambiguity, ambivalence, and heterogeneity in the meanings and experiences associated with computers, it may be more possible to counteract the militaristic and "cyberauthoritarian" biases which are undeniably part of the history of this technology, though not necessarily determinant of its pluripotential futures. Meanwhile the technophiles' need to bolster their egos by conquering and possessing the newest, speediest equipment is an (ir)rationality that serves computer marketeers nicely, certainly better than those more modest and typically feminine desires to understand systems well enough to choose the tool appropriate for the job at hand under principles of scale and utility many women have tried to teach men in more intimate pedagogical scenarios: that it's not what you've got, but how effectively you use it that matters.

CHAPTER 2

The Everyday Aesthetics of Computer Education

ANTHONY P. SCOTT

Concepts and Terminology

Aesthetics and Engagement

What is aesthetics, and what is *aesthetic form?* I am not going to delve into centuries of nuanced argument about the full import of the word 'aesthetics.' I am going to employ a commonsense definition: that aesthetics is that part of knowledge concerned with pattern and appearance, with the look of things and the fitness for purpose of those things, with ideas of beauty and ugliness, and with what it means for something to be called "art." I am going to use 'aesthetics,' 'the aesthetic,' and 'aesthetic form' interchangeably, without making any claims about form versus content debates in the philosophy of art.

I will make two further claims, though, on the meaning of 'aesthetic.' First, aesthetics includes ethics: more precisely, "(e)thics and aesthetics are one and the same thing" (Benjamin, 1977, p. 185). In other words, there is a moral dimension to anything one regards as art. This might be manifest in its form or content, or (most relevant in my context) in the technology of its making. This position would lead me to reject, for example, certain works because of their ontogeny, however elegant their manifestation of design. Second, the history of an artifact or artistic procedure is present in the work. It cannot be otherwise, for artifacts are sediments of cultural history. Together, these two facets of aesthetic valuing give rise to problems when an artist has appropriated procedures with questionable antecedents, and has not differentiated his or her art, as commentary or otherwise, from those procedures. The consequences of these extensions of the commonsense meaning of aesthetics are probably best explained with a personal example.

Virtual reality (VR) is offered as a new horizon for the sciences and the arts. VR development has had and continues to receive extensive military funding. In my view, it depends on an immersive illusion and an abrogation of the identity of the user, whether as consumer, spectator, or interactor. In its most extensive form, it also depends on the technology of the body suit (a kind of diver's wet suit offering total isolation from the elements in which one is immersed). The body suit is a technology which has its origins in a technology, not of sensory enhancement but of sensory deprivation. For VR to work, it is necessary to dispense with physical sensory experiences, to decouple the subject from the world, prior to impressing the senses of the virtual world on the body. One needs to ask, then, of instances of virtual reality as art, whether the artist has overcome, challenged, or even responded to strategies of sensory deprivation condemned by Amnesty International as torture. My primary concerns in this chapter, however, are the negative implications of my extended aesthetic definition for our daily experiences of educational computing; VR is not as yet an everyday experience.

In *Lord I'm Coming Home: Everyday Aesthetics in Tidewater North Carolina*, Forrest (1988) defines the everyday aesthetic as the total aesthetic experience of the community he is observing. He adopts a strategy of including in that daily experience any act of judgment of taste he observes. His emphasis is on aesthetics in practice, in the choices people make, and in the observations they make about their home, leisure, work, and religious activities.

Although he avoids aesthetics-by-definition, believing that "(a)esthetic form is inherently an open concept and cannot be defined in terms of necessary and sufficient conditions" (p. 20), he does provide some orienting concepts.

He asserts that aesthetic forms are:

1. Capable of sensory perception.
2. Open to judgments based on taste.
3. Capable of affecting the perceiver.
4. Capable of disinterested appreciation. (p. 21)

However, he points out that this is not a rigid framework for determining or describing aesthetic forms, but merely a starting point. From here he goes on to catalog the aesthetic life of his informants. It was an ambitious task.

He believes that "nothing less than a survey of the entire aesthetic realm of a community can provide an aesthetic context comprehensive enough for the situating of aesthetic experiences." It is a task he could undertake only, in fact, by adopting a strategy "not to think in terms of art at all. Freed from categorical assumptions," he can claim "the widest possible observation of aesthetic forms and experiences" (p. 28). From this perspective, he reviews human aesthetic activity in the home, work, leisure, and religious life. He demonstrates that the aesthetic is a process which permeates daily life and goes beyond the conscious activity of making art. In the following, I will mention the use of computers to make art only in passing. My focus is on the everyday aesthetic of computer education, by which I mean something both more common and less conscious than art making. Following Forrest, I include in my definition of aesthetic behavior a person's:

1. sensory perception of computer systems, computer screens, and computer-mediated communication processes of various kinds;
2. judgments based on personal taste, preferences held about computer systems, screens, and communication processes; and
3. actions resulting from the effects of those observations and judgments.

I do not believe it is necessary for my purposes to be concerned with the notion of "disinterested appreciation," for if I am talking about students making art on the computer or viewing other computer-mediated art, I believe that to be an interested judgment. And if I am not talking directly about computer art, I am concerned with the *indirect* effects of computer aesthetics.

It is necessary to my argument, though, to address the notions of *engagement* and *flow* as aspects of aesthetic experience. Csikszentmihalyi (1988, 1990) theorizes that we experience moments of total engagement with the world as flow, oneness with our environment, absorption in the task at hand and acceptance of its rules.

The Aesthetic Dimension of Educational Computing

In this section I am concerned with the aesthetic dimension of human-computer interaction, which is a property of our engagement with computing devices, whatever the application. The computer's motivating and engaging character is seen most readily in the addictive qualities of arcade-style computer games and in the instructional designer's attempts to capitalize on this property. However, there are in my view a number of other aesthetic aspects of computer use occurring in education, which I can only briefly touch on here. In addition to the process of engagement with computer-based art making, which I will label as an aesthetic of action, there is also an aesthetic of illusion, an aesthetic of ergonomics, and an aesthetic of folk design.

The aesthetic of illusion. Every day, we are confronted by dozens, hundreds, or even thousands of computer-generated images produced for commercial advertising. The "art" of making these images lies in their going undetected. The total engagement of the spectator is involved with the illusion being created or in an irony about the cartoon reality being depicted by the advertiser. The organization of pixels (the graphic elements of computer-generated images) to promote the understanding of the artificial image as the real is one aspect of the everyday aesthetics of computing. It is the visual version of the embedding of computer chips in the everyday technology of our lives. Televisions, bank machines, programmable household appliances, and others are increasingly built around computer chips. The general population is neither sensitive to the computer mediation of our engineered realities nor fully aware of the extraordinary capacity for illusion of computer-mediated entertainment and information systems.

The aesthetic of ergonomics. Complementary to the everyday aesthetic of the computer, made invisible through processes of embedding and illusion, is the aesthetic of the machine environment itself. This includes the ergonomically designed aspects of the physical presence of the home or office personal computer, the interface through which computing options are presented to the user, and the structure of the software that affords those options. There are, of course, qualities particular to the containers in which computing power is provided. They relate quite closely to consumer electronics design, especially the design of home entertainment systems. Sometimes, computer case design is an uneasy compromise between a functional tradition and user convenience. In the functional tradition, the computer is provided as a set of boxes (computer, monitor, keyboard, printer, and speakers); each box is optimized for a particular function. In the convenience model, speakers are integrated into monitors, and computers are sometimes integrated with keyboards or monitors. Computers are not yet available in appropriate veneers for the study or living room. The technical aesthetic still dominates, and computers have until very recently come in engineering colors rather than household colors. Most of the ergonomic evolution has occurred in terms of pointing devices (such as the mouse) and typing devices (such as the keyboard), though changes in the latter probably are driven by economic convenience or insurance considerations (reduced metacarpal damage) rather than aesthetic ones.

It is also necessary to attend to the design of what appears on the screen. The increased power of personal computers allows the human-computer interface to be presented as a series of holders (folders, windows) and agents (icons). Part of the market segmentation of the two largest personal microcomputer manufacturers, Apple and IBM, is undoubtedly aesthetic preference for the modes of presentation they each adopt and the totality of the combination of those interface styles with the physical style of the computer itself (Harris, 1994). Note that both use a command-and-control instrument aesthetic, in which the user is presented a variety of choices (icons, menus) from which he or she selects. Primarily, the act of interfacing with the computer is one of selection.

The command-line-interpreter approach, wherein the user issues a sequence of commands to the computer, has been automated to become both more transparent and reserved for the "expert" in computing. What has been automated out in this design process is any significant degree of control by the user over the machine. Even in its military applications, the containment of the user as a consumer, as a chooser of the options marketed, is the primary aesthetic principle of the computer-human interface (Noble 1991).

The aesthetic of folk design. In the home environment, when one wakes up one's personal computer from its screen sleep, it may not be to do his or her taxes or word process a term paper. It might be used to run one of a growing number of programs of a genre I call "folk design": garden design, home design, or interior design. One might also create and illustrate stories for one's children using computer graphics programs that do "real" art without one's having to learn to paint. There is an encapsulation in computer programs of certain sets of values concerning the organization of nature, the proper disposition of the domestic hearth, and the use of appropriate decorative arts and crafts. These values all stem from *an aesthetic of containment.* If there is to be wilderness in the garden, it must be a managed wilderness. Computer programs concerned with house design do not offer radical alternatives to the balloon-frame dwelling first made available through the Sears catalog. Energy-efficient under-earth houses are not provided in the clip-art repertoire. All of these programs are embedded in a strategy of selection from given alternatives. Clip-art is about more than providing a copyright-free source of imagery; it is also about providing a risk-free source of ideas.

Transparency and Engagement

Each of the previously noted aspects of the aesthetic of computing comes with certain degrees of transparency. The first, the aesthetic of action, foregrounds the act of art making through the medium of the computer. The second, the aesthetic of illusion, is characterized by transparency as a goal. The third, the aesthetic of ergonomics, is characterized by product identity as a goal. The fourth, the aesthetic of folk design or containment, is characterized by presenting to the market an encapsulation of "doing art without the work."

All these aspects of the everyday aesthetic of computing are also at play whenever one uses computers for teaching or learning. The everyday aesthetic of computing operates throughout the use of the computer as a vehicle for instruction, both in formal schooling and in the home. Students encounter with increasing frequency an instructional technology that organizes their learning into a series of small, digestible items of knowledge. Even where interactive media are used, the multimedia presentation of knowledge is still organized in hierarchical fashion. The use of technology in this way is advocated for the superior motivating effect of the engagement of the individual in the task of learning. It is no longer, and probably never really was, valued for the empowerment of the individual and the democratization of learning that was originally promised in the advertisements that accompanied the personal computer revolution.

Writers about computing in education are concerned primarily with instructional efficiency and the presentation of content. Occasionally they are concerned with social aspects of the computing medium, such as the dynamics of gender relations or equity of access to computing resources (Bowers, 1988). They do not usually address the process of engagement with the computing environment itself. Yet the capacity of the computer to invoke a total engagement, as evident in video games, is what led many educators to advocate the use of computers in education in the first place.

This situation leaves us with a number of problems: What set of values underpins the affordances of these everyday computer aesthetics? What should educators, particularly those who teach about the media in contemporary society, be doing to make visible these aesthetics and their implications? What strategies can be used to reveal these values? These are important problems, but before they can effectively be addressed we need to develop our understanding of how computing generally, and educational computing specifically, is grounded in cultural and social institutions.

The Sociohistorical Context of Educational Computing

Computers have been integral to the sociocultural and socioeconomic changes in the last fifty years. They are, and have been, seen as the engine of the third machine age, the central metaphor of the information society, and an automatic generator of success. Many influential educational technologists have taken quite a narrow view of the purposes and potential of this particular technological revolution and its economic and educational impact: not only are computers an unquestioned engine of economic change, they are also an engine of educational improvement. Bromley's (1991) statement to Congress is a clear exemplification of the dangers of the conservative view:

> Imagine a classroom in which each student obtains self-paced, individualized instruction from his (sic) own terminal, rich in graphic imagery, which provides reinforcement when appropriate, and repetition using different words and con-

cepts when appropriate. All this will be made possible by a single optic fiber cable no bigger than your thumb. (Allan Bromley, Evidence to Congress on the Proposal for a National Research and Education Network, March 7, 1991)

At the time of this statement, Bromley *[no relation to the editor of the present volume]* was an official of the Office of Educational Research and Innovation, which is the U.S. Congress' own agency for advice on educational technology. He advocated the application of a multimillion dollar project to the preservation of a behaviorist view of education which is much enamored in military training tradition.

The commercialization of the Internet and its use as an instrument of (certain kinds of) educational change are part of the National Information Initiative of the Clinton administration. The national communications network, which has its roots in the military's need for a failsafe command-and-control system, had threatened to break away from its roots and become an open system, especially in higher education. Once more it has been contained. Technology may be used to amplify traditional training practices in education, or it may (and should) be used to amplify cooperative constructive practices. Eraut (1991) pointed this out in a review of the implications of the New Information and Communication Technologies (NICT) for European education systems.

> Education should now take a more proactive stance towards changes in society. The new information and communication technologies . . . should not be rejected but accommodated through a more critical approach based on the fundamental human values of personal choice, equity, and the protection of cultural life. In the words of the Finnish Minister of Education, Mr. Christoffer Taxell, "modern technology is a good servant but a poor master." (p. xi)

What one should pay careful attention to is the partnership of the military and education establishments to support a particular set of values. Noble (1991) cogently expresses this concern:

> Recent technological excursions in the classroom reflect not so much the use of technology in the service of education as the usurpation of education in the service of technology. While new technologies, most notably computers, are increasingly viewed as tools in the service of education, it is rarely noted that education itself is now conceived, ideally, as a tool, a sophisticated supply system of human cognitive resources, in the service of a computerized, technology-driven economy. Attempts to wed education to advanced technology, as in computer-based education (CBE), have not been driven, in the final analysis, by the real and pressing needs of education. Instead, forces external to education, but integral to technological development, have forged this coupling, remodeling education in the process.

What are these forces? Commercial enterprise, of course, has played a significant role in this unlikely union, as has often been noted. But on a deeper, more historical and cultural level, efforts to align education with technological development have, to an unrecognized extent, been driven by another exercise, one quite alien to education. This enterprise has not only captured the collective imagination of educational policy makers; it has shaped and redefined the very contours of economic, political and scientific institutions in postwar American society. This enterprise is military research and development. (p. 1)

Noble goes on to catalogue the various strategies through which the military agenda is achieved. The next section will examine some items in that inventory.

The Military Provenance of The Computer Aesthetic

The word 'computer' originally referred to a person who computed numbers. Urgent military necessity to calculate enormously complex equations led to the turnover of such computations to machines, displacing the human computer, who became the programmer of the machine, that is, of the electronic computer. The widespread use of electronic computers in recent times for many nonmilitary applications disguises the continued influence of its origins in military-sponsored research. However, as Weizenbaum (1976) comments, "The computer in its modern form was born from the womb of the military" (p. 568). Recent historical research seems to support this conclusion (Noble, 1989, 1991; Edwards, 1996; Williams, 1996; Winegrad, 1996). It is important to point out in the current context that many developments in the educational uses of computers have had their origins in research on creating man-machine systems for military purposes and in research to improve military performance.

For example, Competency-Based Education (CBE) emphasizes mastery learning assessed by batteries of performance tests. Its focus on task analysis and skills training to achieve those tasks is a marker of its military origins. Behavioral objectives, and more recently, Total Quality Management (TQM), stem from a particular approach to task analysis that accepts hierarchical views of the world. Much CBE instructional software available in the schools is couched in a drill-and-practice philosophy that takes its very terminology from Boot Camp. Noble (1991) points out, "The Army, Navy and Air Force were the first to express interest in Skinner[ian] teaching technologies and sponsored and developed them" (p. 23). This occurred prior to the computer's more general introduction to public schooling. The function of the education system, in this view, is to produce a new kind of cannon fodder, a new kind of Tayloresque artisan who can make complex decisions when necessary from a predetermined menu or (in the case of highly able engineers) structure his or her own decisions based on acceptance of the values returned by cost/benefit/risk analysis, but not question the moral framework or ecological import of such decisions. In such circumstances, teaching humans to promote the formation of questioning minds, as Postman and Weingartner (1969) advocated, is indeed a subversive activity. Using computers to assist in the formation of such minds is then a double subversion of the military program.

It is important that educationists be aware of the military value system and its expression through the everyday computer aesthetic as it has a presence in the classroom opposed to the liberal ethic espoused in the 1960s by Postman and Weingartner, and in more recent decades by several analysts of the malaise of the educational system.

An Intelligent Computer-aided Tutoring System

The issue of military provenance can be most clearly seen in the use of computers as "intelligent tutors." A recent issue of the *American Educational Research Journal* carried an article by Schofield, Eurich-Fulcer, and Britt (1994), which sought to explain an apparent paradox: "students who readily assert that a teacher provides better assistance in learning how to do geometry proofs than an artificially intelligent computer-based tutor nonetheless prefer using the tutor to learning in the more traditional mode. In addition, students appear to work harder with the tutor than in the traditional situation, and they may even end up learning more" (p. 580). The student, despite his or her affiliation to the teacher and his or her knowledge that the teacher's understanding of the student is both profound and sympathetic compared to any ITS model, is nevertheless seduced by the machine. The process of seduction in operation here works through what I described earlier as the aesthetics of engagement. The phenomenon of students' rapport with the computer program is common. This is underlined by the researchers' own review of the relevant literature (Schofield, Eurich-Fulcer, and Britt, pp. 580–81):

> An emerging literature on the impact of computer assisted instruction (CAI) suggests that this is the case with the various kinds of computer applications subsumed under this rubric. In fact, one large-scale survey of microcomputer-using teachers found that they were five times as likely to report that using computers increased students' general enthusiasm than to indicate it helped students to learn more (Becker, 1983). . . . Another theme that has emerged in several studies is the idea that the use of computers in the classroom increases student motivation and interest (Campbell, 1984; Ferrell, 1986; Johnston, 1987; Podmore, 1981; Ritter, 1989; Sandholtz, Ringstaff, and Dwyer, 1990). This is evi-

denced by the fact that studies often report students exhibiting high levels of task involvement and persistence (Johnston, 1987; Podmore, 1991). In addition, the use of computers seems to increase the amount of time students spend on task. (Johnston, 1987; Sandholtz and Dwyer, 1990)

There is nothing wrong with motivating students. Motivation is an important part of learning and an essential part of the social fabric of schooling. But what the research literature does not highlight is the trade-off involved in much computer use, that the greater motivation is accompanied by a narrower definition of the task at hand. Students are, indeed, spending more time on task, but each task is likely to be more highly specified, and in a more closely defined domain, due to its computerization. This can be seen in the physically oriented arcade game, where one's motor skills are devoted to the task of "zapping" some enemy and avoiding being zapped. It can be seen in the drill-and-practice programs, which increase students' motivation by rapid feedback and some reward system, over a very tightly specified, multiple-choice but not open-choice domain. It can also be seen where *intelligent* computer assisted instruction (ICAI) is used in place of CAI. Schofield, Eurich-Fulcer, and Britt comment that ICAI is more likely to change the social context of the classroom because "it is possible that such tutors, through their ability to provide significant amounts of help and information to students, will create a kind of challenge to the teacher's expertise-based authority" (p. 582). It may well be that there is some redefinition of expertise, but the domain-expertise knowledge of the ICAI system will always be outweighed by the social and personal insights of the teacher. The students in the study acknowledge that the teacher could provide better, more insightful assistance to their problem solving. But the control effected through the display mechanisms, the illusion of open choice presented by ICAI systems, or the smaller range of choices more directly offered by CAI/drill-and-practice systems, all motivate the students to prefer the game-like domain of the computer. In this choice-bound and rule-bound system, they are more likely to achieve engagement and flow than in the more challenging, more open environment of the teacher-mediated classroom.

The Fifth Dimension

An alternative aesthetic might be found in the after-school use of computers, as the number of computers in homes rises past the point where their presence is special, extraordinary, or even a marker of middle-class parenting. Children's use of home-based computers extends from the construction of multimedia reports through explorations of the Internet to engagement with computer games, often of the shoot'em up variety.

What about more formal after-school activities? Play must be a key ingredient in any form of educational activity if it is to engage the child in more constructive after-school activity than such games. One such effort is organized around a "utopian" environment called "The Fifth Dimension" (LCHC 1989; Nicolopolou and Cole 1993; Vasquez, 1996). A Fifth Dimension is a deliberately constructed mixture of educational, play, and peer-oriented activities, in which computer-based games and writing through telecommunications play a central role. The elements of the Fifth Dimension may appear trivial when they are looked at separately; it is the combination of elements, including carefully designed adult support, that makes them effective. The linear nature of the present medium (text), however, forces a narrative description of each element in turn.

First, a Fifth Dimension can be considered as a kind of adventure game. The child enters a maze on a quest. In this case, the maze is not secret but is an explicit map of twenty "rooms." The child has access to both a diagrammatic map and a three-dimensional model to locate his/her position in the maze, the content of the adjoining rooms, and the positioning and difficulty of the doors leading to each adjoining room. Second, a Fifth Dimension can be considered as a net or web of assignments to be tackled. In each room, a child has a choice of two activities; both of these activities have three levels of difficulty. The higher the level of difficulty of the activity, the more doors are open, and the more routes to reach whatever the child's goal happens to be. That goal might be to transform (in a "Dungeons and Dragons" sense) by entering the maze from one door and leaving from a different door after only a short journey; or it might be to reach a favorite game; or it might be to become a Wizard's Assistant. (The Wizard is a mythical entity, based in the computer network, who "controls" the Fifth Dimension.) Third, one could consider a Fifth Dimension as a kind of amusement arcade that caters especially to children but also allows adults and young adults to enter.

Conclusion

What should educators, particularly art educators and others who teach about the media in contemporary society, be doing to make visible these aesthetics and their implications? There is an overwhelming amount of current exploration in the use of new technologies to enhance human capacities for experiencing the world, and hence for organizing them to experience the world more deeply. Consequently, while one admires new forms of potentially educational activities which are being created on relatively high-powered devices, either standalone computers or combined computer and television/film media, one worries about provenance, accessibility, and the continued dominance of the military in educational research (in work on computer-mediated education in particular). In so far as militarily constrained task environments also organize computer-based versions of computer-as-substitute teacher, it is likely that they contain, in some measure, the top-down control system that is the military's special dispensation in the name of national defense.

Computer games may be addictive. That addiction is expressed in terms of total absorption in the microworld presented by the game and by the achievement of expertise within it. It was the observation of the regard in which game experts were held by their peers, as they played during a coffee break, that led Michael Cole and his colleagues to reorganize a remedial math/reading project. They realized that the peer-to-peer counseling that they were struggling to create during the project was taking place in the coffee breaks, as expert gamesmen exchanged tips and hints with their lesser brethren. Other than a demonstration to educators of the power of the computer to provoke *engagement*, and the ability of adolescent males to go with the *flow*, arcade games have seemed to be a purely leisure occupation, that is, a purposeless means of passing (real) time with no goal outside the (virtual) gameworld. To the contrary, media coverage of the Gulf War revealed military targeting systems which owed more to *PacMan* than to Clausewicz. The incorporation of the aesthetics of engagement, immersion, and flow into such systems should give one pause for thought—a pause that the pilots operating/playing the weapons control systems/games don't get. Which is what led me to write this essay.

CHAPTER 3

Telling Tales Out of School:
Modernist, Critical, and Postmodern
"True Stories" about Educational Computing[1]

MARY BRYSON and
SUZANNE DE CASTELL

> All our truths are, in a sense, fictions—they are stories
> we choose to believe.
>
> —Hilary Lawson, 1989, p. xxviii

> Both science and popular culture are intricately woven
> of fact and fiction. . . . Scientific practice may be con-
> sidered a kind of story-telling practice—a rule-gov-
> erned, constrained, historically changing craft of narrat-
> ing the history of nature. Scientific practice and
> scientific theories produce and are embedded in particu-
> lar kinds of stories. . . . Scientific practice is above all a
> story-telling practice in the sense of historically specific
> practices of interpretation and testimony.
>
> —Donna Haraway, 1989, p. 4

As "Talking Head" David Byrne tells us in the film "True Stories," our task
at the present time, that is, the postmodern project, in his words, is to "Stop
making sense." This chapter is an attempt to do just that. And this, contrary to
what one might imagine, is not so easy to do. For the discursive context of
research and practice in relation to educational computing[2] is one in which
"sense" is doggedly (even if often contrafactually) made, in which seamless
narratives attempt to tell "true stories" of how and why new technologies are
to be harnessed in the service of educational ends, and about the prospects and
pitfalls therein.

    Alarmist rhetoric, reminiscent of earlier debates about the so-called liter-
acy crisis (see Graff, 1988), survives today in a wide range of educational pol-

icy documents (see, for example, British Columbia Ministry of Education, 1990) that urge educators to grapple with the implications of an "explosion in knowledge, coupled with powerful new communication and information processing technologies" and, therefore, to promote widespread "technological literacy." Arguments that enthusiastically promote the widespread implementation of educational computing typically predict that these technologies will (a) facilitate teaching processes, and (b) promote significant positive gains, both academic and vocational, for students. However, evaluation studies suggest that unreflexive and unabashed optimism about the necessarily transformative nature of new educational technologies is both naive and historically unfounded (see Cuban, 1986).

Historical analyses of documentary evidence from times "when old technologies were new" (Marvin, 1988) suggest that, generally speaking, the implementation of new technologies begins in documentary (or in virtual) reality with wild projections of massive transformation by futurologists and with descriptions of high hopes for the realization of widespread social and economic reform, and end up in actual reality with failed predictions and quashed hopes. It comes as no surprise to discover, then, that the "official" story of the impact of new educational technologies, like film or television, on teachers' practices or on students' accomplishments is a resolutely disappointing one. A similarly resilient gap between predictions and outcomes has routinely been reported in studies of the educational implementations of computers (Cohen, 1987; Cuban, 1986; Ragsdale, 1988). Additionally, sociological studies have documented systematic gender, class, and race inequities in both white-collar computer occupations and educational uses of technology (for an excellent summary, see Sutton, 1991).

This chapter comes out of an attempt to "make sense" of the disorienting terrain of educational computing, necessitated by (the first author) having assumed the role of principle co-investigator in a multisite longitudinal study of the implementation of computers in elementary school classrooms (Bryson, 1993), and discovering, with great dismay, that those accounts and incidents which, to this researcher, appeared to hold out the greatest potential educational benefits often were regarded by teachers and administrators as "irrelevant," "impractical," "too radical," and the like, or as prescribing or constituting "low-level" or "illegitimate" computer uses.

Like Scheherazade, in the 1001 Tales of the Arabian Nights, educational theorists are allowed to extend their livelihood in the publish-or-perish world of the ivory tower by virtue of the degree to which their tales serve valued institutional purposes (Lather, 1990). The analysis offered here, then, construes the discourses of educational research as being made up of an eclectic inventory of tales whose primary purpose is to provide a regulative, or sense-making, technology.[3] Postmodern inversions, deliberate uses of irony, and distortions of chronological linearity aside, these tales prototypically are made up of a predictable range of elements,[4] including: intransigent conflicts ("Why Johnny still can't read"), laudable intentions ("We aim for full and eager participation in literacy activities by all children"), persistent obstacles ("Low self-esteem hampers girls' performance in mathematics"), notable successes ("LD child composes entire novel on word processor!"), and a host of central characters ("the at-risk child" or "the primary teacher").

It is argued here that in an ongoing dialogical process of co-construction, university-based researchers' narratives both constitute and are constituted by necessarily partial and "interested"[5] accounts generated by teachers, ministry-based education workers, students, and others within the broader educational community. Researchers' accounts about new educational technologies, then, are seen here as a species of metanarrative which informs and is informed by practitioners' first-order accounts (also construed as stories) of the nature and proper function of computer technology in the classroom. Such accounts are given to teachers and, through teachers, to students themselves, in curricular resources and curriculum guides, in the teachers' guides and publishers manuals accompanying educational software packages, in policy directives, in-service workshops on implementation, in casual conversations among teachers themselves, in teachers' magazines, and, not least of course, in the tales told "out of school" about educational computing. The burgeoning discourses of academic research itself, then, define for educators, and indirectly for students, the limits and possibilities of computers. Accordingly, they both shape and constrain the ways in which teachers can teach and learners can learn using that technology, as well as what and how researchers can investigate these classroom practices.

In this chapter, we describe three kinds of stories that are told about educational computing. Making use of a text-based interpretive strategy, which we have described elsewhere in a metatextual analysis of the discourses of "gender differences and educational computing" (Bryson and de Castell, 1995), we argue here that it is productive to analyze stories about educational technologies in terms of how these embedded narratives contribute to the constitution of distinct "textual communities" (Stock, 1983). These communities involve authorized interpreters whose function it is to generate theoretical accounts (and related research strategies and pedagogical practices) for the purpose of situating computers appropriately within educational environments. The kinds of stories that are told about educational computing, we suggest, reflect differently ordered sets of assumptions about the nature of knowledge, the purposes of schooling, investments in specific constructions of gender/race/class identity politics, and the scope and limits of computer technology in the classroom. We argue that it is principally the interpretive constraints imposed by these stories, and only secondarily the material capacities and constraints of the technology itself, which differently construct possibilities for pedagogic relations among students, teachers, and educational technologies. It is these stories, then, which preconstruct human subjects, that is, teachers and learners, in terms of their possible relations to the technologies at their disposal, and delimit accordingly the prospects such technology holds out for the improvement of educational practice.

On the basis of our ongoing field study and in conjunction with a review of research and "lay" discussion of the uses and abuses of computer technology in education, we have found it possible (and, we hope, productive) to discriminate three paradigmatic types of accounts, here construed as "stories" about educational computing. They are, first, the modernist/romantic tale, second, the critical/tragic tale, and third, the postmodern/ironic tale (after Van Maanen, 1988, and White, 1973). We briefly characterize each of these in turn, then go on to try to specify some ways in which each "story" shapes in quite different ways what teachers can do and how students can learn with computer technology, and how these in turn both shape and constrain what and how researchers can learn from these classroom practices. The chapter concludes with some remarks about possible implications for researchers, in particular, with some warnings about how "making sense" is always in danger of making nonsense of well-meaning attempts to advance educational goals through the implementation of computer technology in the classroom.

Technicism/Modernism: Romantic Tales about Computers as "The Thinking Man's Tool"

A dynamic way of dealing with intellectual abstractions over time, unbounded by the circumstances of any given facts but adaptable to new facts, new data, change. Well-structured problems that would require children to use a variety of computing tools at appropriate places would teach perhaps the most valuable skill of all, which is problem solving. Beyond that, students acquire the confidence to deal with complexity, for even the simplest programs can transform a certain degree of messy, muddy detail into more clearly structured intellectual representations. (McCorduck, 1985, p. 229)

Romantic tales of modernist technicists prescribe "computer literacy"—the systematic inculcation of specific skills and dispositions which allow for successful adaptation to the inexorable demands of relentless progress toward a "space-age" society—as a necessary rite of passage for youth born into the "information age." These tales are here characterized as romantic in the sense that their authors demonstrate a consistent, uncritical, and zealous faith in (a) the possibility of accessing, measuring, and manipulating original and organic "truths" about "human nature" and (b) the necessarily salutary role to be played by reason, new technologies, and the technics of the natural sciences in fueling "progress" and thereby resolving significant social and empirical problems and generally improving quality of life.[6] The views of Jean-Jacques Servan-Schreibner, former president of the Paris-based World Center for Microcomputer and Human Resources, construct the technicist's vision of the relationship between technology and pedagogy:

> The computer is the first intellectual revolution in 500 years. It is bound to transform every aspect of the human endeavor—agriculture, industry, the office, medicine, education. To ignore this revolution is to make oneself irrelevant. . . . Every characteristic—creativity, imagination, talent—that makes a human being different from a machine can be enhanced by the computer revolution. . . . [With regard to education], when computer and telecommunications networks are sufficiently developed, the lectures, research, and new findings of important intellectuals and academics can be made available to students around the world. (quoted in Bowers, 1988, p. 117)

Within this view, a shift is posited from investing considerable effort in learning facts and mastering bodies of knowledge to strategically locating up-to-date information as a means to an end—the solution of significant problems—which is seen here as the key mechanism that underlies scientific progress. Educational uses of computers, typically characterized within the technicist's view as our most powerful information-processing technology, take center-stage since the central aim of education, on this view, is to prepare students for effective participation in an economy that trades in "knowledge" and "solutions" as key forms of "cultural capital."

Technicist visions of educational technology present computers as value-neutral tools which, however, *can* become educationally valuable but only insofar as one can distinguish between optimal and suboptimal implementation and pedagogical strategies. Accordingly, technicist accounts make contrastive use of metaphors such as 'boob-tube' vs. 'Proteus of machines' (e.g., Papert, 1980) or dichotomies between "drill and practice" vs. "learning environments" (e.g., Brown, 1985; Shute, Glaser, and Resnick, 1986) in order to privilege as properly "educational" certain forms of computer-based pedagogical activities and to relegate others, seen as idle entertainment or "busy-work," to the margins.

The 'boob-tube' metaphor, for instance, constructs a particular kind of educational use of computers which is usually construed as negative since it is supposed to replicate the child's passive assimilation of insignificant or harmful images during televiewing. Drill-and-practice software, videogames, and computer-automated worksheets are the most common kinds of educational computing relegated to this undesirable category. Most texts on educational computing suggest that teachers avoid relying on this kind of educational software. The Foundation Document for the new Primary Program in British Columbia (B. C. Ministry of Education, 1990) suggests, for example, that "Evaluation of software is necessary to ensure that the child is actively engaged in learning and not merely focusing on decontextualized drill and isolated skills" (p. 36).

The 'Proteus of machines' metaphor, by contrast, was coined by Seymour Papert, whose LOGO-based research is widely acknowledged to be the most influential amongst technicist computer educators (see Bowers, 1988; Broughton, 1984). 'Proteus' refers to the sea god who could change shape depending on the unique exigencies of any given situation. In an elaboration of this metaphor, Papert (1980) wrote that "The computer is the Proteus of machines. Its essence is its universality, its power to simulate. Because it can take on a thousand forms and can serve a thousand functions, it can appeal to a thousand tastes" (p. viii).

This view that there exists a privileged form of educational computing presupposes that educationally fruitful and empowering environments can be designed which are responsive to individual differences and which therefore are able to support self-directed, independent, intellectual activity. As Papert (1984) argued, "The computer allows us for the first time to match the subject matter and learning style to the personality type" (p. 425). Technicist metaphors for educational computing are consistent, then, with parallel dualistic notions of "higher-order" or abstract vs. "low-level" or concrete learning in cognitive-developmental psychology. In educational applications of cognitive-developmental psychology, the goal of pedagogy is to provide instruction which goes beyond training in basic skills.

> Research from cognitive science questions this assumption [about teaching and basic skills] and leads to a quite different view of children's learning and appropriate instruction. . . . Researchers are developing models of intervention that...provide access to explicit models of thinking in areas that have traditionally been termed "advanced" or "higher order." . . . Cognitive research on comprehension processes has shown the importance of trying to relate what you read to what you already know, checking to see that your understanding of new information fits with what you have already read, setting up expectations for what is to follow and then seeing whether they've been fulfilled. (Means & Knapp, 1990, pp. 1–7)

Technicist researchers in educational computing posit a relation between children's acquisition of particular "higher" forms of thinking, such as hypothetico-deductive reasoning, and their engagement with computers in activities like LOGO programming (e.g., Papert, 1980) or word processing (e.g., Joram, Woodruff, Bryson, and Lindsay, 1992). Papert, for example, describes the goal for engagement with computers as "intellectual model building." Hence his focus is on facilitating the attainment of abstract, logico-deductive reasoning as a high-priority pedagogical goal. One of the main themes in Papert's characterization of the significance of LOGO programming is that it instantiates a pedagogical approach that is "ego-syntonic," that is, it is in tune with how children "naturally" learn. As such, it is supposed to represent an approach to educational computing that is both revolutionary and superior to traditional methods. As Papert (1980) wrote:

> In many schools today, the phrase "computer-aided instruction" means making the computer teach the child. One might say the computer is being used to program the child. In my vision, the child programs the computer. . . . And in teaching the computer how to think, children embark on an exploration about how they themselves think. (pp. 5–19)

It is interesting to note that although Papert's more recent accounts (e.g., Turkle and Papert, 1990) of the role of new technologies in education now include explicit commitments to the goals, broadly conceived, of social equity (such as the ongoing program of research on LOGO, educational computing, and minority students' learning processes in Project Headlight, an inner-city school in Boston), the investigative methodology continues explicitly to target putative relationships between certain "thinking styles" (exhibited by minority students and women), such as "narrative" or "concrete" thinking and "low levels of educational achievement" (see also Motherwell, 1988).

Other studies reporting actual implementation of the LOGO language reveal that the construal of this kind of educational computing as somehow natural or ego-syntonic is highly problematic. Emihovich and Miller (1988), for example, reported a study where they argue that the instructional value of LOGO in educating children "at risk" for failure in traditional educational contexts was that it enabled them to match minority students' so-called learning styles with a "suitable" form of computer-based instruction. Following Papert, they suggest that "Ethnic differences are an important determinant of students' learning styles" (p. 474). The purpose of this study was to remediate what the authors construed to be a lack of "higher-order thinking" in black American children. Citing a report from the Carnegie Corporation, which invokes Shirley Heath's (1986) ethnographic study of variations in the functions and uses of literacy across three Appalachian mill-town communities, the authors write that

One way for the United States to retain its competitive edge is for children to use a highly prized learning style called metacognitive thinking . . . minority children from communities like Trackton often lack opportunities to display metacognitive skills. . . . *Programming builds upon the learning strengths of black students, such as high responsiveness to visual and auditory stimuli and desire to collaborate with and pass on information to peers* (italics added for emphasis). By encouraging minority children to talk and share their ideas and to use the "turtle" as a concrete representation of their thinking, a learning environment can be constructed that may make these students more aware of their thought processes. (p. 476)

Stories of this kind, it is to be noted, persistently conceptualize equity issues as questions of psychological "styles," of individual (albeit perhaps culturally induced) "differences" in what are called "thinking styles." The metaphor of thinking 'style' here takes the contextually variable differences in functions and uses of literacy of the sort explicitly discussed by Shirley Heath in her *own* account of her work with minority students from Trackton, and rhetorically reduces what are clearly socioeconomic inequities to matters of fashion and preference, even matters of individual taste. Such "ways of telling," to adopt one of Heath's own expressions, manage to obscure significant critical observations, for example, by the likes of John Ogbu (1981). Ogbu argues that the failure of institutional schooling adequately to respond to the unique and pressing needs of students from oppressed groups, which he refers to as "subordinate minorities," has far more to do with their "caste-like" status, than with their thinking styles. Indeed this rhetoric of "thinking styles" functions to constitute essentialist ontological categories out of what are far more plausibly seen as vastly unequal access to power in school, as in society (and in school, not coincidentally, *because* this is the case in society).

Technicist accounts of technology, just like skills-based accounts of literacy, are thus construed here to be incapable of acknowledging sociopolitically grounded differences which create for different learners quite different and indeed inequitable relations to educational technologies. Because they adopt an "artifactual" view of such technologies, severing them from the normative contexts of social practice with which they have their uses, such accounts make possible the production of abstract generalizations enabling the construal of material inequality in terms of equal access to new educational opportunities.

Critical Theory: Tragic Tales about Computers as Technologies of Normalization

Knowledge is always inescapably complicit with the first-order myths and enabling fictions that underwrite its claims to truth. (Norris, 1985, p. 23)

Critical discourses about educational technology, by contrast with technicist/romantic discourses, are explicitly concerned with what is problematic about the value-neutral role accorded to the use of computers by technicist educational reformers. We have characterized critical stories as tragic, because their primary aim is typically to provide an opportunity for a cautious and sobering "stepping back from the fray" so as to see more clearly the potentially destructive and oppressive network of unequal social and material relations within which new technologies are typically constituted. In constructing a critical analysis in terms of what is "problematic" about the educational uses of computers, we refer specifically to a method of inquiry usually associated with Michel Foucault, that is, to bring to the center of the stage those issues which are traditionally left in the wings and to transform what is usually accepted as a set of givens into a set of questions. As Foucault (1983) wrote, "What I want to do is not the history of solutions. . . . I would like to do the genealogy of problems, or problematiques. My point is not that everything is bad, but that everything is dangerous. . . . I think that the ethico-political choice we have to make every day is to determine which is the main danger" (p. 147).

In critical theorizing, this process of problematizing the "taken for granted" in pedagogical discourses about institutionalized learning is often referred to as one of exposing the "hidden curriculum" (Bowles and Gintis, 1976; Freire, 1971; Giroux, 1981; Weiler, 1988). The hidden curriculum includes a wide range of ideological and marginalizing dimensions of schooling that are not typically acknowledged or discussed in state-sanctioned educational discourses—restrictive constructs that might include, for example, gender roles, class-based epistemologies, and non-standard language codes.

A significant proportion of critical discourses on educational computing deal explicitly with the task of making explicit the implicit hidden curriculum inscribed in technicist applications of educational technologies (e.g., Bowers, 1988; Broughton, 1984). In *The Cultural Dimensions of Educational Computing*, Bowers argues that computers are not, as is commonly believed, value-neutral educational tools. Indeed, he goes on to say, technocrats focus on educational uses of computers as a potentially transformative technology precisely because their own goals are themselves ideologically skewed in the direction provided by modernist views of progress. This view of progress includes (a) increased control over access to and manipulation of information, (b) abstract rationality as the most effective form of human thinking, and (c) individualism and entrepreneurship as constituting the most effective models for human commerce.

According to critical theorists, hegemonic or oppressive relations between dominant and marginalized groups are unlikely to change with the advent of computers unless we understand how it is that value-neutral accounts of this new technology actually play a key role in reifying education as a systematic process of acculturation to the values and normative practices of dominant groups. Broughton (1984), for example, exposes the epistemological underpinnings of Papert's LOGO culture, in constructing a critical discourse for educational computing. Tracing Papert's particular view of learning to cognitive/developmental models, such as those associated with Jean Piaget (with whom Papert studied for six years), Broughton criticizes the ways in which these models serve to lend an aura of scientificity or systematic rationality to models of human thinking that place the ability to reason, or to make use of inductive/deductive logical operations, at the highest level of human intellectual achievements. The construction of these theories draws directly on the historical context of Cartesian notions of rationality as the most privileged form of thinking and on notions of universal, cross-cultural accounts of learning. As Valerie Walkerdine (1989) points out:

> This fixed sequence takes us from pre-logical to logico-mathematical reasoning at first concrete and then abstract. The assumed pinnacle of abstract reasoning is rarely if ever questioned. And yet of course it is precisely that which various groups are routinely accused of not being able to reach: girls, working class children, blacks, third world children, etc. . . . This sequence is itself an historical product of a certain world-view produced out of European models of mind developed at a moment in the development of a European capitalism dependent on the colonization and domination of the Other, held to be different and inferior. (p. 5)

Critical theory stresses that covertly entrenched in the technicists' processes of categorizing, and thus hierarchizing, different types of software or different types of learning are existing social norms and relations of power. Foucault (1978), in analyses of the nineteenth-century construction of the domains of knowledge which we now know as psychiatry, statistics, medical science, jurisprudence, and education, argued that hierarchical classificatory schemes of the kind central to the modernist tale serve to define, to subjugate, and thereby to regulate what comes to be regarded as normal behavior. Foucault (1980) refers to these practices as the "technologies of normalization" and argues that the invention of these schemes is an essential component of the exercise of power.

Critical research on educational computing documents systematic inequities in both access to and utilization of technology by members of marginalized groups (see Apple & Jungck, this volume; Damarin, 1993; Noble, 1991; and Sutton, 1991). Critical discourses typically focus at the first level on technology as a material commodity which is unequally distributed and therefore differentially accessible—the "political-economic" critique of educational technology. At a second level, broadly speaking, the "sociology of knowledge" critique, critical discourses focus on how those in power adapt and channel innovation in order to retain control over emerging forms of knowledge, thereby reproducing (see Bourdieu and Passeron, 1977) existing oppressive social structures during periods of potentially liberatory social transformation. Kathleen Weiler (1988) describes this process as follows:

> As state institutions, they [public schools] reflect the logic of state power within a certain economic formation, in this case, capitalism. Their hierarchical structure, the content of the formal curriculum, the nature of the hidden curriculum of rules and social relationships all tend to reproduce the status quo. In this society, that entails the reproduction of existing class, racial, and gender divisions. Those who are in control, who dominate and benefit from this structure, attempt in both conscious and unconscious ways to shape the schools so as to maintain their own privilege. (p. 150)

In a national survey of 1,082 computer-using schools conducted by the Center for Social Organization of Schools (1983–84), for example, it was reported that:

1. More computers are being placed in the hands of middle- and upper-class than poor children;
2. When computers are placed in schools for poor children, they are used for rote drill and practice instead of the cognitive enrichment that they provide for middle- and upper-class students;
3. Female students have less involvement than male students with computers in schools, irrespective of class or ethnicity. (quoted in LCHC, 1989, p. 74)

Likewise, Persell and Cookson (1987) report a study of the prevalence and uses of computers in a range of American schools, including coeducational, boys', and girls' elite boarding schools. With respect to the "political-economic" critique, their findings suggest that (a) larger, better-endowed schools were more likely than smaller, less well-endowed schools to have computer centers, (b) boys' schools and coeducational schools were more likely than girls' schools to have computer facilities, and (c) white boys were much more frequent computer users than were any other subgroup. With respect to the (broadly so described) "sociology of knowledge" critique, it has been argued that both in form and in content, educational computing privileges dominant assumptions and practices in very much the same ways that the traditional textual curriculum does, indeed to worse effect, given the relative accessibility of textual as opposed to technological educational resources.

Hence, there is a tendency on the part of adherents to critical theory accounts to minimize both teachers' and students' expectations of what the technology can do for them and what they can do with the technology.

Moving from critical theory to postmodernism, we find that the traditionally "gloomy posture" of the essentially tragic critical tale of preordained and hence inevitable misfortune has been mitigated in recent years by postcritical stories about the pedagogic "possibilities" (e.g., Aronowitz and Giroux, 1991) opened up in virtue of the "contradictory and contested" terrain of educational praxis. The critical tale's tragic predictions of inevitable reproduction of educational inequities are disclosed as a species of mechanistic determinism which construes human subjects as the unwitting dupes of an inexorable hegemonic process. Contestation and resistance by both teachers and students are proposed within a "logic of possibility" capable of transforming traditionally reproductive education into a new, postmodern pluralism. This "leveling" of all traditions, even the previously sacrosanct, holds out the promise of a new educational equity where educational technology, because of its unique capacities for blurring human/machine boundaries, plays a central role.

Whose interests are served by such accounts and the practices that follow from them? Paradoxically, those best served are conservative teachers, intellectuals, and the already privileged. For teachers need not alter their practices to accommodate educational technologies if these are rightly seen to be inherently inequitable; intellectuals can bask in the rosy glow of their emancipatory intents, secure in the presumption that knowledge and rationality will set us free to become wise and critical consumers, not unwitting dupes of the marketplace; and the already privileged maintain that status, since *their* children, but not those denied access to new technologies at school *or* at home, will develop technological knowledge and skills which, like it or not, are valued as indispensable, not only in the modern workplace, but indeed in the academy as well. This presumption that rational analysis fuels the engine of emancipation is doubly problematic, ignoring as it does the elements of power, pleasure, and desire so central to our relations to new technologies. The critical tale thereby removes from children of lesser privilege what might be their only opportunities to participate in a technological culture seen as a critically important route to decent jobs and higher education, thus entrenching existing inequalities in the name of emancipation.

Postmodernism: Ironic Tales about Computers as "Transformers . . . More than Meets the Eye"

Is there life after poststructuralism, and if so, what form might its institutionalization take? How may we carry on our critical and pedagogical practice under the pitiless gaze of deconstruction in particular, a doctrine that desanctifies our once sacred texts, destabilizes our secure hierarchies of authors and readers, classics and criticism, out of reliable relations, and demystifies our humanist vision of high cultural and moral purpose? With the cat so far out of the bag, what is our best strategy for survival? (Felperin, 1985, pp. 216–17)

Not so many years ago, any given Saturday morning of televiewing might find countless North American children watching with fascination their favorite cartoon heroes—Transformers—fight for their survival by endlessly de/reconstructing their embodied characteristics. Transformers assumed a myriad of features not satisfactorily accounted for by recourse to conventional binary categorization schemes purporting to enable a rational distinction between humans and machines. One might well argue that the Transformers characters satisfactorily incarnate a truly postmodern response to Turing's (1964) question, "Can machines think?"

Postmodernist accounts (see Barthes, 1977; Baudrillard, 1983; Derrida, 1978; Fraser, 1989) are discourses of montage, rupture, and dislocation. The fixed subjects (both human subjects and subject-matters) of modernist and critical discourses are rearticulated in new relations of displacement; images, ideas, and the like are deleted from their original context and the fragments reinserted into other contexts which they thereby disrupt. This has been criticized as engendering a species of paralysis or as excluding agency; or it can be represented as constituting a form of retooling, and hence, re-configuring, of praxis. A kind of ecologically sound "recycling" movement is the too-often overlooked real-world analog to postmodernism's primary implications for re-thinking pedagogy. We have characterized postmodern tales as "ironic" because, as the philosopher Richard Rorty (1989) has persuasively argued, irony seems a possible and plausible tentative relation to "truth" after a thorough-going deconstruction of all and any previously held notions of epistemological or ontological stability.

Any attempt to define 'postmodernism,' then, is necessarily at cross-purposes with its own discursive practices, which eschew all finite and self-confident attempts at constructing grand narratives, truths, or ontological schemes. As Hutcheon (1989) explains:

Perhaps this is an appropriate condition, for postmodernism is a phenomenon whose mode is resolutely contradictory as well as unavoidably political. . . . It seems reasonable to say that the postmodern's initial concern is to de-naturalize some of the dominant features of our way of life; to point out those entities that we unthinkingly experience as "natural" . . . are in fact "cultural"; made by us, not given to us. . . . Yet it must be admitted from the start that this is a strange kind of critique, one bound up, too, with its own complicity with power and domination, one that acknowledges that it cannot escape implication in that which it nevertheless still wants to analyze and maybe even undermine. (pp. 1–4)

Postmodern discourses about technology, then, deliberately blur "natural kind" boundaries like 'male and female,' 'teacher and student,' 'the natural and the artificial,' or 'person and machine.' Donna Haraway (1990) suggests paradigmatically that ". . . the boundary between science fiction and social reality is an optical illusion" (p. 191). She writes that

We are all chimeras, theorized and fabricated hybrids of machine and organism; in short, we are cyborgs. The cyborg is our ontology; it gives us our politics. The cyborg is a condensed image of both imagination and material reality, the two joined centers structuring any possibility of historical transformation. . . . This is an argument for pleasure in the confusion of boundaries and for responsibility in their construction. (p. 191)

It has been argued of late that postmodernism's main contribution to theories of "difference" has been the deconstruction of essentialist theories about sites of oppression in traditional theorizing (e.g., Belenky, Clinchy, Goldberger, and Tarule, 1986) as fundamentally raced, classed, and hence as politically unproductive (Bryson and de Castell, 1993; Bordo, 1990; Leach and Davies, 1990). Haraway's postmodern cyborg "women," by contrast, embody fractured identities that are contested on multiple sites of oppression, including age, race, and sexual orientation.

Haraway's somewhat abstract and obtuse allegory about cyborgs finds a "real-world" analog in the fascinating story of the now-famous Minitel service in France (De Lacy, 1989). Minitel, which is distributed free to French telephone subscribers, was designed in 1978 as the world's first electronic telephone directory. Although viewed as a useful information source, De Lacy argues that Minitel was not widely used in its first incarnation. However, when transformed in 1981 into a direct-dialogue messaging system, communicating via Minitel under an infinite range of assumed guises became an instant national obsession. The communicative opacity afforded by Minitel technology has allowed users to play with, deconstruct and reconstruct, the traditional constraints that shape face-to-face discourse, such as biological sex, social class, ethnicity, age, and body size. Minitel has also provided a direct means for members of traditionally marginalized groups, such as gays and lesbians, people living with AIDS or cancer, and the elderly, to form effective coalitions for political organization and action. De Lacy reports that Minitel has also provided a medium for the development of unique dialects, or "Minitel patois," thereby providing an accessible medium for the deliberate reconstruction of the French language, which has heretofore been strictly guarded as the purview of the elite Academie Francaise.

Postmodernist theorists (e.g., Gore, 1993; Lather, 1991; Luke and Gore, 1992) have of late challenged many of the axiomatic assumptions of critical theorists of education. Perhaps the most serious challenge has been to cast doubt on the implicit claim of critical theorists (e.g., Aronowitz and Giroux, 1991; Bowles and Gintis, 1976; Freire, 1971; or Giroux, 1981) that so-called liberatory and/or reflexive practices enable one to identify, and thereby to manipulate, the ideological bases of oppressive pedagogies. Elizabeth Ellsworth's (1989) "Why Doesn't this Feel Empowering? Working Through the Repressive Myths of Critical Pedagogy," describes her experience of the contradictions inherent in actively engaging with liberatory pedagogy as follows:

> Our classroom was the site of dispersing, shifting, and contradictory contexts of knowing that coalesced differently in different moments of student/professor speech, action, and emotion. This situation meant that individuals and affinity groups constantly had to change strategies and priorities of resistance against oppressive ways of knowing and being known. The antagonist became power itself as it was deployed within our classroom—oppressive ways of knowing and oppressive knowledges. (p. 322)

Ellsworth's and Haraway's accounts of shifting and unstable subjects do not lend themselves to easy extrapolations into the traditionally conservative and stable domain of educational computing. We may, however, make a preliminary attempt, extrapolating from research which, it must be noted, does not necessarily present itself in these terms.

Griffin and Cole (1987), for example, report results from a computer-mediated literacy project with minority children that offer promising insights into the ways in which technology can act as a catalyst for reconfiguring relations between children, tasks, and teachers in educational contexts. In this concluding section of the chapter, we treat that research as a species of postmodern tale and sketch out some of the perils and prospects of such a tale as these seem to follow from such critical analyses as Ellsworth's and, if far more generally, Foucault's.

The authors begin their account with a description of the well-documented findings of both unequal access to technology and an exclusive focus on low-level or "basic skills," which they term the "parts problem," characterizing both traditional literacy pedagogy and computer-supported instruction when these are provided to members of marginalized cultural groups, such as female students, working-class children, and ethnic minority students. Results from evaluation studies conducted since the arrival of computers in educational settings, they report, seem to indicate that (a) education is not thereby made more equally accessible to all parts of the population, and (b) some children's (that is, minority students') interactions with computers aren't ever getting to the more open-ended and challenging parts of complex tasks. Griffin and Cole argue that in order to address the "parts problem," educators need to abandon the notion that competencies can be hierarchically organized in terms of higher- and lower-order skills and the notion that each individual child has to master all aspects of a complex task in order to demonstrate competence. Rather, the authors "propose to admit many different first-level activities into computer use in schools" (p. 208) on the assumption that what are usually thought to be "lower-order" skills can serve "higher-order" purposes, depending on culturally and historically specific contextual conditions.

What we see here is an example of the kind of thinking characteristic of postmodernism, specifically, practices of appropriation and recycling, salvaging icons, images, and artifacts resurrected from within their original sociohistorical context, and reinserted into another context within which this "detritus" can take on a new, significantly greater cultural value (Thompson, 1979; Ulmer, 1983). It is a characteristically postmodern montage of previously unconnected events which we see instantiated in this pedagogic strategy, with its unprecedented and often unlikely juxtapositions of what, in its origins, might have been both scarce and highly valued with what, in its original context, might conversely have been at best commonplace, ordinary, and seemingly without value. As cigarette cards, green glass coke bottles, those dreadful melmac plates, and padded plastic covered tables and chairs in whose metal studded backs were the diamonds, clubs, hearts, and spades of playing cards are today found in exclusive furniture stores at phenomenally inflated prices, so, conversely, originally prized and costly commodities like turntables and self-correcting typewriters are today relegated to the trashcans of second-hand stores and junk dealers.

In the Griffin and Cole project, students who had been identified as being in the bottom 20 percent of their elementary school population were provided with computer supports for engaging in literacy activities that included real-time electronic mail dialogues with Italian pen-pals and written rap exchanges with same-age and adult interlocutors. The authors assert that the problems that surfaced during the implementation of these activities, such as code-switching between English, Spanish, and Italian or dealing with time differences between San Diego and Pistoia, actually contributed to the students' active engagement in these exchanges and to their sense of authorship or ownership of the discursive medium. They conclude by arguing that "discord may be harnessed for growth," and genres like rap, which might traditionally be dismissed as "street talk," can serve as valuable "beginning points that can be appropriated for the development of writing" (p. 229). Griffin and Cole conclude that this technology provides a means for reconstructing the division of labor in classroom tasks and for restructuring power relations between participants in educational contexts who typically occupy very unevenly positioned discursive roles with respect to power.

Even in the postmodern tale, notwithstanding its avowed intents to disrupt traditional hierarchies of skill, knowledge, and social/instructional power, there remains an implicit metanarrative of trials and failed attempts, as illustrated in Griffin and Cole's discussion of "low performance in a new mode." They report that, although children "playfully" reversed the "social power relations and discourse roles" between them and their adult interlocutor, "Nothing of substance was developed as a topic. . . ." But what their study also showed, and what they might perhaps more profitably have emphasized and explored, were the ways in which the technology made possible new forms of resistance, made it possible for students to reverse intended reversals, to refuse, to evaluate and judge adult performance, to criticize the thinly veiled authoritarianism of both the agendas they were set and the adult interlocutors charged with the responsibility of carrying these out. Griffin and Cole mention in passing that when the adult made designs by using nonalphabetic symbols (# : | %), the children entered the activity with great fluency and invented non-modeled strings. They also initiated this kind of play without invitation or instruction or request from the adults. It was only in response to an entirely meaningless set of coded symbols that students entered uninvited into the interaction, as if perhaps even educators' implicit metanarratives remained all too obvious to these students. Whether this is an inevitable failing of any "postmodern pedagogy" (Aronowitz and Giroux, 1991), given its unavoidable subordination to traditional educational purposes of "enlightenment," remains to be seen. Clearly, however, postmodern conceptions of the educative prospects of new technologies can effect a pedagogic variant of a Nietzschean "transvaluation of values" in a manner and to an extent nowhere considered with either technicist or critical accounts. If only for that reason, it seems a direction worth pursuing.

Concluding Thoughts: So/Now What?

Surveying the vast array of literature that is available today on the topic of educational technology reveals that there is a great deal more disagreement than consensus concerning the optimal purposes and uses of computers in educational contexts. This conflictual intellectual terrain, it turns out, poses significant problems for both researchers and for practitioners. Their respective problems, though rather different, are importantly related. Setting up a horse race between the truth value of competing accounts of the likely educational impact of educational computing and of the appropriate relations between computers and learners does not seem a particularly promising undertaking. Nor can differences in pedagogical methods or implementation strategies that issue from these various accounts be resolved by recourse to the kinds of empirical contrasts provided by traditional positivistic experimental studies. Rather, we have argued here that the divisive playing field of educational technology is populated by various teams telling altogether different "true stories" having quite different settings, characters, and plots, with very different impacts for both educational outcomes and appropriate relations. But they are telling these very different stories, it is essential to note, about the very same technology. Thus it becomes important to discover which tales are told in which classrooms and how student computer use is accordingly delimited, as much as it is important to discern what is—and dangerously so—common to all these accounts. As Foucault (1980) suggested, the purpose of theorizing is not to answer questions about truth and rightness, but rather to ask *how things could have come to be this way* and to try to discover, at any given moment, wherein lie the greatest dangers within the various discourses which are accepted and made to function as "true."

We have suggested here that there is *no* master narrative to be found or made in educational discourses about educational computing. There is no single true story, no grand synthesis. There is instead a *set* of stories, each with its distinctive scope and limits, each of which imposes, in different ways, a different system of constraints, prescriptions, and prohibitions, a different set of "limit situations" defining the boundaries beyond which teachers and learners cannot go. If it is indeed, as we've supposed, principally the constraints imposed upon educational technology by the stories that are told about it, and only secondarily the capacities and limitations inherent within the technology itself, which define and delimit how such technologies are used, then it follows that the greatest danger in research practice in educational computing is the danger of setting arbitrary limits and imposing premature closure on what can be done; that is to say, it is in normativizing *any* one particular account as "the account" and prescribing any particular set of practices as "the practices" appropriate to the educational use of computers. What is essential here is the recognition of the centrality of stories in contemporary discourses, both academic and practical, on educational technology. What we argue, therefore, is that it is the very fact of the unreflexive and uncritical telling of the tales themselves, whether told in school by teachers and learners, or out of school by policy makers and researchers, that confronts us with the greatest danger.

This is precisely because the efficacy and rhetorical appeal of the "true stories" told in relation to "solving" long-standing "educational problems" conceal their constitutive effects behind the emphatically present, visible, and seductive corpus of the technology itself.

What are the implications, then, of our "tale" for a reconstruction of the role of the "externally located" (Goodson & Mangan, 1991) researcher whose uniquely privileged role in the field of educational computing is defined in terms of the provision of resources in exchange for a normatively determined form of accountability—perhaps most importantly, the provision of the exclusive authority to construct definitive accounts? We have argued that the researcher is not to compose, like Scheherazade in her "ivory tower," endless stories of how educational technology ought to work—a thinly veiled activity of intellectual self-justification which in the end serves only to preconstrain and to limit what she is able to see. For that reason especially, she is not to believe the "true stories" that she herself recounts. But it is important to note here that admitting of the diversity, contingency, and constructedness of tales told about educational computing does not imply a kind of relativistic "separate but equal" notion that any old story will do. This is an explicit argument for rhetorical responsibility in the weaving of tales and for an ethics of narration with the focus squarely on the possibilities for agency and equity as these are enabled and constrained within particular "emplotments" (White, 1973).

Nor should researchers expect that teachers' or students' own stories correspond with theirs, and this in turn requires that researchers pay explicit and serious attention to which stories are accepted/acceptable by various groups within the educational field—teachers, administrators, journal editors, university-based tenure/promotions committees, boards and ministries of education—and which are denied, overlooked, or prohibited. As researchers, we need first of all to understand what it is that participants in educational settings are attempting to do before we can attempt to study how they are doing it. We need, that is, to become privy to their understandings and their intentions as these necessarily shape the actual public practices and outcomes which are accessible to and observable by the researcher. In the process of our own research, what has hitherto confounded our attempts to "make sense" of what we were seeing in classrooms and hearing from teachers has been the disparity between and among accounts, a disparity which this analytic device of implicit, embedded stories is gradually enabling us to understand and to work with.

We have found in our own research that, to this end, one useful exercise involves paying particular attention to accounts which (a) detail what has "failed" about educational innovation, and/or (b) are deemed by teachers and/or administrators to be educationally irrelevant, unsound, nonsense, inconceivable, extreme, biased, and the like. For to a large extent, this process of recognizing and rewarding only a subset of activities or accounts tells us at the same time both how 'success' is defined and why such definitions are arbitrary. What will count as failure from within a given story tells us, for example, what that story will exclude in terms of the prospective uses of that technology. And, perhaps most importantly, here it is that we see how educational technologies can become "technologies of normalization" and at what educational cost such normalization is achieved.

We suggest, then, that probably the most important job for researchers concerned to understand the scope and limits of the educational uses of technology is to seek out those stories that are not being circulated, to stop "making sense," to look for educational technology's version of Foucault's "subjugated knowledges" within which the complications, contradictions, and complexities of this new educational domain are most likely and most productively to be discerned. For it will most likely be in *these* tales, we suspect, that radically innovative possibilities for the transformation of hegemonic practices might best be found. But we will have to leave that story for another day. Perhaps novelist Jeanette Winterson (cited in Suleiman, 1990, p. 191) put it best when she wrote, "The vital thing is to have an alternative so that people will realize that there is no such thing as a true story."

CHAPTER 4

Computer Advertising and the Construction of Gender

MATTHEW WEINSTEIN

Introduction: Theory and Method

Responding to the often exuberant and downright utopian discourses around the impact of technology on society, Mary Ann Doane (1990, p. 163) notes,

> Although it is certainly true that in the case of some contemporary science fiction writers—particularly feminist authors—technology makes possible the destabilization of sexual identity as a category, there has also been a curious but fairly insistent history of representations of technology that work to fortify— sometimes desperately—conventional understandings of the feminine.

This chapter is an investigation into the "desperately" conventional understandings not only of femininity, but of masculinity as well, that are circulated by the computer industry. I wish to examine computers as technologies of gender using Teresa de Lauretis's semiotic theory (de Lauretis, 1987). Gender to de Lauretis is a representation that is carried out in our practices and our institutions. To her there are no essential characteristics of men and women apart from how science, law, art, theory, and common practices conceptualize them. Furthermore, to de Lauretis "the representation of gender *is* its construction." That is, gender, how we understand what attributes are masculine and what are feminine, is produced by the way that images of men and women are assembled. "[S]ocial technologies, such as cinema, and . . . institutionalized discourses, epistemologies, and critical practices, as well as practices of daily life" all produce gender, that is, they represent what constitutes being male and female, and as such they are "technologies of gender" (p. 2).

This chapter considers the home computer as a specific technology of gender. My question concerns how computers are represented in magazine advertisements as sites where masculinity and femininity are defined, that is, where women come to be identified with certain practices and men with others, and how these effects are related to those at other sites of gender production. On the one hand, computers are artifacts of the same patriarchal, capitalist society that fetishizes cars, women's bodies, and aerospace technology, and, at the same time, they are unique sites and signs of struggle, and their rules of use must be actively written anew.

My choice of *home,* rather than business, computing magazines was made because I hoped that the multiple representations of the home as a technology of sexuality and gender, for instance, as a site for heterosexual activity, as the site of women's unpaid labor, as man's castle, would lead to a richer semiotic field. In retrospect, I was wrong. The representations in these magazines are as conservative, if not more so, than those produced in other parts of the computer industry.

In my analysis I have focused on advertisements in two magazines: *PC Home Journal* and *Amiga World.* I have excluded looking at articles, in part because the ads provide a view of how the computer industry itself views the technology, whereas the articles represent a much broader coalition of computer hackers, publishers, and editors. My method has been to treat each ad as a syntagm, and I have used advertising handbooks to establish the paradigm from which each was formed (Kleppner, 1986; Nelson, 1985). I chose the ads I did because these most clearly linked the computer with gender.

My claim in this chapter is *not* that these representations lead directly to specific practices. Certainly gender is embodied in practices. This is the sense of Judith Butler's (1990) theory that gender is performance,[1] which does not contradict de Lauretis's fundamental proposition since performance is essentially a representation in action. Nevertheless, there is a diversity to practice that these representations do not communicate. Furthermore, practice, as many have noted, (de Certeau, 1984; Fiske, 1989b; Hebdige, 1988) is oppositional as well as compliant. Finally, there can be a sense within a community or individual that actions are not performances, that they are spontaneous and ephemeral embodiments that play to no audience. In this way, practice exceeds representation (or performance). This chapter is *not* about practice. Nor is it a representation of practice, that is, an ethnography. It is instead an examination of static representation itself. My purpose is to examine the discourse that floats above and behind the practices that men and women actually engage in.

But this study of advertising reveals more than just background noise before which practice plays in apparent disregard. It reveals how products and practices are linked with anxiety and desire. And while some reject the connections, others accept them uncritically. For some consumers the links are harmonious and for other dissonant.

This break between discourse and practice also reemphasizes de Lauretis's distinction between men and women and Man and Woman (p. 2), the latter being the abstract categories in which membership by real people is doubtful. In examining representation I am focusing on the latter binary pair in an attempt to see how the categories reflect and refract their definitions in other quarters.

Before carrying out the analysis, some caveats need to be made about the limits of this study, especially concerning the lack of consideration of class and race. Race, for instance, has a significantly different representation from representations of gender in these magazines. Whereas masculine and feminine are set against each other in the images I studied, whiteness is projected as the world *tout court,* that is, these magazines embody Richard Dyer's conceptualization of whiteness, which is ". . . to be everything and nothing" (1988, p. 45). In these magazines whiteness is everything in that there are *no* images of people of other races, and it is nothing in that, to the great majority of white Americans, this glaringly racist construction would go unnoticed.

Given this disclaimer, the conclusions that I reach need to be tempered. First, the masculinities and femininities that these magazines engineer are specifically for whites of the managerial class. This can be seen in the conflation of play and work seen in these constructions of masculinity. As Basil Bernstein notes in his discussion of the *new* middle class, "In essence, play is work and work is play. . . . [F]or certain subgroups of the middle class, work and play are weakly classified and weakly framed. For these subgroups, no strict line may be drawn between work and play" (Bernstein, 1977, p. 122). Second, the computer industry is conceptualizing minorities as being absent, that is, that nonwhites should not use computers as props in identity formation, and that their identity is unspecifically being represented as not tied to the computer. Certainly, what I describe here in no way captures the multiple masculinities and femininities that circulate in our society and that fragment along these and other axes of power.

Finally, I want to clarify my reason for carrying out this analysis. I am interested in using semiotics and this sort of interrogation of images to disassemble and reveal the politics of my own desires as an expert computer user. In trying to sort out what might be reappropriated from the technology in the cause of democratic struggles, I want to come to understand how unwittingly I have become a part of practices that reproduce hierarchy. This sort of deconstruction is aimed at accomplishing just those ends.

Gender and Cybernetics

Men and masculinity are the constant presence of home computing magazines. Despite attempts in the articles that fill these magazines to include images of wives and daughters, it is sons, fathers, and men detached from family that fill the advertising pages.

Masculinity is constructed in two ways in these ads: through images of men and through the construction of the reader as a male viewer. The former is accomplished through ads that generally show men using the technology. By portraying only men as actively engaged with the technology, an identification is established in which masculinity becomes the engagement. But these ads also interpellate their audience as male by the use of women as passive objects.

1. Men Children in the Promised Land

Spectrum HoloByte's advertisement presents the most bold example of how masculinity is produced. This ad appears in the most hallowed spot in the magazine, inside the front cover (see Figure 4.1). The advertisement is expertly designed, keeping a constant tension between a formal balance in which objects on the left side of the center line are symmetrically offset by objects on the right side—the green plant balances the green clock, the game player balances the computer screen, the keyboard balances the mouse, and the face balances the foot of the conquered—while simultaneously creating a sense of motion through the use of informal balance created by (1) the displacement of the photo from the center of the two-page ad, (2) the misalignment of the optical center of the photo with the optical center of the page, and (3) the strong diagonals made by the half-height partitions. Two men are playing a game against each other. One of them has won by destroying the other's plane, not only in cyberspace, but in the physical space as well, leaving the trash can burning and the computer destroyed. The man who has been vanquished and is falling out of his seat, his computer left in rubble, is a strong, handsome, probably younger employee. The victor is double-chinned, his hair and skin are darker, and nose and cheeks are not as romanesque as the loser's. The victor stares at us with his face in a childish grin, oddly out of place for the sterile office environment. The ad is unique among game ads in using explicitly gendered language. While most game ads are clearly directed at men, usually their language strives at gender neutrality. But, as Spectrum HoloByte says, "It's no longer *man* vs. machine. It's you against them." What follows the headline implodes friendship and enmity, which is a significant mark of masculinity as constructed here. Thus in these games you will be "smashing your friends off the track," "smoke your enemy in Falcon 3.0," "blow 'em to smithereens," and "commanding an M-1 Tank and *firing* on someone. . . ." This firing is significant since the victor in the picture clearly wishes that his opponent were fired (the pun being picked up again by the

Figure 4.1. Masculinity as Play
Reprinted courtesy of Spectrum HoloByte, Inc. All rights reserved.

burning trash can). R. W. Connell has noted that violence is "implicit in the physical construction of hegemonic masculinity" (1987, p. 86). This is the hyperreal (Baudrillard, 1983) version of the ritual Connell describes of boys in South London hitting each other with vigor when they are in their friendship peer group. But the violence has been removed from the physical power of the body, permitting a group of men who have lacked the muscle power to exercise masculine violence in the real to exercise it in the cyberreal.[2] Thus, in this ad the more handsome and physically endowed is destroyed by the nerdish hero with whom we are to identify, hence the comradely glance to us, the reader. In giving access to traditional masculinity to this new group of men, what constitutes skill and power is redefined/remapped into the hyperreality of cyberspace. Thus the traditional whole-body physique needed to crush an opponent in football or war is translated to the slightest gestures of the hand. This collapse of physical activity to simulation is part of an entire postmodern elision of the real and cyberreal that runs throughout the ad. ("You'll experience *real* competition," ". . . down the streets of San Francisco against a *real* opponent!" ". . . games so *realistic* they're used in *actual* flight training *simulations*.")

The concept of play is also important in the conception of cybermasculinity. Just as friend/enemy and space/cyberspace are collapsed, so are the categories of work and play. Here in the setting of work is play, and the walls are adorned with signs of other games. Whereas many men bring their work home, which for them is the site for leisure at the expense of the women in their lives (either by hire, slavery, or marriage) these men have brought their leisure to work. But again playing the game is also accomplishing the work of eliminating competition among themselves.

Finally, this blurring of play and work is part of a larger blurring between children and adults. The game promises for men perpetual childhood. The absurd grin on the victor's face is one sign of this. These games are continuous with the ones marketed to children in their emphasis on mixing violence with skill. What childhood computer games promise is both physical power and a world in which to exercise it; in the adult world the physical power remains contained within the machine, though the world in which to exercise it has become dangerously real, most ominously in techno-nuclear weaponry.[3]

2. The Cybernetic Gaze

In the last section I analyzed how masculinity is constructed by the representation of men in ads. Masculinity and femininity are more complexly and oppositionally constructed through the images of women in computer advertising in that an understanding of how gender is produced requires not only an analysis of the syntagm of the advertisement but also of how the advertisement works to position its reader.

John Berger (1972) notes that "Men look at women. Women watch themselves being looked at. This determines not only most relations between men and women but also the relation of women to themselves" (p. 47). The power/pleasure men gain by viewing is exercised ubiquitously from the street to the film. de Lauretis quotes Laura Mulvey describing classical narrative film: "[Woman] is isolated, glamorous, on display, sexualized. But as the narrative progresses she falls in love with the main male protagonist and . . . her eroticism is subjected to the male star alone" (p. 99). de Lauretis adds that "the apparatus of looks converging on the female figure integrates voyeurism into the conventions of storytelling, combining a direct solicitation of the scopic drive with the demands of plot conflict, climax, and resolution" (p. 99). This process is two way; male exercise of gaze constructs films as sites for male voyeurism, but film also constructs audiences as male voyeurs. That is, it counts on the practice of men looking "at women."

As computers become increasingly capable of manipulating images in sophisticated ways for little expense, the gender construction of the technology increasingly becomes tied to how women are used as objects of glamour. A key question in understanding computers as a technology that produces gender is understanding how manufacturers represent technology as extending the gaze. Bill Nichols notes that "cybernetic interaction emphasizes the *fetishist* rather than the fetish objects" (1988, p. 32). The power has been magnified by the computer so that the emphasis shifts from looking to reconstructing images. This puts the computer user in control of the script and staging of what is seen. There is a "(predominantly masculine) fascination with the control of simulated interactions [that] replaces a (predominantly masculine) fascination with the to-be-looked-at-ness of projected image."

One genre of software that has appeared in the American underground over the last ten years is computer pornography. This includes static pornographic images that can be altered in "paint" programs like Adobe Photo Shop and more explicit simulations like MacPlaymate in which the user "interacts" with the pornographic images.[4]

Many manufacturers of video/computer interfaces take advantage of the desire by men to use the machine to manipulate images of women, that is, many manufacturers of screens and other computer-video equipment exploit the gaze in hawking their wares. For instance, in an ad for Colorburst, a video board/image control package, several images, presumably produced by this package, are shown in a column. The central image features a glamorized woman who has turned towards the camera, thus offering herself to us as an object of possession. Onto this image has been scanned the image of a man, probably the user of the computer, with his arm leaning forward so that it appears that he is touching her and causing her to turn. There is something both aggressive and possessive in his gesture. The user of the computer has rewritten the text so that the woman becomes explicitly his property. (The fact that this is a scanned image is dramatically emphasized by placing it right below an image [same ad] that integrates a picture of Ben Franklin, a fractal landscape, and a photo of the moon.) The promise of this ad is that the technology will permit us, the male viewer, to share in this power over the image and over women. Masculinity, the power to look without being looked at, is actively constructed in this ad. The viewer of the ad is assumed to be masculine, that is, is assumed to want to participate in violating women, or at least women's images.

This construction of the viewer is made even more explicit in the ad for the Video Toaster, a technology that has *made* the market for the Amiga computer in large part (a computer represented explicitly as feminine by its name). This product allows images to be captured and manipulated from video (see Figure 4.2). Where the Colorburst ad crudely uses the computer as a stage for white het-male fantasy, here a *relatively* sophisticated construction is made with the viewer "out of sight." The male voyeur, however, is made explicit reference to. The O of toaster, in the product logo, contains a man's eye staring out. Hence the camera is constructed as masculine; the user of the computer, masculine; the computer, feminine; the image, feminine.

This is a copy-heavy ad that scatters little micro-images off the Video Toaster throughout the text, which is divided into three columns. Two images sit in the optical center of the page. First, going from left to right, we see a weather woman, already a glamorized image, taken supposedly off a live newscast. In case the image of the weather woman is too neutral, it is placed side by side with a picture of an F-15 fighter bomber, also from the Video Toaster; this links the coercion implied in masculinity with heterosexual desire. Two additional images appear mixed with the text. Each is a demonstration of how the face of the weatherwoman can be manipulated with this technology. On the left, we see her face multiplied 9 times, filling the screen. On the right, keeping the formal balance of the ad, is her face transformed into a psychedelic topographic map.

Scattered through the ad are subheadlines and tiny one- or two-sentence amplifications extolling the technical power of the Toaster to manipulate images. The amplification for subheadline 7 (Toaster Digital Video Effects), for instance, states: "[t]he Toaster lets you warp, spin, zoom, trail, and squeeze any of four live video sources in real-time and in 24–bit color." The emphasis is on technical power, which is again being sold as part of the masculine regime.

Figure 4.2. Masculinity as Voyeurism
Reprinted courtesy of NewTek, Inc. All rights reserved.

Finally in the action to take ("Call now for the Video Toaster Demo Tape & See for yourself!") explicit reference is made to classical film and the role of the starlet as an object of desire. "See the incredible results possible with the Video Toaster. *Starring NewTek's own Kiki Stockhammer,* and featuring animation by 3D artist and LightWave programmer Allen Hastings. Like the Toaster itself, this videotape will knock your socks off." Ms. Stockhammer is marked strongly as female by the fact that, unlike Allen Hastings, she has no credentials that would indicate why she is in the video tape other than that she is the property of NewTek corporation.

In the cybermasculinity of the Video Toaster, the voyeuristic gaze of film is given the power to transform its object. Through the technology the male user can force captured images to enact his fantasies in a way that no previous technology has enabled. The violence between men, made real in the cyberspace created by Spectrum HoloByte, is recoded by the Toaster into the violence that men exercise against women. What holds constant is the extension of skill through the technology and the exercise of violence which marks the dominant construction of masculinity.

3. Femininity as Silence, as Object

The prevalent images of women in these magazines portray them on a screen as an object, as in the Video Toaster and the Colorburst ads, but even these glamorized, manipulated images of women are rare. The primary construction of women is as an absence. Even the simplest measure, a head count of images of men and women in these magazines, highlights this fact: there are fifty-nine images of men in the main part of the magazine, compared to sixteen of women, and this count tells us nothing about how the images of men and women differ in construction and use; for example, the three images of the weatherwoman are counted in those sixteen.

The absence of images of women in these magazines is viciously ironic. Since most users of computers are clerical workers (seven to ten million) and 80 percent of them are women, in fact, more women use computers than do men (Machung, 1988). Those women, however, are not using the computers to manipulate text, images, or information for their own pleasure or profit. Instead they are often manipulated through the technology, like the images on the screen, by their male supervisors. In Shoshona Zuboff's (1984) *In the Age of the Smart Machine*, a study of how computers have changed the nature of work, for instance, the sites where computers were most aggressively and explicitly used to control workers were those where women comprised the majority of the work force. These gendered labor relations become sort of a sadistic, hyperreal Video Toaster: women being manipulated by computers while being remotely monitored by their male employers.

These advertisements are actively re-presenting, if not constructing, a world that excludes women. This effort on the part of computer manufacturers to re-create a boys club suggests that a reexamination is needed of studies that blame women, as not having been socialized the right way, for their failure to "love the machine." These cultural deprivation studies, such as Sherry Turkle's article *Computational Reticence: Why Women Fear The Intimate Machine* (1988), fail to examine how constructions of masculinity and femininity work together to exclude women, and how practices of male hackers objectify women to the point of identifying women with the machines they use, such as the Amiga computer.

4. Femininity as Lobotomy

Given the few images of women that exist in computer magazines, those that do appear take on an excessively powerful significance. One of the few non-digitized images of women is in the ad for DesignWorks by New Horizons. The layout is a picture window, but the picture is of some cybernetic space in which photographic (real) images are mixed with computer graphic (cyber real) images. In front of a uniform black background are shapes in bright computer colors: vivid reds, greens, and blues. The shot of the woman's face holding a tight-lipped smile is in bright, cheerful colors. A trail of circles runs in an S from the lower-left corner through her hoop earring, by the optical center to a point at the top of the woman's head which is off (optical) center. The last circle is on a computer screen, and has been transformed into the New Horizons logo (a red sphere floating in a computer-generated landscape), its shadow and glare having been added using the graphics program. The headline is right justified in the window and declares, "Unleash the artist within— No natural talent required." Like the Spectrum HoloByte ad, the copy is placed to the right of the picture window. The first part of the text stresses the artistic capabilities of the program and the simplicity of its interface; the end stresses the technical capabilities of the program.

The primary discourse that saturates this ad is one of *Woman as idiot*. The point is made in the headline: "No natural talent required." The woman's lobotomized smile, reminiscent of the first image in the film *Killing Us Softly* of the perfect image of Woman, restates visually the headline. The point is driven home by the fact that the graphic image is shown popping out of her head like Athena fully grown: no keyboard, no mouse, no effort needed. The text restresses the Woman's lack of skill by placing its emphasis on the "simplicity" and "ease-of-use" of the program; again, technical details are listed last.

Significantly, what this Woman lacks is artistic skills. Her aspirations are

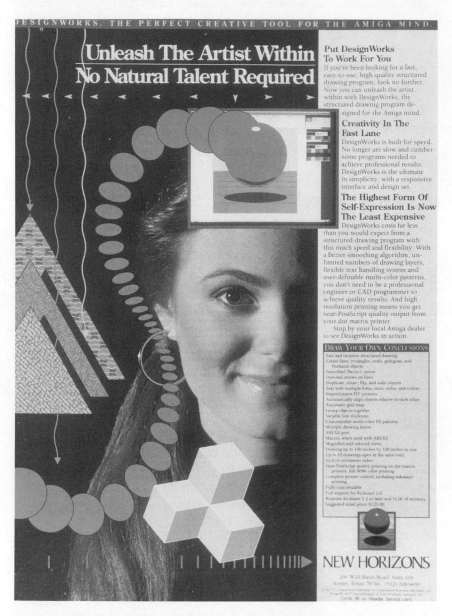

Figure 4.3. Feminity as Vacuousness
Reprinted courtesy of Steve Cockwell. All rights reserved.

reemphasized by her all-black attire (people in black, a.k.a. pibs, are known to have artistic souls) and huge hoop earring, which complements her pib attire. Unfortunately, as the headline implies, her muse is leashed within, she has no natural talent.

Thus the technology is presented as saving the Woman from herself. It possesses the talent she lacks. When the first subheadline says, "Put Design-Works To Work For You," the suggestion is that the program will proceed automatically. In reality, unfortunately, the talent must lie with the user of the program, though the specific nature of the skills needed may have been altered by the technology. The representation that the machine and not the user embodies the needed skills ironically parallels management fantasies that computer automation would do away with the need for a skilled work force (Noble, 1984). In fact, those fantasies could never be realized, just as using the computer as a design tool does not obviate the need for talent.

The implication that women would use this for artistic rather than technical work recreates the traditional male-mechanical female-expressive dichotomy.[5] This linking of femininity with emotional/artistic expression, together with the representation of the technology as providing the missing feminine skill, constructs femininity almost identically to the way in which the Spectrum HoloByte ad constructs masculinity. Where in that ad men without physical prowess were able to gain it through the computer, here women without artistic talent are able to have the machine exercise it for them remotely. Both ads suggest that the technology gives access to traditional forms of gender capital to those who lack the physical/natural ability to express it. However, the differences in the two ads are equally significant. For men the technology *enables* action and physical prowess, for women it acts *for* them in the area of emotional/artistic skill, further constructing femininity as passive.

To understand how this ad functions paradigmatically, consider briefly the syntagm of the Canvas 3 by Deneba Software, a similar type of drawing program. Without exploring the layers and details of this ad, one can see that it is striving for a masculine appeal with its racing-car mentality and violent imagery ("Blow the doors off the competition"). In many ways the ads are inversions of each other—even the layout of the text is reversed left and right. Where the DesignWorks ad starts with descriptions of ease of use and ends with a list of its features, the Canvas 3 ad stresses power first, through a detailed description of its features, and ends with the statement, "It's incredibly easy to use. . . ." Furthermore, there is nothing in the Canvas 3 ad to imply that the user lacks talent. Instead it is implied that the program has the incredible power to match and enhance the skill of the person using it. "Why drive some sedate sedan when you can own the road. . . ?" This program promises

Figure 4.4. Masculinity as Competence
Reprinted courtesy of Deneba, Inc. All rights reserved.

not to do the drawing for you, but to give you the power to do the drawing.

The contrast between these two ads, then, is the difference between a construction of a masculine and feminine reader, one with power and skill, and one without either. As R. W. Connell has noted, the link between skill and masculinity is tight, to the point that femininity lands up being defined as the lack of skill. "Prowess . . . becomes a means of judging one's degree of masculinity" (1987, p. 85).

The two ads also point up how the technology is constructed differently for men and women (just as women and men themselves are so constructed). For men the computer is a tool that enhances their power. For women it is a machine that possesses the skills they lack.

Conclusion

This analysis is not meant to detail the entire construction of femininity and masculinity in computer advertising. Among the images that I have chosen not to deal with here are those of women as managers which have appeared in advertisements for products from companies with women CEO's, such as MacConnection, T/Maker and and SoftView. To my knowledge, this genre has only appeared in Mac magazines; it is certainly absent in these home computing magazines. More remarkable are the advertisements that invert the male gaze—again I have only seen these in Mac magazines. One such ad for a scanner shows a woman's hand holding a photo of a hyperdeveloped male body (head cropped) about to be scanned into the computer for her own cyber porno pleasure.

The images I have analyzed, however, are salient ones. They represent the largest genres of gender representation in the magazines I examined. These images show the ways that computers are conceptualized as absurdly conservative in regard to their construction of masculinity and femininity. First, constructions of Man and Woman are wholesale transfers from other discourses, or in another light, these are merely extensions of the gendered discourses that exist around other technologies, such as film and weaponry. Second, computers are represented as tools which allow men who have been excluded from the dominant form of masculinity to partake of it, be it male/male or male/female violence, and allow women, in a far more limited way, to have access to the artistic aspects of femininity with which they may not be "naturally" endowed. Third, the user-of-the-computer (reader-of-the-magazine) is taken to be white and, to a lesser degree, male. Even when women are constructed as the audience of the magazine, they are not shown using the technology. Instead it is implied that they are feeble-minded and lacking in technical know-how.

Finally, returning to the metaphor of gender as performance, these ads can be seen as providing more than just hardware and software. They are providing props and, more importantly, scripts, which allow men and women to distinguish themselves from each other. But in advocating these particular scripts, the industry is also advocating the use of the computer as a tool to maintain male hegemony and to manipulate women. As Zuboff has shown, these performances are realized in regular business practices; computers are used by male managers as panopticonal tools to monitor the work and bodies of women. In a larger consumer market, computers promise to men, on the one hand, the ability to manipulate and sexualize, if not actually to engage in sex with images of women, and on the other, to annihilate and murder, and to women, only further marginalization.

Classroom Practices:
Pedagogy and Power in Action

"I Like Computers, But Many Girls Don't": Gender and the Sociocultural Context of Computing[1]

BRAD R. HUBER and
JANET WARD SCHOFIELD

It seems more logical to call them *computadoras* [feminine form for 'computers'] than *computadores* [masculine] in light of the subtle and mysterious enchantment found in all feminine words.[2]

—Alvaro Montoya Gomez, author of
"El eterno feminino," an article
that appeared in a Costa Rican
computer journal (1990:22)

Introduction

This paper examines differences in the way boys and girls think about and use computers at Escuela San Juan,[3] a Costa Rican primary school. Students at Escuela San Juan generally have positive attitudes toward LOGO programming, computers, and the computer lab. However, girls as a group like LOGO less, are less confident of their ability to use computers, and are more anxious about the lab environment than boys. Student competition in the lab, stereotypes about programming, the level of assistance students receive, and amount of prior computer experience are related to these gender differences in attitudes.

San Juan's "computer culture" is best understood within the broader context of pervasive gender-linked stereotypes and social patterns found at this school and in Costa Rican society at large. As is the case with cultures around the world (Williams and Best, 1982), the idea that males and females have different personalities and aptitudes is fairly widespread in Costa Rica. These gender stereotypes are transmitted by socialization practices, the radio, television, popular magazines, school textbooks, and other means. They shape patterns of political office holding, familial roles, occupational choice, and scientific and technical training.

In this chapter, anthropology's holistic perspective is used to understand the complex ways in which these variables are interconnected and interrelated (see Mehan, 1989; Motherwell, 1988; Papert, 1987; Turkle, 1984; Turkle and Papert, 1990). It is clear that student attitudes toward computers are profoundly influenced by the cultural and social forces mentioned above. Moreover, this study suggests that the computer labs in Costa Rica's schools may help to maintain and reproduce this country's gender status quo.

The research reported below has a number of theoretical, methodological, and practical implications. First, our work represents an effort to determine whether theory and findings based upon research undertaken primarily in the United States generalize to a somewhat different cultural setting. As Huberman (1987:12) found, research conducted in the United States may be "right on the nose" in helping to elucidate certain phenomena in other cultures but prove to be unproductive in others. Second, journals such as the *Logo Exchange* give every indication that educational computing programs similar to Costa Rica's will have a significant impact on students in Latin America. Social scientists, educators, and policy makers who are developing and implementing programs for these students may find our work useful for practical reasons. Third, previous research on gender and attitudes toward computers has for the most part been exclusively quantitative. This research has been very fruitful. Frequent reference is made to it as well as to a quantitative time allocation study and survey research conducted at a second Costa Rican primary school. Nevertheless, the qualitative research undertaken at Escuela San Juan allows us to "flesh out," evaluate, and clarify previous explanations for gender-related differences in this domain.

This paper is organized in the following manner. First, the research methods employed in the study reported here are discussed. This is followed by an overview of Costa Rica's educational computing program in primary schools and the sociocultural context in which it is embedded. The main body of the paper examines in detail the attitudes San Juan's girls and boys have toward LOGO and some of the reasons girls have less positive attitudes than boys. The conclusion discusses the findings and the more general conceptual and pragmatic issues they raise.

Research Methods

Escuela San Juan is a twenty-five year old public primary school located in a working and middle class suburban neighborhood in the city of Heredia.

Heredia, with a population of approximately 79,500 people (Trejos, 1991, p. 243), is one of three small cities surrounding San Jose, Costa Rica's capital. There are approximately 945 students who attend this school's morning and afternoon sessions. Ethnically, almost all of San Juan's students and teachers identify themselves as white. Thirty-three teachers, twenty-nine of whom are women, teach kindergarten and grades 1–6. The school has a male principal.

San Juan's students started using the Spanish version of LOGOWRITER during the fall of 1989, approximately seven months before research was begun. LOGOWRITER (Version 2.01) has both programming and word processing capabilities. Some of the most capable older students develop fairly sophisticated projects that combine color graphics, animation, and text, such as representations of the hydrological cycle with clouds, rain, mountains, and the sun; diagrams of different types of triangles with accompanying descriptive captions. Younger, less accomplished students create simple geometric forms, houses, flowers, cars, and soccer fields.

In general, students are given considerable freedom to develop projects of their choice (Aguilar, Alvarado, Calderón, Fallas, Hernández, Pereira, Ramírez, and Vargas, 1989; Chacón, 1989). During the course of working on LOGO projects, it is hoped that students will become familiar with the computer and some of its applications, acquire a positive attitude toward science and technology, better understand mathematics, the sciences, and Spanish, and develop new reasoning and problem-solving skills. Learning to program in LOGO is seen as a means to achieve these goals rather than as an end in itself (Badilla-Saxe, 1991; Fonseca, 1991, 42, p. 75).

San Juan's LOGO lab has twenty computers. Generally, the thirty to forty students in the lab work in pairs. The students' lab work is facilitated by a lab teacher and their regular classroom teacher. Typically, the lab teacher introduces new LOGO commands to students during the initial five to ten minutes of class. Afterwards, students enter their passwords into the computer and begin programming. They are allowed to work at their own pace, though the teachers do reprimand students when they are making little or no progress on their projects.

During the summer of 1990, the first author observed student-teacher and peer interactions at Escuela San Juan. Computer labs and classrooms were observed four days a week for eight weeks. On each of these days, one eighty-minute session in the computer lab was observed. A kindergarten, second, fourth, and sixth grade class were selected for observation. In addition, the same groups of students were observed once each week for eighty minutes in their regular classrooms, where they learned about mathematics, Spanish, and the natural and social sciences. Field notes on lab and classroom interactions were made at the time they were being observed. These notes were written up in expanded form one to three hours after each observation.

In addition, semi-structured interviews were administered in Spanish to San Juan's three lab teachers, and to six sixth grade and six fourth grade students. Three boys and three girls were interviewed from each grade. An additional sixth grade boy who assisted a lab teacher with one or two classes each week was also interviewed. According to other students and the lab teachers, the students who were interviewed were among the best programmers at San Juan. The criteria used to select these students included: (1) the boys and girls should be roughly comparable with respect to their level of programming proficiency, and (2) their attitudes must be solidly grounded in experience.

The majority of the students interviewed came from middle-class households, consistent with the preponderance of middle-class students in the student body. Although the sample of students interviewed here is too small to permit meaningful comparisons between students from different social class backgrounds, it is striking that the gender-linked patterns discussed in the later part of this paper were very apparent in the interview data, since scholars have noted that the *machismo-marianismo* complex, a constellation of gender-related stereotypes and behaviors discussed in more detail below, appears to be somewhat less pronounced among the middle than the working class (Biesanz, Biesanz, and Biesanz, 1988, pp. 96–97, 108; Méndez Barrantes, 1988, p. 40).

Clear and consistent patterns emerged upon analysis of the lab observations and interviews. San Juan's girls and boys think about and use computers differently. This conclusion, derived from analysis of the qualitative data gathered at San Juan, is also consistent with quantitative data collected during a ten-week period in 1992 at Escuela Pérez, another primary school in Heredia with the same program and very similar facilities (Huber and Scaglion, 1995). At Escuela Pérez, a time allocation study was undertaken to determine how lab and regular classroom teachers allocate their time with computer lab students. Four groups of fifth graders and five groups each of first, second, third, fourth, and sixth graders were observed in the lab. Observations of teacher-student interactions were made every five minutes for each of the twenty-nine groups, for a total of 388 observations. Student attitudes toward LOGO programming and Escuela Pérez's lab environment were also investigated by administering a questionnaire to 262 students: two groups each of third, fourth, fifth, and sixth graders. Although a detailed report on the complete findings of this study is beyond the scope of this paper, some reference will be made to this study when it clarifies issues that arose at San Juan.

Costa Rica's *Programa de Informatica Educativa*

Democracy, peace, and education have long been cherished in Costa Rica, a small Central American nation of approximately three million people. "We have more teachers than soldiers" was frequently heard even before Costa Rica's armed forces were officially abolished in the late 1940s (Biesanz et al., 1988, p. 9). By the mid-1980s, a large percentage of children regularly completed nine years of schooling, and many new public and private schools and universities with modern facilities were operating in rural and urban areas (Pacheco, 1986; Wahab, 1983, p. 2). Costa Rica engages 27 percent of its population as teachers and students, assigns a sizable proportion of its national budget to public education, and has a 93 percent literacy rate (Asociación Demográfica Costarricense, 1984; Biesanz et al., 1988, pp. 114, 220; Institute of International Education, 1986, p. 34; *The Tico Times*, 1989, p. 21).

The integration of computers into the primary school curriculum is one of the most visible ways in which Costa Rica is attempting to enhance its educational system (Biesanz et al., 1988, p. 220; Wahab, 1983, p. 4). After Oscar Arias Sanchez became president in 1986, Costa Rica began to create computer labs in nearly two hundred of its primary schools. Its educational computing program,[4] known as the Programa de Informática Educativa, is financed through private enterprise and national and international agencies, supported by Costa Rica's Ministry of Education, and coordinated by the private, nonprofit Fundación Omar Dengo (FOD). It is under the tutelage of Seymour Papert, a leading figure in computers and education, and developer of LOGO (Dyer, 1988, p. 12; Fonseca, 1991, pp. 69–84).

In 1988, computer labs of twenty IBM PS-2 computers were set up in sixty primary schools. An additional seventy labs were established by 1990. Thirty more are scheduled for the near future. When the third set of laboratories are in place, computers will be located throughout the country and be accessible to 134,500 students—32 percent of the elementary school population[5] (Chen Quesada, 1992; Fonseca, 1991, p. 55; Harper, 1991, p. 43; *La Nación*, 6 July 1992, p. 8A).

Gender Roles in Costa Rica:
Escuela San Juan's Sociocultural Context

In Costa Rica, male and female roles and relationships are strongly influenced by the machismo-marianismo complex. Machismo is the belief that males will excel in intellectual matters and dominate social relationships involving the opposite sex. Males are often characterized as dominant, authoritative, rational, independent, and interested in politics, sports, mathematics, and science. Marianismo refers to female submissiveness and superiority in spiritual and moral matters. Women are frequently seen as soft, sweet, obedient, intuitive, interested in the home and child care, compassionate, pious, decent, and pure (Biesanz et al., 1988, p. 90; Méndez Barrantes, 1988, pp. 36–37; Romero, Osorio, Piza, Crespo, León, and Montero, 1986, pp. 44, 170).

These gender stereotypes are transmitted in many ways. Men and women are often portrayed in a manner consistent with the images described above in Costa Rican radio programs, television shows, commercials, popular magazines, and programs and materials developed by governmental and non-governmental agencies. Gender stereotypes are also found in primary school textbooks. Over 70 percent of school book illustrations and textual material is devoted to male historical figures, professionals, scientists, and technicians. Women most often appear as teachers or housewives; illustrations of girls playing house or with dolls are also common. Stereotyping is found in textbooks for all elementary school grades but is most evident in fourth, fifth, and sixth grade books (Abramovay, Ramírez Quirós, and Damasco Figueredo, 1991, pp. 83, 229–44; González Suárez, 1988a, pp. 603–07, 1988b, pp. 19–22; Quirós and Larrain, 1977, p. 78).

Popular computer magazines available in Costa Rica also often portray women and girls using computers in a stereotypical manner. In July 1992, Costa Rica's two largest retailers of books and magazines (La Universal and Librería Lehmann) sold titles familiar to those interested in computing in the United States, such as *PC Magazine*, *BYTE*, *PC World*, and *Personal Computing*. Relatively recent studies of such computing magazines, including *BYTE* and *Personal Computing*, have concluded that women appear in illustrations with computers less frequently than men, and when they do appear, they are often depicted as clerical workers and sex objects. In contrast, men are more often depicted as managers, experts, technicians, and in active "hands-on" roles. These studies conclude that students, teachers, and parents who read these magazines are likely to come to associate the use of computers with males (Demetrulias and Rosenthal, 1985, p. 93; Levin and Gordon, 1989, p. 86; Sanders and Stone, 1986, p. 7; Ware and Stuck, 1985, pp. 211–13).

The placement of these magazines in Costa Rica's book stores reflects this association. For example, at Librería Lehmann they are found next to magazines dealing with cars, stereo equipment, electronics, science, skin diving, and model building, rather than near magazines on topics such as cooking, sewing, and parenting, clearly reflecting the retailer's association of computers with males.

Gender stereotypes influence many kinds of behavior, such as political office holding and occupational choices, with men in Costa Rica typically being much more likely to hold positions of power and authority. Although Costa Rica recently had a female vice president and a female president of its Legislative Assembly, men continue to hold most political posts. From 1953 to 1986, 91–99 percent of the fifty-seven deputies in the Legislative Assembly were men. A similar level of male office holding is found in Costa Rica's political parties, municipal councils, and community associations (Hernández, 1990–91, p. 125; Méndez Barrantes, 1985, p. 42; 1988, p. 41; Romero et al., 1986, pp. 191–94).

Turning to occupations, we find that over 75 percent of women are classified as housewives. Of the approximately 25 percent classified as economically active in 1980 (that is, female wage earners), most worked in personal services (such as cooks, maids, waitresses, janitors, seamstresses) or were employed as primary and secondary school teachers, nurses, typists, secretaries, beauticians, and hairdressers. The average wage earned by women is substantially less than that earned by men, even when men and women perform the same work (Abramovay et al., 1991, pp. 49, 60; Casasola, Morera, and Obando, 1983, pp. 32–33; González Suárez, 1977, p. 32; Guzmán, 1983, pp. 14–16; Méndez Barrantes, 1985, pp. 41–42; Romero et al., 1986, pp. 196–97).

A similar pattern is found in Costa Rica's educational system. Most preschool (98 percent), primary school (79 percent), and secondary school teachers (54 percent) are women. Higher paying and more prestigious roles in the educational system, such as university professors and administrators, primary and secondary school principals, and regional directors, are typically filled by males (Abramovay et al., 1991, p. 82; González Suárez, 1977, pp. 33–41; Méndez Barrantes, 1988, p. 38).

Gender also helps to shape enrollment patterns for Costa Rica's students. More men than women pursue an advanced degree at Costa Rica's major universities. Male and female university students also tend to select different majors. Men predominate in the natural sciences, law, engineering, economics, business, and educational administration. Women tend to major in the social sciences, arts and letters, nursing, and education (Chavarría González, 1985, p. 92; Méndez Barrantes, 1985, p. 41; 1988, p. 38; Mendiola, 1988, p. 87).

With respect to computer science, 70 percent of the 1991 graduates of the Universidad de Costa Rica's computer science programs were men (Oficina de Registro, Universidad de Costa Rica, 1991, p. 24; cf. Chavarría González, 1985, p. 92). Of the 471 students enrolled in July 1992 at the Universidad Nacional's School of Computer Science, 68 percent were male (Floyd Gray, personal communication). Approximately 54 percent of the 1075 students recently admitted to the Instituto Nacional de Aprendizaje's Computer Science Center were men (*La Nación*, 24 July 1992, pp. 34A–35A).

Differences in the proportion of men and women enrolled in these computer science programs may reflect a division into a higher status tier dominated by men and a lower status tier populated by women. The Universidad de Costa Rica and Universidad Nacional are two of this country's most prestigious universities, from which many top scholars, administrators, and educators come. The Instituto Nacional de Aprendizaje provides students with one to two years of training in a number of technical fields.

An emphasis on gender as an important attribute which can appropriately be used in organizing activities is apparent in Costa Rican secondary and primary schools in general, and at San Juan in particular, although the formal school curriculum is very similar for males and females. For example, secondary school boys are much more likely than girls to enroll in industrial arts and technical schools, while girls are more likely to take family life and art classes (Abramovay, Ramírez Quirós, and Figueredo, 1991, p. 83; Romero et al., 1986, p. 198). In addition, Costa Rica's Ministry of Education has a dress code that requires male secondary and primary school students to wear shirts and pants and girls to dress in blouses and skirts. At Escuela San Juan the division by gender is also apparent in a wide variety of contexts. For example, the physical education teacher often forms same-sex basketball teams and may have girls and boys play against each other. Teachers also give blue report cards to boys and pink cards to girls.

Numerous practices of the students' teachers encourage sex segregation of San Juan's computer lab (and most classrooms). Teachers transferring students between their regular classroom and the lab have students form two lines, one of boys and another composed of girls. In addition, students who were interviewed mentioned that they were allowed to select their own lab partners. Since Costa Rican students of this age generally have same-sex friends, the pairs working in the lab virtually always had gender in common. Furthermore, students were allowed to decide where they would sit in the lab, resulting in a seating pattern with boys on one side of the lab and girls on the other.

In sum, San Juan's students and teachers are living in a society which perceives males and females as having quite different personal abilities and personalities and which encourages males to hold political and administrative posts, work outside the home, and acquire advanced scientific and technical training, including training in computer science. Since many of the patterns are similar to those documented in the United States, it should not be too surprising that this study uncovered a number of parallels between the way in which boys and girls in the two countries view computers.

Gender Differences in Students' Attitudes
Toward Computer Activities

A considerable amount of research has been undertaken in the United States, Canada, the United Kingdom, Australia, and Israel on gender and attitudes toward educational uses of computers. Findings from these studies are generally quite consistent regardless of the nationality of students and teachers. However, it must be pointed out that the range of cultural variation covered in these studies is quite limited, since the vast majority have been conducted in English-speaking countries which share strong historical ties and cultural roots.

Most researchers report that girls have more negative attitudes towards computing than boys. However, this does not mean that the girls' attitudes toward computers are negative in an absolute sense nor that boys' and girls' attitudes are radically different. As will be discussed in more detail below, a careful examination of the findings of prior research shows that both boys and girls generally like computers, are confident of their ability to use them, and experience little anxiety performing computer-related tasks. Thus, it is more accurate to say that most boys and girls have positive attitudes toward computing, with the girls' attitudes being somewhat less positive than those of boys. This general finding was parallel to our findings at San Juan primary school for the three attitudes discussed below: computer liking, confidence, and anxiety.

Computer Liking

Computer liking—how much one enjoys and is interested in computing—has been investigated by a number of scholars. Hawkins (1985, p. 172) found that third and sixth grade girls in the United States like LOGO programming less than do boys (see Mawby, Clement, Pea, and Hawkins, 1984, p. 8). The majority of researchers who have investigated other educational uses of computers report a similar pattern (Abler and Sedlacek, 1987, p. 166; Chen, 1986, p. 273; Colley, Gale, and Harris, 1994, p. 132; Collis, 1985, p. 33; Collis and Williams, 1987, p. 22; Johnson, Johnson, and Stanne, 1985, p. 674; Kay, 1989, p. 312; Krendl, Broihier, and Fleetwood, 1989, p. 90; Levin and Gordon, 1989, p. 75; Miura, 1987, pp. 307–08; Okebukola, 1993, p. 184; Shashaani, 1994, p. 438, 1995, p. 35; Wilder, Mackie, and Cooper, 1985, p. 218; Woodrow, 1994, p. 319).

Some studies, including an analysis of the Computer Attitude Scale administered at Escuela Pérez, have found no statistically significant difference in how much boys and girls like computers (Busch, 1995, p. 151; Colbourn and Light, 1987, p. 134; Dyck and Smither, 1994, p. 246; Francis, 1994, p. 286; Hawkins, 1985, p. 177; Loyd and Gressard, 1984, p. 76; Robertson, Calder, Fung, Jones, and O'Shea, 1995, p. 77). However, Loyd and Gressard (1984, p. 75) did find that the boys' mean score was somewhat higher than the girls'. Further, students who participated in Colbourn and Light's (1987, pp. 138–39) and Hawkins's (1985, pp. 177–78) research were found to have collaborated extensively while using computers at school. Since investigators report girls prefer collaboration and cooperation to competition, their finding of no difference is not surprising. This issue is discussed in more detail below.

A few researchers have suggested that girls as a group have more positive attitudes toward some computer activities than boys (DeRemer 1989, p. 45; Hawkins, 1985, p. 177; Loyd, Loyd, and Gressard, 1987, p. 18; Williams and Rosenwasser, 1987–89, p. 59). However, Loyd et al. (1987, p. 18) report that girls with one or more years of computing experience actually like computers less than comparably experienced boys (cf. DeRemer 1989, p. 48). In Williams and Rosenwasser's (1987–89, p. 59) behavioral measure for computer interest, how frequently students approach and work on the computer may account for their unusual finding. Since students often had to wait in line to use the classroom computer, "it may be that willingness to wait, or patience, was being measured in addition to computer interest *per se*." Thus, we conclude, as does Sutton (1991, p. 490) in a review of this literature, that the preponderance of the evidence suggests boys tend to like computers better than girls.

The majority of the boys and girls who were interviewed at San Juan primary school like LOGO programming. With the exception of two sixth graders, a boy and girl, students say they prefer computer programming to their regular class work. Humberto, a sixth grade boy, was one of the most enthusiastic computer users. "I like computers a lot. . . . Anything that has to do with the computer and learning about the computer is very interesting. How it functions interests me. [So does its ability] to do so many things by itself [and] the way it stores so many things in memory." Some additional things students report enjoying include: (1) having the freedom to develop a wide variety of computer projects, (2) being creative and artistic, (3) being able to talk more in the lab, and especially (4) writing less and not having to take exams. Interestingly, features of the lab which students like are neither inevitable results of using LOGO nor, in principle, unobtainable changes in classrooms which do not use LOGO. Nonetheless, the utilization of computers in the classroom often seems to lead to such changes, even when achieving them is not part of the underlying rationale for use (Schofield, 1995).

Although all students expressed enthusiasm about using computers in the lab, the girls seemed to like LOGO somewhat less than the boys. For example, when asked to indicate their favorite subjects, four boys named computing and a fifth included computing among his top three subjects. This contrasts sharply with the responses of the girls, none of whom said computing was their favorite subject. In fact, only one girl, a sixth grader named Laura, mentioned computing at all, and it was her third choice. She liked home economics best, with religion a close second.

Observational data gathered in the computer lab are consistent with the view that boys like lab work more than girls. Boys are generally more eager than girls to begin working on the computers. The following observation of kindergarten students is typical of students entering the lab.

> [The kindergarten students] line up outside the door. Maestra Andrea lets the girls enter first. The boys enter second. The first five or six boys run to their seats. The [lab] teacher scolds them and makes them go back to the door. She says they must walk to their seats.

In general, boys are also more reluctant to stop working on their lab projects than girls. They are usually the last to leave the lab. In addition, it is not uncommon for some boys to remain after class to continue working on their projects. In contrast, it was frequently observed that some girls quit working on their projects five minutes before the lab period ended. The following observation of a fourth grade class illustrates these general points.

> Before the bell rang, several girls grabbed their notebooks and stood about a meter [inside the lab] door, milling around and talking. When the bell rang, [they and most of the remaining] students . . . filed out of the room. [However], Nestor was one of [several] boys who remained working. Maestra Victoria went around the room preparing the computers for the next class and saving the students' work [to disk]. Javier and Randall came into the lab to work, but [on this occasion] the [lab] teacher asked them to leave.

In contrast, no gender differences were observed with respect to students entering or leaving their regular classrooms or remaining in them during recess.

Boys also more frequently go to the computer lab during recess than girls. It was rare for a girl to be among the one to eight students present in the lab during recess. Moreover, boys and girls reported going to the lab during recess for different reasons. Boys often reported working on their projects during recess. The two girls who go to the lab do so for other reasons. Johanna confides, "I go to the computer lab during recess because I have almost no one else to be with. Sometimes [my friends] gossip and [this] angers me. [Recess] is boring, so I go to the computer lab." Milena appears to go to the lab because she's curious, not because she wants to program. "Sometimes I go to the lab during recess to see the designs the other groups [of students] are making." Jokingly she adds, "Their designs certainly are ugly."

As was previously indicated, an analysis of the Computer Attitude Scale administered at Escuela Pérez found no statistically significant gender differences in liking computer lab activities. Differences in the way students used computers at these two schools may account for this inconsistency. For example, the word processing feature of LOGOWRITER was used more extensively by Pérez's students than by San Juan's. The work of Hawkins (1985, p. 176) and Wilder et al. (1985, p. 219) suggests that girls like writing and word processing as much as or more than boys. Another difference between San Juan and Pérez concerns the use of the computer lab during recess. At San Juan, boys dominated the lab during this time. This undoubtedly contributed to their being more confident and interested computer users than girls. It would also tend to confirm stereotypes that link computers with boys. In contrast, Pérez's lab was closed during recess. As a consequence, girls had a somewhat more level "playing field" at this school than they did at San Juan.

Computer Confidence

Female students of all ages have generally been found to be less confident of their ability to use computers than males (Busch, 1995, p. 151; Chambers and Clarke, 1987, pp. 513–14; Chen, 1986, p. 273; Clarke and Chambers, 1989, p. 424; Colley et al., 1994, p. 132; Collis and Williams, 1987, p. 22; DeRemer, 1989, p. 45; Hattie and Fitzgerald, 1987, p. 10; Johnson et al., 1985, p. 674; Levin and Gordon 1989, p. 75; Miura, 1987, pp. 307–08; Robertson et al., 1995, p. 77; Shashaani, 1994, p. 438, 1995, p. 35; Smith, 1986, p. 341; Temple and Lips, 1989, p. 221; Wilder et al., 1985, p. 226; Woodrow, 1994, p. 319). Several researchers, including DeRemer (1989, pp. 45–46), Dyck and Smither (1994, p. 246), Francis (1994, p. 286), Koohang (1989, p. 141), Loyd and Gressard (1984, pp. 75–76), and Loyd et al. (1987, p. 17) found no statistically significant gender differences in computer confidence. However, males who participated in the first three of these studies did have higher mean computer confidence scores than females. In addition, Loyd et al. (1987) found that among those students with six or more months of computer experience, girls were less confident than boys. We are not aware of any study that found girls to be more confident of their computing abilities than boys. Thus, existing research suggests a gender-linked difference in computer confidence.

The Costa Rican students who were interviewed are generally confident of their ability to program in LOGO. However, boys are generally more confident than girls. All of the boys who were interviewed think using LOGO is very easy. The comments made by Nestor, a fourth grade boy, are typical. "Computing is easy because I like it. [In contrast], when I don't like a subject, I don't want to learn it . . . I always know what I'm doing [in the computing lab]." Humberto, a sixth grade boy, was the only boy to acknowledge he ever found lab work difficult. "In the beginning, [computing] was difficult, but now it's easy."

In contrast, girls are far from unanimous in claiming confidence in their computer abilities. Although two of the girls asserted LOGO programming was easy, including one who thought it was very, very easy (facilisimo), the majority rated their computing abilities more modestly than the boys. They perceived computing to be "more or less difficult," "difficult, but interesting," and "easy, more or less." None of the boys acknowledge that LOGO programming is difficult, though all of the students, regardless of gender, say they make mistakes or need assistance from time to time.

An analysis of the Computer Attitude Scale administered at Escuela Pérez also shows that students are generally confident of their ability to program, but that boys are significantly more confident than girls. Specifically, girls are more likely than boys to indicate that they experience difficulty in developing computer projects. Additionally, girls are more likely to report having problems entering text.

Computer Anxiety

The final type of computer attitude to be discussed here is that of computer anxiety—fear of using or learning to use computers. Research on gender differences in computer anxiety most often shows that females are more anxious than males. This has been found for primary and secondary school students and undergraduates (Abler and Sedlacek, 1987, p. 166; Busch, 1995; Chen, 1986, p. 273; Colley et al., 1994, p. 132; Hattie and Fitzgerald, 1987, p. 13; Igbaria and Chakrabarti, 1990, pp. 232–33; Liu, Reed, and Phillips, 1992, p. 460; Okebukola, 1993, p. 184; Wilder et al., 1985, p. 225; Woodrow, 1994, p. 319) and for elementary school children using LOGO (Siann, Macleod, Glissov, and Durndell, 1990).

Campbell (1988, p. 115), Dyck and Smither (1994, p. 246), Francis (1994, p. 286), Kinnear (1995, p. 32), Koohang (1989, p. 141), Loyd and Gressard (1984, p. 76), Robertson et al. (1995, p. 77), Robinson-Staveley and Cooper (1990, pp. 175–76), and Schumacher, Morahan-Martin, and Olinsky (1993, p. 188) found no statistically significant gender differences in the level of computer anxiety for elementary, secondary, and college students. However, the mean anxiety scores of the males are lower than the females' in Koohang's, Loyd and Gressard's, and Robinson-Staveley and Cooper's research. In addition, Campbell (1988, p. 109) notes that computers were not used extensively by the majority of students with whom she worked. Thus, the sorts of in-school experiences that may lead to girls being more anxious about computers could not have been very frequent.

Campbell (1990, p. 496) and Loyd et al. (1987, p. 17) conclude that secondary school girls are less anxious about computers than boys. However, Campbell's conclusion would appear to be mistaken since the computer anxiety scores reported in her paper support the opposite conclusion (1990, p. 492, Table 1). With respect to the Loyd et al. (1987) study, it is once again worth noting that girls with the most experience using computers are actually more anxious than boys with similar levels of experience. In conclusion, when there are gender differences in this domain, boys tend to be less anxious about computers than girls.

There was little evidence of computer anxiety, as it is usually conceptualized, in the students interviewed at San Juan primary school. However, the reasons two girls gave for not using computers during recess do indicate some anxiety about the lab. Laura, a sixth grader, said, "I haven't gone to the lab during recess. I don't like doing that because afterwards they'll say a diskette was lost or something like that, and then the person who came to the lab during recess will be blamed. The teacher and students say things like this. They're lies." A fourth grade girl also reported reservations about going to the lab during recess. "I haven't gone to the computing lab during recess. I don't know if the teacher would allow that or if she would scold me." It is important to note that these girls' anxieties are not about programming *per se* but about possible interpersonal difficulties or criticism which might result from using computers outside of regularly scheduled lab periods.

Analysis of the Computer Attitude Scale administered at Escuela Pérez clearly indicates that girls are somewhat more anxious than boys about lab work. Though boys and girls report feeling very good in the lab and are not nervous about developing projects, girls are more anxious than boys when they correct programming errors. They also report being somewhat more afraid of damaging the computer than boys. Thus, like students in the United States, there is reason to conclude that Costa Rican girls are somewhat more anxious about computer-related activities than boys.

Factors Contributing to the Girls'
Less Positive Attitudes Toward Computers

All educational computing programs, no matter how innovative and constructive, are implemented within a particular social and cultural context. Program administrators and teachers have little direct control over this. Costa Rica's computerization program is no exception. In Costa Rica, cultural images of males and females embodied in the machismo-marianismo complex and reflected in the social and occupational structure of Costa Rican society impinge on students and shape their attitudes and behavior in many ways. Of course, it is also possible that the girls' less positive attitudes are due to specific attributes of the LOGO programming language itself, although no direct evidence supporting this view emerged from this study. This latter point is addressed first.

Male Biased Software

Much of the educational software currently used in classrooms contains features which make it more appealing to boys than girls. For example, software designers often devise game-like educational programs that use metaphors of war, sports, and space. These are areas in which males have traditionally had more involvement and interest than females (Huff and Cooper, 1987, pp. 527–30; Wilder et al., 1985, p. 223; see also Hawkins, 1985, p. 178; Hodes, 1995, p. 6).

Many boys at San Juan develop projects related to domains traditionally more of interest to males than females, such as sports. Similarly, girls often create images traditionally linked to female interests and domains, such as flowers or homes. However, the ways in which LOGO can be used and the kinds of designs and texts students can create are nearly unlimited. They depend more upon the student's imagination and preference than any limitation of the software program (Kiesler, Sproull, and Eccles, 1985, p. 460). A large number of case studies conducted in the United States by Motherwell (1988), Papert (1987), Turkle (1984), and Turkle and Papert (1990) shows that LOGO can appeal to many girls and boys as long as students are given an opportunity to program in a manner with which they feel comfortable. Moreover, Sanders and Stone (1986, p. 61) recommend that primary school instructors use LOGO in their classrooms precisely because of its appeal to both girls and boys. This is significant because, as their book shows, they are clearly aware of the gender biases often found in educational software.

Having said this, it is still possible that the LOGO programming language may be more appealing to boys than girls. Bowers (1988, pp. 62–63) contends that learning mediated by many kinds of educational software, including LOGO, emphasizes digital thinking. Digital thinking refers to storing, manipulating, and retrieving "mind-size bites" of information that have been abstracted from their context. Bowers argues that students use this mode of thinking during the course of mastering LOGO's commands and ordering them in a linear and logical manner. Bowers also cites evidence that males more so than females are socialized to value and be comfortable with digital thinking. If it is assumed that students using LOGO must employ this style of thinking, then boys would be expected to have more favorable attitudes than girls. They would be engaging in their preferred way of thinking and knowing (Bowers, 1988, pp. 91–92). Although we have no evidence from this study which bears on this thesis, if Bowers is correct, this would be one other possible factor contributing to the differences we observed.

Competition and Domination of the Programming Process

A number of authors have suggested that girls develop unfavorable attitudes toward computers when they are used by students to compete. In contrast to boys who seem to enjoy a competitive lab environment, female computer users often appear to prefer collaboration and cooperation (Chambers and Clarke, 1987, p. 512; Clarke and Chambers, 1989, p. 425; Hawkins, 1985, pp. 176–77; Hoyles and Sutherland, 1989, p. 224; Johnson et al., 1985, p. 676; Kinnear, 1995, p. 35; Motherwell, 1988, pp. 48, 142; see Hativa, Lesgold, and Swisa, 1993, pp. 376, 395–98). These preferences are presumably the outcome of socialization patterns that lead boys to enjoy competition, control, and dominance, and girls to enjoy cooperation, negotiation, and nurturance (cf., Turkle and Papert, 1990, pp. 132, 150). Stereotypes and socialization practices prevalent in Costa Rica encourage similar gender-linked preferences in members of the socioeconomic groups under consideration here (Biesanz et al., 1988, pp. 90–98; Méndez Barrantes, 1988, pp. 37–38).

All three of San Juan's lab teachers acknowledged there was competition in the lab, even though Costa Rican educators may not value competition as much as their United States' counterparts[6] (see Marín and Marín's, 1991, pp. 11–12 discussion of allocentrism). It is probably for this reason that the lab teachers felt they had to justify this competition by pointing out its beneficial effects. When Maestra Pamela was asked whether there was competition in her lab, she began by saying that competition was indeed a problem. However, she immediately changed her mind and said, "No, it's not a problem. It's normal. For some students competition is beneficial. They're improving themselves. It's not a problem." The other two lab teachers agree with Maestra Pamela that competition in the lab is beneficial. Maestra Victoria added that the level of competition is not very pronounced but suggested that it could account for the fact that students sometimes copy and erase the designs of others. Maestra Andrea indicated that there is competition in some of her groups but not all.

The students are somewhat less willing than their teachers to acknowledge that they or others were competing with each other. Five of the students, two boys and three girls, maintain there is no competition in the lab. Humberto's view is typical of this group. "For me, [programming] is not competitive. I am trying to do my best, but it's not because I'm competing. Rather, [doing my best] is something that I enjoy."

On the other hand, five students assert there is competition in the lab. Four students, two boys and two girls, gave specific examples of boys competing. For example, Juan Carlos, a sixth grade boy, pointed out, "There are students competing. They're making very nice designs, like Johnny. He calls the teacher over to see [them]. Those who are competing are Jorge Alonso, Jimmy, and Esteben. I'm not competing." Only one student gave an example of competition between girls. Laura, a fourth grade girl, remarked, "I'm trying to do my best in the computer lab and in class. Sometimes two of us see who can finish [a project] first. The first one done wins." This kind of competition is somewhat less intense than that reported among boys.

Laura also refers to a behavioral dynamic related to competition, domination of the programming process, that had a negative impact on her enjoyment of lab activities. Her regular computer was down one day and the teacher placed her at another computer with a boy.

> But it wasn't the same. He didn't allow me to do anything. He said, "I'm going to write everything." I wasn't able to do anything. Sometimes I got angry and told the teacher. The teacher told us that we have to share the work between the two of us. My partner said he was sharing, but it was a lie. He made the entire design. Francisco didn't allow me to do anything.

In a number of pairs, one student tends to get control of the keyboard. Maestra Andrea, a lab teacher, thought this was a problem. "Working in pairs is problematic. Very few pairs function [well]. . . . The pairs that function well are those [consisting of students] who are friends outside [the lab]. [When they're not friends], one of the pair always works and the other watches." It is worthwhile noting that Siann et al. (1990, p. 188) report boy LOGO programmers tend to dominate consoles in mixed-sex pairs.

One student dominating the console can clearly affect the level of student enjoyment of LOGO programming. For example, consider these observations of two pairs of fourth grade girls drawing houses:

> [Cindy and Miriam's] roof was only partially drawn and slightly off center. Their neighbors, Milena and Lupita, had also drawn a house. However, its roof was [even more poorly drawn]. Cindy and Miriam commented to Milena and Lupita as they viewed their drawing, "What a roof Milena!" [By doing so, they] acknowledged that Milena is in charge of her and Lupita's project and that their

roof was poorly drawn. It is worth noting that earlier, Lupita told me that one of the reasons she didn't enjoy using computers was that Milena didn't allow her to use the keyboard.

Both boys and girls were observed trying to gain control of the keyboard. However, this was observed more frequently in male than female pairs. In fact, some girls adopted a more cooperative and collaborative programming style. Consider these observations of two fourth grade girls.

Maria Fernanda and Ana Patricia [are] drawing [a] Costa Rican flag. . . . Both type in information: Maria Fernanda the numbers and Ana Maria the letters. Maria Fernanda discusses [with Ana Patricia] what they might do. Ana Patricia . . . either accepts or rejects Maria Fernanda's suggestion. Sometimes . . . just the opposite [occurs with Ana Patricia making a suggestion and Maria Fernanda accepting or rejecting it].

In sum, a number of students contended that peer interaction in the lab was somewhat competitive and that students were occasionally excluded from participating. Teachers' comments generally supported this conclusion, although it is clear both from their comments and from observation that neither competition nor practices that exclude girls from participating were constant or extremely strong. Balancing the competition was the fact that students did work in pairs, which girls seemed to do somewhat more comfortably and smoothly than boys.

Teacher and Student Stereotypes of Computer Use

In the United States, Wilder et al. (1985, p. 218) found that both boys and girls from kindergarten through twelfth grade stereotype computers as a male domain. Other researchers have found stereotyping to exist but to be somewhat less robust, concluding that: 1) boys more strongly associate computers with males than do girls; 2) boys stereotype computer use as a male activity, girls do not; or 3) both boys and girls believe computers are for both sexes, though boys feel less strongly about this than girls (Campbell, 1990, p. 492; Chen, 1986, pp. 273–74; Colbourn and Light, 1987, p. 134; DeRemer, 1989, p. 48; Hattie and Fitzgerald, 1987, p. 13; Johnson et al., 1985, p. 673; Kinnear, 1995, p. 32; Levin and Gordon, 1989, p. 79; Shashaani, 1994, p. 438, 1995, p. 32; Smith, 1986, p. 341; Smith, 1987, p. 487; Temple and Lips, 1989, p. 221; see Francis, 1994, p. 287). Studies of LOGO programming that examined stereotyping report Type 2 (Bernhard, 1992, p. 183) and Type 3 results (Siann et al., 1990, p. 188).

This research, which taken as a whole suggests that computing is often seen as a predominantly male activity, has been used to argue that the stereotypical association of computers with males causes girls to like computers less than boys, have less confidence using computers, and experience more anxiety. This contention is supported by research conducted in the United States which suggests that many individuals avoid activities which have traditionally been associated with the other gender, even when this results in passing up the opportunity to gain valued rewards (Bem and Lenney, 1976; Bem, Martyna, and Watson, 1976). Such behavior is not too surprising. Individuals tend to discourage others from engaging in behavior associated with the other sex and to disapprove of others who evidence interests or behavior traditionally associated with those of the other sex (Feinman, 1974, 1981; Martin, 1990).

However, the view that existing stereotypes cause females in the United States or Costa Rica to have less positive attitudes towards computers is but one possibility. It also seems likely that girls' less positive attitudes toward computers leads to their using computers less frequently and less enthusiastically than boys. Students who observe this in the lab then come to stereotype computing as a male activity on the basis of their own experience. It is important to note that even if these stereotypes reflect actual gender differences in computing behavior and attitudes, they also serve to maintain them. Girls come to understand that computer use does not "fit" their gender, which may well make them reluctant to become skilled in computer use, even if their own initial personal attitudes about computers did not inhibit this.

The stereotypical association of computers with males was evident at San Juan in students of both sexes as well as in the lab teachers. Both groups seemed quite willing to generalize about the computer-related interests and capabilities of boys and girls as a group, rather than speaking just in terms of individual preferences and aptitudes. Consider some of the comments made by the three female lab teachers. One lab teacher stated that, "Boys are more interested in computers than girls. It's a very, very, very marked difference. . . . Boys are more creative. . . . Boys are interested in math and social studies; girls in Spanish." Another lab teacher believed boys are more interested in computers "because, in general, boys are more analytical; they reason with more persistence." The third lab teacher agreed with her coworkers. "Boys [are more interested in computers]. They are more creative and scientific."

Since teachers frequently evaluate students and have considerable power over their students' school activities, their stereotypical association of computers with males would be expected to strongly influence lab interactions and student attitudes toward computers. In addition, the division of the lab into male and female sections and differences in male and female dress would tend to make this gender-linked association salient (see Deaux and Major, 1987, pp. 373–74). Not surprisingly, the students' attitudes mirror their lab teachers' (cf. Hawkins, 1985). The majority of boys think boys, as a group, are better programmers than girls. For example, Javier, a sixth grade boy, reported, "Girls don't like the lab. Girls work very slowly and make simple things. [In contrast], boys pay more attention in the lab. [Even] the teacher says boys are better at computers than girls. Girls are best at family life (hogar), religion, and music; boys are best at computers and physical education." Nestor, a fourth grade boy, had a similar attitude toward girl computer users. "Computers interest boys more because they have more ability. Girls play with dolls like Barbie. Computers aren't for girls."

Many of the girls agree with their male classmates, attributing greater liking or aptitude for computers to boys as a group than to girls. Yorlenny, a fourth grade girl, said, "I like computers, but many girls don't. Computers interest boys more. . . . Boys make boats . . . , many things. I believe boys like computers more." Some of the girls base their opinions upon what they had observed in the lab. Yenori, a sixth grade girl, remarked, "Computers interest boys more because they're the ones who play the most with computers, who go crazy over them."

There are a few exceptions to this general tendency for students to see computing as a male domain. Four of the thirteen students interviewed (two boys and two girls) thought girls are as interested and as capable programmers as boys. However, none of the students thought that computers are more appropriate for girls than boys.

There is also evidence of students stereotyping lab work as a male activity at Escuela Pérez, although such stereotyping is more evident in boys than girls. Boys were much more likely than girls to indicate that learning to work with computers is more important for boys, that computers interest boys more, and that boys make the best projects. In addition, boys are less likely than girls to believe that girls are just as capable as boys using the computer.

The fact that San Juan's teachers explicitly link LOGO programming to math may have reinforced the idea that boys are better at computing than girls. Although it is FOD policy that the students' lab work not be graded, the lab teachers had reservations about this policy and decided to consider the quality of their students' lab work when calculating their math grades. The knowledge that LOGO programming affects a student's grade in mathematics is widespread among students.

Linking LOGO lab work to math seems likely to reinforce the perceived similarity between these two activities. It has been shown that Costa Rican sixth grade boys achieve a higher level of proficiency in math than do their female classmates (Esquivel and Brenes, 1988, p. 4). Although to our knowledge no researcher has examined gender and its relationship to attitudes toward math in Costa Rica, there is a large body of evidence suggesting that females in the United States show less confidence in their math ability and less interest in math than males (Chipman, Brush, and Wilson, 1985; Hyde, Fennema, Ryan, Frost, and Hopp, 1990). If this pattern holds in Costa Rica, as is likely given the preponderance of males among those pursuing technical education and careers in fields which require mathematics, the link between LOGO and math at Escuela San Juan may well have reinforced the gender-linked patterning of attitudes discussed above (see Clarke and Chambers, 1989, pp. 412–13).

Before we leave stereotyping, one important issue must be addressed. In explaining the stereotyping of computing as a male activity in the United States, one factor which is often invoked as a contributing factor is the relative paucity of female role models (Beynon, 1991, p. 288; Chen, 1986, p. 279; Fish, Gross, and Sanders, 1986, p. 184; Hawkins, Sheingold, Gearhart, and Berger, 1982, p. 371; Levin and Gordon, 1989, p. 86; Miura, 1987, p. 305; Schofield, 1995; Temple and Lips, 1989, p. 224). Yet all of the lab teachers at Escuela San Juan were female, as were most of the other teachers who assisted in the lab, and these teachers performed their duties in ways which daily demonstrated clear competence (see Gutiérrez, 1994, pp. 127–28).

The question then arises as to how the presence of these positive role models can be reconciled with the clear stereotyping discussed above. First, it must be pointed out that role models are seen as important in leading to change, but not so overwhelmingly important that supplying them will immediately undo the impact of all the other forces which may still foster the maintenance of stereotypes. Second, since teaching, especially elementary school teaching, is so overwhelmingly a female profession in Costa Rica, it may be that students just expect their teachers to be female. If this is the case, then students would not necessarily conclude that females like using computers because they have female lab teachers.

One fascinating example of the way students think about their lab teachers comes from an interview with a boy who was a skilled computer user himself. When asked if any student knows more about LOGO than his teacher did, he replied, "There are no students who know more than the lab teacher because Maestra Victoria has more experience and took a course. We [students] didn't. In comparison to us she's a 'superman.'"[7] Interestingly, the teacher's prowess on the computer conjured up a prototypically male image of Superman. Furthermore, the teacher's skill was clearly attributed to her training rather than to any particularly outstanding aptitude in this domain.

In addition, certain of the regular classroom teachers' behaviors in the lab conveyed the impression that women were not really interested in computing or that boys were better at computing than girls. Thus, even though the lab teachers modelled competence personally, the regular classroom teachers may have inadvertently reinforced the impression students gained from other sources that computing is a male domain. For example, instead of working with students in the lab the full eighty minutes, regular classroom teachers sometimes attend administrative meetings, grade homework in the lab, chat with teachers passing by, or go to the teachers' lounge.

At Escuela Pérez, where quantitative data were collected on this topic, regular classroom teachers, who were female, spend only 54 percent of the lab period interacting with students. In contrast, the lab teachers, who were also female, spend 74 percent of their time with students.[8] Clearly, the presence of female teachers in the lab does not assure girls will always see enthusiastic adult female computer users (see Hoyles and Sutherland, 1989, p. 161; Sanders and Stone, 1986, p. 16).

San Juan's lab teachers also tend to encourage boys rather than girls to assist other students when they are busy, thus reinforcing the image of boys as especially skilled in this domain. Johanna, a sixth grade girl, remarks, "Maestra Victoria . . . calls over Jose Carlos when I don't understand something. He explains it to me." Maestra Victoria actually formalized the role of student lab assistant. She selected a sixth grade boy, Carlos Andrés, to help her with students in the lower grades. Carlos Andrés helps out his lab teacher once or twice each week. He does not view himself as a full-fledged lab teacher. Rather, he sees himself as his teacher's "right hand." He says he enjoys his work immensely. "I feel really good around [the students] because I'm always helping those who don't understand. I'm very happy because I'm helping the children to learn." He hopes to teach computing in the future. Although the teachers may single out boys as formal or informal assistants because of their competence and enthusiasm, this pattern nonetheless reinforces the image of computers as associated with males. Lab teachers also sometimes appear to focus more student attention on boys' projects than on girls' projects, thus emphasizing male expertise as discussed in the next section of this paper.

Differential Assistance In LOGO Programming

To our knowledge, Huber and Scaglion (1995) are the only researchers to have examined gender-linked patterns in the level of assistance students are offered by teachers in computer labs. However, Guntermann and Tovar (1987, p. 324) found that boys using LOGO request more assistance from classmates than do girls. It is also worth noting that in the United States, math teachers generally spend more time with males than females, praise boys more, give boys more academic help, and are more likely to accept boys' comments during classroom discussions (Campbell, 1986, p. 517; Fennema, 1980, p. 169; Leinhardt, Seewald, and Engel, 1979, p. 432; Sadker and Sadker, 1985, p. 54). Female mathematics teachers are just as likely as male teachers to give more assistance to boys (Fennema 1980, p. 169).

Allowing segregation of the classroom by sex, a common practice in San Juan's LOGO lab, may well increase the likelihood that teachers will help boys. In classrooms where boys and girls sit in different sections, Sadker and Sadker (1985, p. 56) suggest that after a student answers a question, teachers tend to question students in the same general area. Because boys are often more assertive than girls, the teacher interacts with the boys' section longer. Giving so much assistance to boys communicates to them that mathematics is very important. In addition, of course, it often provides extra instruction directed specifically at their needs.

There is some evidence that San Juan's girls receive less assistance and guidance from their lab teachers, regular classroom teachers, and classmates in the LOGO lab than their male peers. The three lab teachers were asked who they helped the most in the lab. Maestra Andrea said, "I help both [boys and girls] but because boys are more interested, I'm with them more." She also says she tends to spend more time with students in the upper grades and with the most capable students, because they stimulate her the most and show the most interest. The other two lab teachers said that they thought they gave the same level of assistance to boys and girls. However, Maestra Victoria also stated that she spent more time with the most capable students, "because they call me over to see their designs." Since she also believes that boys are the most capable computer users, it is reasonable to infer that she too assisted boys more than girls. Therefore, it is very likely that San Juan's lab teachers actually spend more time with boys in the lab than with girls.

Several of San Juan's students (two boys and two girls) reported boys receive more help from the lab teachers than girls. Yenori's explanation for this is similar to that of Maestra Andrea, her lab teacher. "The teacher helps boys more because they know the most [about LOGO]." Only one student, Juan Carlos, thought the lab teacher helped the girls in his sixth grade computer lab more than boys.

Lab and regular classroom teachers at Escuela Pérez clearly interacted more frequently with boys than girls in the computer lab (Huber and Scaglion, 1995, pp. 15–16). Observations of lab and regular classroom teachers interacting with individual students and student pairs show that lab teachers spend 59.6 percent of their time with boys and 40.4 percent of their time with girls. This difference is meaningful in light of the fact that almost exactly 50 percent of the students from the twenty-nine groups observed in the lab were girls (554 girls and 551 boys). Classroom teachers, who tend to play a more secondary role in the lab, allocate their time somewhat more equitably in the lab. They interact with boys 53.9 percent and girls 46.1 percent of the time. This disparity does not go unfelt by students. Specifically, the girls were more likely than the boys to indicate on the Computer Attitude Scale that they would like the lab and regular classroom teachers to spend more time with them in the lab.

In order to better appreciate these quantitative differences, consider these observations of a group of kindergartners using LOGO at San Juan. On this particular day, the lab teacher (Maestra Andrea), the students' regular classroom teacher (Grace), and a regional tutor from the Fundación Omar Dengo (also a woman) were present in the lab.

> Grace and the tutor spend most of their time helping the boys. Maestra Andrea spends [a roughly] equal amount of time with boys and girls. At one point [though], all three were helping boys. Three girls got out of their seats and asked Maestra Andrea to help them. "I'm coming now," says Maestra Andrea. . . . [At the end of class], I observe that most of the boys have "nice" well-formed box shapes. Few girls do. I believe this occurred because Grace and the tutor helped the boys with their boxes much more than they did the girls. Maestra Andrea confirmed my analysis but added that the girls' figures were more creative and free, and corresponded more closely to their real capabilities.

With respect to students assisting other students, both sexes report receiving more help from boys, at least under certain circumstances. When students were asked what they did when they had a problem and both teachers were busy, nine students volunteered names of student helpers. Seven of these students, four girls and three boys, reported receiving assistance from boys. Yorlenny, a fourth grade girl, gave this reason for calling over a boy. "Yes, a classmate helps me when both teachers are busy. [When both are busy] then I say to him, 'Alan, how is this done?' Since he has a computer a home, he tells me." Only two students, both girls, named girls who give them assistance.

Extra-Curricular Computer Experience

Yorlenny's comment just above suggests another factor which may contribute to the attitudinal differences under discussion in this paper. Consistent with findings in the United States (Brady and Slesnick, 1985; Chen, 1986; Hess and Miura, 1985; Sanders, 1984), boys at Escuela San Juan were more likely than girls to report that their parents actively encourage them to develop their computing skills in various ways. Humberto, a sixth grade boy, said, "My parents encourage me. When I tell them I want to know a bit more [about computing], they help me to find teachers from whom I can learn more and by buying me diskettes." Laura, a fourth grader, was the only girl to report that her parents actively encourage her to learn more about computers. It is interesting to note how she responded to their advice.

> I've told my parents I'm in computing. My mother thinks that's very good and my father says I may be able to take computer courses [outside of school]. I've told them that's good. . . . They encourage me. They always say, "Laura, why don't you take computer classes?" But I don't know, because I'm in the school chorus. To be in both at the same time would be difficult.

There is considerable evidence that, like boys elsewhere (Busch, 1995, p. 151; Chambers and Clarke, 1987, p. 513; Chen, 1986, p. 271; Hattie and Fitzgerald, 1987, p. 10; Levin and Gordon, 1989, p. 791; Loyd et al., 1987, p. 18; Sanders and Stone, 1986, p. 4; Siann et al., 1990, p. 186; Wilder et al., 1985, p. 223; Woodrow, 1994, p. 329), boys who were interviewed at San Juan use computers outside of school more frequently than do girls. This extracurricular experience helps to foster their skills and puts their female classmates at a relative disadvantage. For example, boys were more likely than girls to report using a computer at a relative's or friend's house. Nestor's out-of-class use undoubtedly contributed to his acknowledged expertise in school. "The first time I used a computer was two and one-half years ago at my cousins' house. I made designs with LOGO." Carlos Andrés, the sixth grade boy who served as Maestra Victoria's lab assistant, was the only student to have reported taking a computer course outside of school. Note his level of confidence. "I was in a computing course in the fourth grade. After two months, I was programming. It turned out well. I was a very capable boy. I liked computers from the very first." Humberto, a sixth grade boy, was the only student interviewed who reported having a computer at home. "The first time I used a computer was at a computer exposition. My father purchased one and we have it at home. I started using it about a year ago whenever the teacher assigned written work."

Though there are a few exceptions (e.g., Krendl et al., 1989, p. 91), most investigators have concluded that the more computer-related experience students have, the more positive their attitudes toward computers become (Badagliacco, 1990, p. 48; Campbell, 1988, p. 115; Chambers and Clarke, 1987, p. 503; Chen, 1986, p. 278; Colley et al., 1994, pp. 133–34; DeRemer, 1989, p. 48; Dyck and Smither, 1994, p. 243; Igbaria and Chakrabarti, 1990, p. 233; Koohang, 1989, p. 148; Levin and Gordon, 1989, p. 84; Loyd and Gressard, 1984, p. 73; Loyd et al., 1987, pp. 17–18; Miura, 1987, pp. 308–10; Robertson et al., 1995, p. 77; Robinson-Staveley and Cooper, 1990, p. 174; Sacks, Bellisimo, and Mergendoller, 1993–94, p. 266; Smith, 1986, p. 343; Wilder et al., 1985, pp. 221–23; Woodrow, 1994, pp. 318, 330). However, we agree with Chambers and Clarke (1987, p. 498), Chen (1986, p. 279), and Levin and Gordon (1989, p. 85) that scholars need to be critical of broad generalizations about the positive impact of computer experience. Specifically, the social dynamics of extra-curricular computer experiences, the meaning students attach to them, and their impact on attitudes can be somewhat different from the dynamics, meaning, and impact of in-school computer experiences. For example, computer use outside of school is likely to be voluntary rather than compulsory. In addition, with the exception of enrolling in a computer course, students using computers outside of school probably work individually or in very small groups rather than in groups of thirty to forty students.

Many extracurricular computer experiences, especially using a computer at home or at a friend's or relative's house, would be expected to have a positive impact on attitudes (see Campbell, 1988, p. 113; Levin and Gordon, 1989, p. 79). Both sexes would tend to become more skillful, confident, and favorably disposed toward computers with experience. In contrast, it is at least possible that the more time students use computers in milieus which support and maintain the traditional linkage between gender and computer use, the wider the gap will become between boys' and girls' attitudes. To the extent that work in a computer lab is competitive, that boys exclude girls from programming, that students and teachers explicitly associate computers with boys, and that boys receive more assistance from teachers and classmates, boys are likely to develop more positive attitudes than girls over time.

The findings of two studies are consistent with the last point. Chambers and Clarke (1987, p. 503) found that after using computers at school for a year, the attitudes of elementary and secondary school girls were significantly less positive than the boys', although boys' and girls' attitudes did not differ initially. Collis (1985, p. 34) examined the impact of a school computer literacy course on the attitudes of eighth and twelfth graders. Compared to their respective same-sex control groups, boys had more positive attitudes after completing the course, while girls had less favorable ones.

Discussion of the Findings and Concluding Remarks

Theory and findings based upon work in educational settings in the United States and elsewhere were clearly supported by the research undertaken in Costa Rica. In general, San Juan's students have favorable attitudes toward computer-related activities and become quite skilled in using LOGO. However, girls report liking lab work less than boys and are less confident of their programming ability. They were also less likely to use the computer lab outside of regularly scheduled lab periods, at least partly because of their anxieties about the lab environment. Thus, the situation at Escuela San Juan was remarkably similar to that reported in earlier studies in the United States and elsewhere.

Qualitative research at Escuela San Juan, with its emphasis on "thick description," has allowed us to flesh out and interpret findings from earlier studies. For example, San Juan's students overwhelmingly reported liking working in the computer lab, as have students in many previous studies. However, the reasons students gave for this often had very little to do with the LOGOWRITER software *per se*. They enjoyed the absence of tests and having the freedom to talk more and write less. Similarly, girls at San Juan (and Pérez) were found to be somewhat more anxious than boys. However, girls tended to be anxious not about computer use *per se* but about interpersonal difficulties with peers and lab teachers. A recently published qualitative study of computer use in a high school in the United States suggests yet another factor creating positive attitudes toward computers: changes in the teacher's role that led to more individualized instruction and less lecturing (Schofield, 1995).

Most quantitative research has not examined in great detail the computer cultures that develop after educational computing programs are implemented. Computer cultures such as San Juan's are extremely complex. The elements of these cultures "work as a web of mutually supporting, interacting processes" (Papert, 1987, p. 26). Recall that Javier reported that he believed LOGO was best suited for boys because his teacher told him so and because he observed the complex designs some boys create with the assistance of their teachers and peers. Nestor's confidence in his ability to program was a major reason he liked LOGO. The fact that he had two and one half year's experience using LOGO prior to programming in school contributed to his high level of confidence. Girls such as Lupita got discouraged about programming because they did not like being excluded from participating in lab work.

Some aspects of San Juan's computer culture appear to have a greater impact on student attitudes than others. The stereotypical association of LOGO, and computers more generally, with boys appears to be particularly important. As a consequence of this stereotype, teachers, parents, and students behave toward boys in ways which encourage them to do things like enrolling in computer courses outside of school, using a computer at home, and spending time in the LOGO lab during recess. These experiences build the boys' confidence and ability to program well. Because boys are confident and experienced computer users, teachers and girls turn to boys for assistance. Since girls have relatively few girlfriends who are expert programmers or who encourage them to value computing, they conclude that boys are best suited for programming. This is something girls have observed first-hand and have been told by others. The belief that boys are most suited for programming becomes a self-fulfilling prophecy.

The view that all parts of San Juan's computer culture are interrelated has implications for educators who wish to encourage girls to view computers more favorably. We suggest that educators implement strategies that involve all relevant groups: students, teachers, parents, and administrators (see Sanders and Stone, 1988). Strategies that focus on one group to the exclusion of others address only part of the problem. San Juan's LOGO lab had three well-trained and dedicated women teachers. Their presence as positive role models would be expected to encourage girls to view LOGO positively. However, their teachers' positive example was offset by several mitigating circumstances. The lab teachers believed and occasionally even stated to students that LOGO programming was more appropriate for boys than girls. In addition, they spent more time assisting boys and encouraged boys to formally or informally serve as lab assistants.

Gender differences in attitudes and behavior in San Juan's LOGO lab should be viewed in their broadest possible context. As was indicated at the beginning of this paper, many roles and relationships between the sexes in Costa Rica are defined by the machismo-marianismo complex. Males are expected to acquire the requisite scientific knowledge and technical skills that prepare them for authoritative positions in business, government, and education. Similar sorts of roles, skills, and knowledge are thought to be less appropriate for females. These gender-linked differences are depicted in and reinforced by school textbooks, television and radio programs, magazines, and socialization practices. In a very real sense, San Juan's computer lab is a microcosm of Costa Rican society.

Research was undertaken less than a year after San Juan's lab became operational. Since the lab was observed during its initial phase of operation, it makes sense to view lab interactions and student attitudes toward computers as having been strongly influenced by more general aspects of Costa Rica's culture. However, it also seems likely that computer labs like San Juan's will play a role in helping to reproduce Costa Rica's gender status quo in the future (see Apple, 1986, pp. 170–71; Krendl et al., 1989, p. 85). When fully implemented, Costa Rica's computerization program will reach one-third of this country's public school children. Children whose attitudes towards computers will be based upon six year's experience will soon be graduating from schools. If the attitudes of San Juan's students are an indication of things to come, we would expect more boys than girls to gravitate toward educational programs in which knowledge of and training in computer applications are important: computer science, engineering, economics, business, the natural sciences, and educational administration. These are exactly the sorts of programs that will allow young Costa Rican men to attain influential positions in government, private enterprise, and universities. Since gender-linked aspects of San Juan's computer culture are remarkably similar to those documented in research in the United States and elsewhere, this prediction may very well apply to many other societies around the world.

"You Don't Have To Be a Teacher To Teach This Unit": Teaching, Technology, and Control in the Classroom

MICHAEL W. APPLE and
SUSAN JUNGCK

Teaching in Crisis

With all of the rhetoric about teaching and professionalism, about enhancing teachers' power, and about raising pay and respect, the reality of many teachers' lives bears little resemblance to the rhetoric. Rather than moving in the direction of increased autonomy, in all too many instances the daily lives of teachers in classrooms in many nations are becoming ever more controlled, ever more subject to administrative logics that seek to tighten the reins on the processes of teaching and curriculum. Teacher development, cooperation, and "empowerment" may be the talk, but centralization, standardization, and rationalization may be the strongest tendencies. In Britain and the United States, to take but two examples, reductive accountability and teacher-evaluation schemes and increasing centralization have become so commonplace that in a few more years we may have lost from our collective memory the very possibility of difference. Indeed, there are areas in the United States where it has been mandated that teachers must teach *only* that material which is in the approved textbook. Going beyond the "approved" material risks administrative sanctions.

An odd combination of forces has led to this situation. Economic modernizers, educational efficiency experts, neoconservatives, segments of the new right, many working- and lower-middle-class parents who believe that their children's futures are threatened by a school system that does not guarantee jobs, and members of parts of the new middle class whose own mobility is dependent on technical and administratively oriented knowledge have formed a tense and contradictory alliance to return us to "the basics," to "appropriate" values and dispositions, to "efficiency and accountability," and to a close connection between schools and an economy in crisis.[1]

While we need to be cautious of being overly economistic (and indeed have argued at great length against such tendencies in other places[2]), it is still the case that educators have witnessed a massive attempt—more than a little successful—at exporting the crisis in the economy and in authority relations from the practices and policies of dominant group onto the schools. If schools and their teachers and curricula were more tightly controlled, goes the argument, more closely linked to the needs of business and industry, more technically oriented, with more stress on traditional values and workplace norms and dispositions, then the problems of achievement, of unemployment, of international economic competitiveness, of the disintegration of the inner city, and so on, would largely disappear.

In the United States, a multitude of reports have told us that because of the inefficiency of our educational system and the poor quality of our teachers and curricula, our nation was at risk. In Britain, a similar argument was heard. Teachers were seen as holding onto a curriculum that was "ill-suited to modern technological and industrial needs and as generally fostering an anti-industrial ethos among their students. In all respects, schools and teachers were portrayed as failing the nation." Industry was turned into "dirty word," a fact that supposedly contributed greatly to the nation's industrial decline.[3]

As one of us has argued at greater length elsewhere, there is immense pressure currently not only to redefine the manner in which education is carried out, but what education is actually *for*. This has not remained outside the classroom but is now proceeding rather rapidly to enter into classroom life and alter our definitions of what counts as good teaching. As we shall see in the second, more empirical part of this paper in our analysis of what happens in computer literacy classes—one of the newly formed high status areas of curriculum and teaching during the "educational crisis"—this can have a serious impact on the reality of teaching.

Among the major effects of these pressures is what happens to teaching as an occupation and as a set of skilled and self-reflective actions. Important transformations are occurring that will have significant impacts on how we do our jobs and on who will decide whether we are successfully carrying them out. Seeing what is happening will require that we recapitulate a set of arguments about the relationships among teaching, how one's work is controlled (what has been called "proletarianization"), and the struggles over what counts as, and who has, skills.[4]

Teaching as a Labor Process

In order to understand this argument, we need to think about teaching in a particular way, as what might be called a complicated *labor process* that is significantly different from that of working on an assembly line, in the home, or in an office. But even given these differences, the same pressures that are currently affecting jobs in general are increasingly being felt in teaching. In the general sociological literature, the label affixed to what is happening is the "degradation of labor."[5] This degradation is a "gift" our dominant economic and ideological arrangements have given us.

In the larger society, there has been an exceptionally long history of rationalizing and standardizing people's jobs. In industry, a familiar example of this was management's use of Taylorism and time-and-motion studies in their continual search for higher profits and greater control over their employees. Here, complicated jobs were rigorously examined by management experts. Each element that went into doing the job was broken down into its simplest components. Less skilled and lower-paid workers were hired to do these simpler activities. All planning was to be done by management, not workers. The consequences of this have been profound, but two of them are especially important for our discussion.[6]

The first is what we shall call the separation of conception from execution. When complicated jobs are broken down into atomistic elements, the person doing the job loses sight of the whole process and loses control over her or his own labor, since someone outside the immediate situation now has greater control over both the planning and what is actually to go on. The second consequence is related but adds a further debilitating characteristic known as deskilling. As employees lose control over their own labor, the skills that they have developed over the years atrophy. They are slowly lost, thereby making it even easier for management to control even more of one's job, because the skills of planning and controlling it yourself are no longer available.[7] A general principle emerges here: in one's labor, lack of use leads to loss. This has been particularly the case for women's labor. Women's work has been particularly subject to the deskilling and depowering tendencies of management.[8] These tendencies are quite visible in a multitude of workplaces throughout the country, from factories and clerical and other office work to stores, restaurants, and government jobs, and now even teaching. More and more of these seem to be subject to such "degradation."

How is this process now working through the job of teaching? At the outset, it is important to realize that it has taken teachers decades to gain the skills and power they have. Even though in many school systems teachers in reality have only a limited right actually to choose the texts and other curricular materials they use, these conditions are still a good deal better than in earlier periods of our educational history, when text and curricular selection was an administrative responsibility. The gains that teachers have made did not come easily. It took thousands of teachers in hundreds of districts throughout the country constantly reaffirming their right to determine what would happen in their classrooms to take each small step away from total administrative control of the curriculum. This was even more the case at an elementary school level, where the overwhelming majority of teachers have historically been women. Women teachers have had to struggle even harder to gain recognition of their skills and worth.[9]

Yet while curriculum planning and determination are *formally* more democratic in most areas of the curriculum, there are forces acting on the school that may make such choices nearly meaningless. At the local, state, and national levels, movements for strict accountability systems, competency-based education and testing, systems management, a truncated vision of the "basics," mandated curricular content and goals, and so on, are growing. Teaching methods, texts, tests, and outcomes are increasingly taken out of the hands of the people who must put them into practice. Instead, they are legislated by national or state departments of education or in state legislatures and either supported or stimulated by national reports, such as *A Nation At Risk* and more recent reports, which offer simplistic assessments of, and responses to, problems in education[10] and demonstrate the increasing power of conservative ideologies in our public discourse.

For example, at the time of this writing, in the United States nearly forty of the fifty states have established some form of statewide competency testing. Many of these systems are reductive and more than a little unreflective. While their purpose is ostensibly to guarantee some form of "quality control," one of the major effects of such state intervention has been to put considerable pressure on teachers to teach simply for the tests.[11] It is part of a growing process of state intervention into teaching and the curriculum and constitutes another instance in the long history of state intervention into the work of a largely women's labor force.[12]

As has been demonstrated at considerable length in *Teachers and Texts*, much of the attempt by state legislatures, departments of education, and "educational managers" to rationalize and standardize the process and products of teaching, to mandate very specific content and teaching, and to define all teaching as a collection of measurable "competencies," is related to a longer history of attempts to control the labor of occupations that have historically been seen as women's paid work. That is, we do not think it is possible to understand why teachers are subject to greater control and greater governmental intervention, and what the effects of such mandates are, unless we step back and ask a particular kind of question. By and large, *who* is doing the teaching?

Historically, teaching has been constructed as women's paid work. In most western industrialized nations, approximately two thirds of the teaching force are women, a figure that is much higher the lower one goes in the educational system. Administrators are overwhelmingly male, and significantly more so the higher one goes in the educational system. Thus, both statistically and in terms of its effects, it would be a mistake of considerable proportions to ignore the gendered composition of teaching when we discuss the rationalizing ethos increasingly surrounding it.[13]

These rationalizing forces are quite consequential and need to be analyzed structurally to see the lasting impact they may have on teaching. In much the same way as in other jobs, we are seeing the *deskilling* of our teachers.[14] As we noted, when individuals cease to plan and control a large portion of their own work, the skills essential to doing these tasks self-reflectively and well atrophy and are forgotten. The skills that teachers have built up over decades of hard work—including setting relevant curricular goals, establishing content, designing lessons and instructional strategies, "community building" in the classroom, individualizing instruction based on an intimate knowledge of students' desires and needs—are lost. Given the centralization of authority and control, they are simply no longer "needed." In the process, however, the very things that make teaching a professional activity—the control of one's expertise and time—also dissipate. There is no better formula for alienation and burnout than loss of control of one's labor, though it is unfortunate that terms such as 'burnout' have such currency, since they make the problem into a psychological one rather than a structural one concerning the control of teachers' labor.

The tendency for the curriculum increasingly to become planned, systematized, and standardized at a central level, totally focused on competencies measured by standardized tests, and largely dependent on predesigned commercial materials and texts written specifically for those states that have the tightest centralized control and, thus, the largest guaranteed markets,[15] may have consequences exactly the opposite of what many authorities intend. Instead of professional teachers who care greatly about what they do and why they do it, we may have alienated executors of someone else's plans. In fact, the literature on the labor process in general, as well as that specifically related to women's paid work, is replete with instances documenting the negative effects of systems of tight management and control and the accompanying loss of skill, autonomy, craft, and pride that results.[16] As is too often the case, educational bureaucrats borrow the ideology and techniques of industrial management without recognizing what can and has happened to the majority of employees in industry itself.[17]

These kinds of interventionist movements will have consequences not only for teachers' ability to control their own work but also for the kind of content that is stressed in the curriculum.

A simple way of thinking about this is to divide the kinds of knowledge that we want students to learn into three types: knowledge *that*, *how*, and *to*. "Knowledge that" is factual information, such as knowing that Madison is the capital of Wisconsin or Baton Rouge is the capital of Louisiana. "Knowledge how" is skills, such as knowing how to use the library or how to inquire into the history of, say, women or unions in the United States. "Knowledge to" is dispositional knowledge. That is, it includes those norms, values, and propensities that guide our future conduct. Examples include knowing to be honest, to have pride in one's racial heritage, to want to learn more after one's formal schooling is over, to be intellectually open-minded, or to see oneself as part of a democratic community and to act cooperatively. Each of these is important, but if we were to place them in some sort of hierarchy, most of us would agree that knowing an assortment of facts is probably less important than higher-order skills of inquiry. And these in turn are made less significant than they should be if the person is not disposed to use them in educationally and socially important ways.

With control over content, teaching, and evaluation shifting outside the classroom, the focus is increasingly on those elements of social studies, reading, science, and mathematics that can be measured easily on standardized tests. Knowledge "that," and occasionally low-level knowledge "how," are the primary foci. Anything else is considered inconsequential. This is bad enough, of course, but in the process even the knowledge "that" that is taught is made "safer," less controversial, less critical. Not only is it a formula for deskilling, it is also a contraction of the universe of possible social knowledge into that which continues the disenfranchisement of knowledge of women and people of color and labor. This knowledge is increasingly important, given the levels of exploitation and domination that exist not only within nations but between them as well.[18]

So far we have discussed at a very general level certain of the social dynamics that threaten to transform curricula and teaching. This discussion cannot be complete unless we add the idea of *intensification*.[19]

Intensification is one of the most tangible ways in which the working conditions of teachers have eroded. It has many symptoms, from the trivial to the more complex, ranging from having no time even to go to the bathroom or have a cup of coffee, to having no time to keep up with one's field. We can see it most visibly in the chronic sense of work overload. More and more has to be done; less and less time is available to do it. This had led to a multitude of effects.

Intensification leads people to "cut corners" so that only what is "essential" to the task immediately at hand is accomplished. It forces people increasingly to rely on "experts" to tell them what to do, and to begin to mistrust the expertise they themselves may have developed over the years. In the process, quality is sacrificed for quantity. Getting done is substituted for work well done. And, as time itself becomes a scarce "commodity," the risk of isolation grows, both reducing the chances that interaction among participants will enable critiques and limiting the possibility that rethinking and peer teaching will naturally evolve. Collective teaching skills are lost as "management skills" are gained. Often the primary task is, to quote one teacher, to "find a way to get through the day." And, finally, pride itself is jeopardized as the work becomes dominated by someone else's conception of what should be done.

As we noted, with the growth of interventionist styles of management and a focus on reductive accountability schemes in many nations, more and more curricula and the act of teaching itself are dominated by prespecified sequential lists of behaviorally defined competencies and objectives. Pretests and posttests measure "readiness" and skill levels, and prepackaged textual and often worksheet material dominate. The amount of paperwork necessary for evaluation and record keeping is often phenomenal under these conditions. As has been documented elsewhere, situations such as these are increasingly common and often require teachers to be busy with these tasks before and after school and during their lunch hour. Teachers come in very early and leave very late, often to be faced with still more work at home every night.[20]

Given the pressures now being placed on schools, this problem is exacerbated by the fact that not only are curricula and teaching more tightly controlled, but more, not less, has to be accomplished. Nothing has been removed from the curriculum. Instead, elements have been added on. One of the best examples is the addition of "computer literacy" programs in many school systems. In most districts, nothing indeed has been dropped from the already crowded curriculum, and teachers are faced with the predicament of finding the time and physical and emotional resources to integrate such programs into the school day. This may have even greater implications for women teachers, as we shall point out in the following section.

As with other labor processes, one of the effects of deskilling and intensification is the threat they pose to the conception of teaching as an "integrated whole activity." Concerns of care, connectedness, nurturance, and fostering growth—concerns that, because of the socially constructed division of public and private spheres and the sexual division of labor, have historically been linked to skills and dispositions surrounding the paid and unpaid labor of women—are devalued. In essence, they are no longer given credit for being skills at all, as the very definition of what counts as a "skill" is further altered to include only that which is technical and based on a process "which places emphasis on performance, monitoring and subject-centered instruction."[21] As we shall see, such transformations can occur all too easily.

Concepts such as deskilling, the separation of conception from execution, and intensification can remain abstractions unless we can see how they represent processes that have a real and material existence in day-to-day school life. Many teachers are experiencing these dynamics as very real alterations in their lives inside and outside the classroom. In the next section of this paper, we shall situate these processes within the activities of a group of teachers in one particular school that was subject to a long-term and comprehensive ethnographic study by one of us of the growth and effects of a mandate to make all students "computer literate." The introduction of such a new curriculum emphasis was officially to help students and teachers become more technically literate. Yet, it had a number of unforeseen effects that often led to the opposite. The new curriculum mandate to develop computer literacy was a response by this particular school system to the calls from a variety of groups for a more technically oriented curriculum that would teach the skills needed for access and mobility later in life. It occurred in an educational, economic, and political context in which the state department of education, business and industry, and many middle-class parents were placing considerable pressure on schools not only to immediately develop programs that guaranteed a computer-literate school population, but to make such "literacy" a requirement for graduation from secondary school and to establish closer links between educational and economic goals.[22]

As we shall see, gender relations, the changing conditions of the labor of teachers, and the organizational and material realities brought about by the fiscal crisis of the state directly impinged on the construction of classroom life. In this site, the intensification of the teachers' workload, the lack of availability of sufficient resources, the organizational structure of the school as it had evolved over time, and the complicated reality of gendered labor all combined to create a situation in which few teachers were fully satisfied with the outcomes.

Inside the Classroom

Lakeside-Maple Glen School District has decided, in the face of national trends and considerable pressure, to make its curricula more responsive to recent and rapid social and technological change.[23] It wants to ensure that its curricula are more responsive to the "needs of the economy" and the perceived future labor market. Computers are one of the keys in the school district's strategies for accomplishing this. Yet this district has also taken the stance that such curriculum programs should not be imposed from above, even given the considerable pressure being placed on it. Rather, teachers themselves must be deeply involved in the curriculum development process.

All too often, the critical literature has assumed that pressures toward deskilling, the separation of conception from execution, and intensification must be imposed continually from the outside through administrative mandates, centralized curriculum determination, or externally produced and controlled evaluation plans. This is not always the case and, in fact, may ignore the complexity of decision making on the ground, so to speak. Because teachers have always sought ways to retain their day-to-day control over classroom reality and historically are not passive receivers of top-down strategies, complexity must be recognized.[24] In fact, as we shall document in this section, these external conditions do not totally determine the reality of curriculum and teaching. Teachers may indeed still have space to maneuver. However, these external pressures may also make it seem unrealistic and not in their immediate interest for many teachers to do anything other than participate in recreating conditions that foster continued difficulties in their own labor. To a large extent, this is exactly what happened here.

One of the first curriculum programs to be developed and implemented under the District's new Computer Literacy Project was the ten-day Computer Literacy Unit (CLU). It was to be added on in every middle school seventh grade math class.

Mr. Nelson, a middle school math teacher and the district computer "expert," and Mr. Miller, another middle school math teacher, were given summer curriculum compensation to develop the seventh grade unit, which they and three other seventh grade math teachers were expected to implement in the fall. Although Mr. Nelson and Mr. Miller had conceptualized the unit before the fall, they had not specifically planned each daily lesson or assembled the necessary materials to be used. They began in the fall with most of what became their unit outline completed:

Day 1. History of and parts of a computer
Day 2. Operation of a computer and computer vocabulary
Day 3. Interaction with a computer (lab)
Day 4. Input to a computer
Day 5. Output from a computer
Day 6. Flowcharting
Day 7. Introduction to programming in BASIC
Day 8. Writing a program in BASIC (lab)
Day 9. Group activity - a computer simulation (lab)
Day 10. Test and effects of computers upon society

Mr. Nelson and Mr. Miller met frequently during the first six weeks of school to work on the unit, a comprehensive task which consisted of preparing daily lesson plans, rescheduling the computer lab, and procuring worksheets, filmstrips, tape recordings, and audiovisual equipment. The unit was developed with a number of "givens" in mind that bear on our earlier arguments.

One "given" that Mr. Nelson and Mr. Miller considered was that the school's seven computers were being used in the computer lab for the eighth grade computer elective courses and were not available when several of the seventh grade math classes met. Therefore, they recognized that most of the unit would have to be taught without the use of computers, a major obstacle because they believed that "hands-on" computer experiences were very important. Through elaborate planning, the teachers were able to schedule three of the ten days in the computer lab, not very much considering that there would be about twenty-five students sharing seven computers on those Lab days.

Minimal computer access, a problem of considerable moment in many budget-conscious school systems, affected the curriculum and the teaching because skills and concepts most effectively developed through using a computer had to be taught in more vicarious ways, such as observations and lectures, or eliminated altogether. For example, too few computers and too little time in the computer lab meant that most students never were able to write a program in BASIC even though it was a specific objective and represented the general active, hands-on experiences that were consistent with the district goals.

A second "given" which influenced how the unit was developed was stated by Mr. Miller this way: "You have to remember that we have faculty in this department who don't know much about computers. We needed a program that everyone could teach." Mr. Nelson explained that a crucial factor in developing the unit was that teachers who know nothing about computers would be able to "teach it." He said, "You see we really needed to develop a canned unit." The three other math teachers, all women, were uninvolved in developing the unit and only found out about it in the fall. One woman, Ms. Wilson, a recent graduate who was newly hired on a part-time basis, had no computer experience and was quite apprehensive about having to teach a Computer Literacy unit. Another teacher, Ms. Linder, had some computer experience but had just returned from a year's leave of absence and had just learned of the required unit. The third woman teacher, Ms. Kane, was experienced in the department but had no experience with computers. Thus, the unit was "canned" so that these or any future teachers would be able to "teach" it.

A third "given" resulted from the organization of the Math Department.

It was a regular practice in the department to test all seventh graders after the first ten weeks of school and transfer those with "superior ability" to an eighth grade math class. Selection by talent, with all its stratifying implications, was not an invisible process. This schedule therefore determined that the unit would have to be completed in all 7th grade math classes by the tenth week of school. In order to be able to share the computers and other equipment and schedule the computer lab, half of the math classes had to implement the unit during weeks seven and eight and the other half had the unit during the ninth and tenth weeks of school. This schedule placed tremendous time pressures on Mr. Nelson and Mr. Miller to complete the unit quickly.

Given these time pressures and the intensification of their own work, Mr. Nelson and Mr. Miller had to assemble the materials rapidly, and communications with the other math teachers about the unit were minimal. They were able to examine some commercially prepared computer literacy curriculum materials that were available.

The foundation of the unit that they planned consisted of two filmstrips and a prepackaged commercial curriculum consisting of tape-recorded lessons and coordinated worksheets. The topical outline they had partially completed was finalized on the basis of some of these tape-recorded lessons and worksheets. The unit became very structured, detailing the objectives, the equipment needed, and the lesson plan for each day. The plan specified that six days were to be spent in the classroom, mostly listening to the commercial tape recordings and completing the worksheets. Three days were to be spent in the computer lab: two for interacting with instructional software and one for writing a computer program. A unit test was planned for the last day, and after the test a film about the social implications of computers would complete the unit. Due to the bulk of all the worksheets and equipment, the curriculum was usually rolled around from room to room on a cart.

In many ways, the "curriculum on a cart" may be viewed as an efficient and practical solution to the several "givens" within the school. What occurred inside the classrooms, however, demonstrates some of the serious contradictions shaping teachers' lives inside and outside the school.

A Curriculum on a Cart

Students and teachers expressed enthusiasm about the two-week computer unit because it represented something new and popular. There were five teachers teaching a total of eleven heterogeneously grouped seventh grade math classes. Due to the time pressures, the unit was not prepared and ready to go until time to begin teaching it. The women teachers had little or no time to preview the unit. In essence, they experienced it as they taught it.

In all classes the unit began with some enthusiasm and two filmstrips and two worksheets. Students were shown a filmstrip which focused on the history and development of computers and were given a timeline of events for notetaking. The content emphasized terminology and dates of events such as the invention of the transistor. There was little class discussion because the filmstrips took the whole period. Homework consisted of a WordSearch worksheet with hidden names of computer parts.

To give a sense of daily activity, let us focus on Day Five. The daily routine that occurred on Day Five was representative of all days in which worksheets and tape recordings were predominant. Day Five is distinct, however, in that it represents a midpoint in the unit, and events on this day illustrate how the routine use of tape recordings and worksheets was beginning to have an impact on the teachers' and students' initial enthusiasm for the unit, on the teachers' sense of skill, and on the intensification of their work.

Day Five

As the students come into class today, one boy shouts out, "Are we going to the lab today?" The teacher answers, "We've got those sheets again and the tapes. . . ." Invariably when hearing that it was a worksheet day, students would start to grumble, one rather loudly, "that man's dejected," "I hate this, this is boring," "Do we have to do this all the time?" "I cannot stand this class," "This isn't computer class, this is worksheets . . . what do we learn, nothing . . . how to push a button" (referring to the tape recorder). One student turned to one of us and, referring to the worksheets, complained, "We know this stuff already, maybe not these fancy words . . . but we know this stuff." Although the students complained about the tapes and the worksheets, they did not disrupt the class routine. They came into class, made a number of inquiries and remarks, took their seats, and cooperated with the teachers. Their attitudes were for the most part ignored or made light of by the teachers, who appeared to regard a certain amount of negativism and complaining as typical adolescent behavior in school.

The first daily procedure in every class was the distribution of worksheets, which took about ten minutes because there were so many of them. Teachers usually passed around a stapler and this became the occasion for individual entertainment as students dawdled with it, withheld it from the next student, slid it on the floor and generally used it to attract attention and delay beginning the worksheets.

The teachers began the lesson by turning on the first tape-recorded lesson for the students. A man's voice read the captioned information on the worksheets, and students were to follow along. He then explained how to complete the worksheet and said "now turn off the tape and complete the worksheet." Teachers who, given the immense work-load of paperwork, used this time to do independent work at their desks, frequently missed this directive, and the students would shout, "Turn off the tape." After a few minutes the teacher would turn the recorder back on and the narrator would read the answers while students were supposed to correct their worksheet. As the unit progressed, many students would just wait for the answers to be read and would fill in their papers at that time. After a worksheet was completed, the narrator would then say, "If you want to continue . . ." which was an invitation to go on to the next worksheet. This invitation invariably met with responses such as "But we don't!" One teacher in a sing-song voice said, "Oh we do, we do." After one of the first classes, this teacher said, "I don't think this was a good day, the kids didn't really get much out of this. . . ." This was a surprising remark at first because the students had been very attentive, completed the worksheets, and the day had progressed according to the Lesson Plan. It expressed, however, the teacher's intuitive sense that this material, as conveyed through the tapes, was not very effective.

As the tape recorder droned on, students found many quiet and unobtrusive diversions. Students would comb their hair, clean dirt from their sneakers, daydream, doodle, and chip pencils. One girl worked all period getting a piece of candy that was wrapped in crinkly paper out of her pocket, unwrapped, and into her mouth all unnoticed. These activities were generally quiet and private, and students in all classes during this unit were outwardly very orderly. These diversions were rarely disruptive. Most of the students, however, were very quiet and completed their worksheets.

Mr. Miller said that the Math Department had the reputation of being quite strict, and the seventh graders, still new to the school, might be a little intimidated by it. The students were also repeatedly told that (a) after this unit the teachers were going to determine which students would be transferred to an eighth grade math class, and (b) they should complete and keep their worksheets because they would be able to use them during the unit test. For many, the possibility of being advanced to the eighth grade math class—determined by their behavior, their accumulated grades including their test score on this unit, and a math achievement test—contributed to their "good" behavior during this unit.

Teachers also passed the time during the tape-recorded lessons in various ways. Some would correct papers from other classes and catch up on the seemingly endless backlog of routine paperwork. At first these taped lessons seemed to be more tolerated, probably because they gave teachers some extra preparation time, which in this school was limited to only forty-five minutes a day. But by Day Five, it appeared that even the opportunity to catch up on other work was not totally absorbing. One teacher paced around the room, stared at a poster for five minutes, stared out the window, and finally stopped near one of us and said, "I'm so sick of these tapes!" One teacher dozed during a tape. On Day Five, as on most days, the teacher's main role was to distribute the worksheets and manage the tape recorder. If all the daily tapes and worksheets were used and completed as specified on the Lesson Plan, then there was little or no time for questions or discussions. In all classes, other than supervising the use and distribution of the instructional materials, the teachers had little to do as the tapes and worksheets established the content and form of the lesson.

However, teachers did not always passively sit by and watch; they intervened into the planned lessons. Mr. Miller turned off the tape one day to explain a concept. He later told one of us, "We have to discuss and clarify some, smooth the rough edges of these worksheets." However, because of this interruption, he never did get back on schedule and complete the taped lesson. Ms. Wilson lost a day due to a school assembly and tried to consolidate two days by "talking through" some of the lessons herself. "We have to catch up today, so we can go to lab tomorrow." They couldn't catch up, however, and ended up skipping some tapes. Ms. Linder stopped a lesson to clarify a mathematical formula, the inclusion of which irritated her because, as she later said, "If I had seen the lesson first . . . I would have taken that out, seventh graders don't know that, it shouldn't be in there." On Day Six she modified the flow chart assignment by requesting her students to write a flow chart on the topic of "their choice," which, she later explained to one of us, would be "more interesting for the students."

Mr. Nelson explained that computers are "dumb" because they perform on the basis of how they are programmed and cannot reason or use common sense. He gave several examples of the kinds of errors that have been made by computers, such as astronomical billing errors that most humans would immediately recognize as erroneous but which of course a computer could not. Mr. Nelson frequently supplemented the lessons in order to increase student interest and understanding. While he too strove to maintain the schedule, he was sufficiently knowledgeable to supplement and enrich the daily lessons.

Mr. Miller took time one day to illustrate the difference between thirteen- and sixteen-sector disks. The computer program selected for use in the lab was on a thirteen-sector disk. Therefore, the students would have to go through some extra procedures in the lab the next day, and he wanted them to understand why. The point was not that this explanation about sectors was important, but that Mr. Miller's explanation represented an attempt to demystify the computer, to help the students understand why the computer responded the way it did. In fact, it was the "mystical" aura of the computer that the general goals of the CLU were attempting to avoid. Teachers unfamiliar with computers, of course, could not explain these kinds of things, and the men did more of this than the women teachers did. In the other classes, the sector incompatibility was not explained, and the students were just told to "first use this disk, then use the program disk."

The male teachers did more explaining in class than did the female teachers, primarily because they were more knowledgeable about computers and familiar with the unit. However, they too were committed to following the lesson plans, and their diversions to "smooth out the rough edges" invariably lost them time. Completing daily lesson plans was important to all the teachers because (a) the daily lessons were too long to make up the next day; (b) the schedule for the computer lab and the completion of the unit were fixed; (c) some lessons were sequential in nature; and (d) the final unit test was correlated to the information on the tapes and filmstrips. Therefore, the time that it would take teachers to explain the "whys" of computers was inevitably brief or not taken at all. To take the time would jeopardize the completion of the two-week unit.

Two points are important here. One is that while the teachers did to varying degrees stop the tapes and clarify, explain, or enrich the lessons, none attempted to eliminate a lesson, change the nature of the lessons, or change the unit. The second point is that, in the context of a pressured and crowded curriculum and an intensified labor process, when teachers did interject discussions, they invariably fell behind schedule. This made the pace of the unit even faster as they later tried to catch up. Thus, teachers felt that they had to maintain the schedule because the unit was a requirement for which they and the students were responsible. Therefore the completion of the CLU became highly dependent on following the unit plans, and this instrumental goal usually took precedence over teacher- or student-originated activities, even when teachers became more than a little uncomfortable. Knowledge "that," and low-level knowledge "how," dominated almost "naturally" in this situation.

Computer Lab Days: Hands On?

The three days in which the students met in the computer lab were quite a contrast to the classroom days because the students were using the computers. On Day Three the students were to select and use programs from a specially prepared demonstration disk. The general enthusiasm was dampened only by the fact that the students had to work in groups of three or four to a computer, and in the forty-five-minute class period each individual did not get very much "hands-on" computer time.

On Days Three and Nine the plan was to have half the class work with the teacher at one computer using a simulation program while the rest of the class shared the six remaining computers and were to complete a lab worksheet and write their own programs, mainly because, given their workload, the teachers did not have time to give them individual help. Ms. Linder recognized this and later said that she did not like this lesson plan because, by working with the large group on the simulation game, she was not able to circulate and help those students who were trying to write programs.

The computer lab days were by far the most favored by students and were planned to provide "hands-on" experiences. Yet, since there were only seven computers to be shared, students had to work in groups of two, or on Day Three in groups of three and four. Because periods were forty-five minutes long, most students spent more time observing computer use than actually using a computer. Many educators claim that it is preferable to have students work in pairs rather than individually at a computer because it promotes peer interaction and learning. We do not wish to reject that claim. However, in this study when groups became larger than two, they usually became dysfunctional, because individual interest waned as students were unable to sit and observe comfortably around the small computers. Invariably, some students would sit and engage in unrelated conversations while waiting for "their turn," which some never got. Therefore, actual hands-on computer time was very limited.

Even with this problem, however, students were in the Lab and were generally enthusiastic about being there. If their computer use was more vicarious than actual, they were at least observing computers. The computer lab days were active and exploratory in nature, and this provided a major contrast to the classroom days.

The Final Unit Test

The CLU final test on the tenth day was a short-answer summary of the worksheets, tapes, and filmstrips. The students could use their notes and worksheets to complete the test, which was composed of matching, listing, and fill-in-the-blank items such as the following:

Name 3 ways of putting information on printouts _____
The first computer was built in Philadelphia and was named_____ .
Put the outcome of each program on the output line.

Reflecting on the relatively reductive nature of the test, Mr. Nelson said that he questioned whether the test really measured what was most important.

Ms. Linder did not really like the test: "I felt that the final test could be better, some of the items were ambiguous and all the vocabulary stressed at the beginning was too technical." Ms. Kane felt that there should have been a review sheet of the "really important things" rather than having the students study and use all their notes during the test. Ms. Wilson said that the students "did well" on the test, and the other teachers referred to the test scores as acceptable. In general, the teachers did not seem to place much emphasis on the test or its results, although the students, who had been repeatedly warned that "this unit will be tested, and your score will count in your quarter grade," did seem to take it seriously and worked carefully on the test.

Teachers' Reconstructions

In later interviews and a departmental meeting, teachers talked about how they felt about the unit. Mr. Nelson, one of the developers, said, "I felt hamstrung, I would probably do things differently, but I felt that I had to pilot it." Since Mr. Nelson had computer expertise, he was not as dependent on the unit, and he, more than most, expanded the daily lesson plans.

Interestingly, use of the prepared CLU was not felt by all the teachers to be a required or even likely practice in the next years. Mr. Nelson did not feel further pressure to use the unit in the future, and he explained that it now exists as a "resource for those who want it," and that as long as the objectives are "covered" it didn't have to be done the same in every class. This is consistent with everyday practice in the Math Department, where all the teachers use the same standard textbook and cover the same objectives, so, as Mr. Miller said, "you know that each student has been exposed to the same things."

However, it is important to state that many of the teachers may indeed still choose to continue to use the "curriculum on a cart" in its current form, even though they recognize that it is minimizing their ability to affect the curriculum and that they are relatively "hamstrung." As noted earlier, the unit provided some "extra" time that teachers could and did use to catch up on routine paperwork and planning. For instance, when Ms. Kane was asked how she felt about the use of the tapes, she said:

> Well it was good . . . I mean naturally it got boring and monotonous, but I would just tune out during those times. I used that time to work on a new unit, or on [some school committee work], and I'd do other things during those tapes. I'd try not to show boredom to the kids, but I really didn't mind it, after all it was only for two weeks. And during that time I didn't have to prepare, everything

was prepared . . . and I didn't have papers to correct during that two weeks. . . .
If I'd change things next year, I'd lecture more, but I'd still use a lot of those
tapes, maybe not all, but a lot of them.

We cannot understand this response unless we situate it into the reality
of teachers' workloads. Ms. Kane taught five seventh grade math classes in
a row and, while she acknowledged that these tapes were boring for her,
she essentially took advantage of these two weeks to gain time and relieve
the pressures of keeping up with the planning and grading for five math
classes. She was aware of the fact that the unit marginalized her own curriculum autonomy, but she did not overtly resist her designated role in it.
Instead, she interpreted and used the unit to compensate for her otherwise
intense routine. She recognized the unit for what it was; she used the
"extra" time that it gave her, and she was not negative in assessing her role
in the unit.

Her colleague, Ms. Linder, also referred to the intensity of work and said
that she didn't like the daily teaching schedule because "There are no breaks
in the day, not time to correct papers, plan. . . . You don't get to know the students as individuals . . . I have a seating chart." Therefore, the unit that was
all prepackaged, ready to go, and included few assignments to be corrected
provided some benefits to teachers whose normal routine is far more labor
intensive.

For some teachers, a curriculum that separated conception from execution can sometimes then seem to be a benefit, not a loss. In addition to providing some time for teachers, the unit also was seen to provide the pedagogical support and information about computers that Ms. Wilson, a first-year
teacher who was unfamiliar with computers, interpreted as helpful. Ms. Wilson said that the tapes helped her because she learned about computers along
with the students and anticipated using the same lessons again, although she
would "branch out" as she becomes more computer literate. Teaching a unit
for which she was unprepared was intimidating, and she welcomed the prepared unit in which she could turn on the tape recorder and use worksheets.
When asked about how she viewed the content on the unit, she said, "I think
it covered the important things . . . but I really don't know much about computers you know. . . ."[25] Ms. Wilson, in general, was positive in her assessment
of the unit.

Even though all the teachers had equally intensive schedules, they did not
all interpret the form of the CLU in terms of benefits. For example, Ms. Linder was more than a little distressed by the form of the unit, as well as some
of the content. Her main objection was that she preferred to plan her own curriculum. She said:

You didn't have to be a teacher to teach this unit. Just turn on and off tapes . . .
I would have done things a little different. I have enough computer background to have done some things differently if I had had time to prepare it. . . .
I was dependent on their plan, tapes, and worksheets. . . . I kept asking to see
the unit, but it wasn't done and I was told, "Don't worry, there isn't much to
do, just tapes." But I didn't like those two weeks at all, I knew when I was out
those days, the sub would be able to do it, she just had to turn on the tape
recorder.

These comments are echoed in other places and by other teachers, though
perhaps not as strongly. To varying degrees, most felt something was being
lost by relying too heavily on "the curriculum on a cart." Yet by and large, the
teachers accepted these two weeks as they were originally planned and did not
markedly alter the standardized curriculum. How can we understand this?

Gender and the Intensification of Teaching

The rhetoric of computer literacy often turns out to be largely that—rhetoric.
Even given the meritorious aims of the staff and the school district, and even
given the extensive amount of work put in by teachers, the curriculum is
reduced once again to work sheets, an impersonal prepackaged style, and fact-
based tests.

A good deal of this can only be fully understood if we place these
attempts at curriculum reform back into what we have called the fiscal crisis
of the state. School systems are often caught between two competing goals:
those of accumulation and legitimation. They must both support an economy,
especially when it is in crisis, and at the same time maintain their legitimacy
with a wide range of different groups. The fiscal crisis makes it nearly impossible for schools to have sufficient resources to meet all of the goals they say
they will meet; yet not to at least try to meet a multitude of varied goals means
that an educational system will lose its legitimacy in the eyes of the "public."
Given this, many goals will simply be symbolic. They will serve as a political rhetoric to communicate to the public that schools are in fact doing what
concerned groups want them to do.

Yet they will not be totally rhetorical. Many teachers will be *committed*
to the goals, believing that they are worth meeting and worth spending the
exceptional amounts of additional time trying to take them seriously. These
teachers will exploit themselves, working even harder in underfunded and
intensified conditions to overcome the contradictory pressures they will be
under. At the same time, however, the additional workload will create a situation in which fully meeting these goals will be impossible.

This school developed a Computer Literacy Unit under the same conditions and with the same intentions that many schools are currently developing similar curricula. Computer-knowledgeable teachers, ample computers, adequate time, and scheduling flexibility are more like wishes than realities in most school districts. Mr. Nelson and Mr. Miller worked intensively for over a month to develop a curriculum that would provide introductory experiences for all the seventh graders. The CLU they developed was significant because it exemplified how the process of transforming a very general goal like computer literacy into a specific curriculum was mediated by the "given" organizational factors and resources—both human and material—typifying the school, and by the gender divisions that organized it, a point to which we shall return in a moment.

It was apparent that the structure of the unit and its implementation schedule, as well as the heavy load of teaching and paperwork that these teachers had, made it difficult for teachers to contribute more to the unit than brief and occasional additions and clarifications to its content. A "canned" or prepackaged curriculum did emerge. Yet it was valued by some teachers as a practical and sensible solution to the problem of curriculum time, resources, and "skills."

Certainly the major condition here was that of curriculum-planning time, both in the immediate and long-term sense. In this school, only the two men teachers were technically prepared to teach the unit. Because the unit had to be completed within the first ten weeks of school, the other teachers did not have time to prepare themselves to develop the new curriculum for their classes. Paying two teachers to develop the unit for the department was the district's way of compensating individual teachers for their lack of curriculum preparation time. However, lack of comprehensive curriculum-planning time is characteristic of the structure of most schools. Thus, the "curriculum on a cart" solution tends to be a generalized response to the demands of new curriculum projects in many schools, especially since other responses would require more money, something we cannot expect in times of the fiscal crisis of the state.

This practice compensates teachers for their lack of time by providing them with prepackaged curricula rather than changing the basic conditions under which inadequate preparation time exists. In the immediate context, some teachers may interpret this as helpful and appreciate it as a resource. But in the broader context, it deprives teachers of a vital component of the curriculum process. Over time, these short-term compensatory practices function as deprivations, because they limit the intellectual and emotional scope of teachers' work. This deprivation was specifically recognized and articulated by Ms. Linder in her quote at the end of the previous section. As an experienced teacher who was very anxious to resume her full responsibilities, she expressed her feelings of alienation and unimportance when she said, "You don't have to be a teacher to teach this unit," and went on to say that she wasn't worried when she was absent and a substitute had to teach her seventh grade class during the unit. Her skills and her curriculum responsibilities had been usurped, and this angered her. Thus, while in the immediate context the availability of the "curriculum on a cart" was positively interpreted by some teachers, in the long term this form of curriculum functions to compensate for and not to alleviate the problem for which it was viewed as a solution, that of time and "expertise."

The condition of time must be examined in *gender* terms here. It was the women teachers, not the men, in the Math Department who were seen as less prepared to teach about computers, and they were the ones most dependent on the availability of the unit. Typically, the source of computer literacy for in-service teachers is either through college and university courses, school district courses, or independent study, all options that take considerable time outside of school. Both Mr. Miller and Mr. Nelson had taken a substantial number of university courses on computers in education. Given the gendered specificities of domestic labor, many women, such as those with child care and household responsibilities, like Ms. Linder, or women who are single parents, may have considerably less out of school time to take additional coursework and prepare new curricula. Therefore, when a new curriculum such as computer literacy is required, women teachers may be more dependent on using the ready-made curriculum materials than most men teachers. Intensification here does lead to an increasing reliance on "outside experts." An understanding of the larger structuring of patriarchal relations, then, is essential if we are to fully comprehend both why the curriculum was produced the way it was and what its effects actually were.

It is absolutely crucial, however, to say that the commitments to environments that embody an ethic of caring and connectedness—commitments that have been shown to be so much a part of many women's daily experiences and are so critical in an education worthy of its name—may actually provide the resources for countering such rationalized curricular models.[26] The sense of loss, of an absence of community, the struggle to personalize and reduce anonymity, all this enables one to restore the collective memory of difference. The women teachers here may have some of the most important resources for resistance in the long run.

These points about the gendered realities of the women teachers are significant in another way. It would be all to easy to blame the women teachers in this setting for basically following the "curriculum on a cart" and, hence, participating in the degradation of their own labor and a reductive "that" based curriculum. This, we believe, would be a major error.

As a number of commentators have suggested, the real lives of many women teachers, when seen close up, are complicated by the fact that one often returns home exhausted after being in the intensified setting of the classroom only to then face the emotional and physical demands of housework, cooking, childcare, and so on. Since many women teachers are *already* doing two jobs, their caution and "lack of enthusiasm" toward additional work is anything but a simplistic response to "innovation." Rather it is a realistic strategy for dealing with the complications in the objective reality they daily face.[27]

We need to remember that doing nothing is a form of action itself. Though it is not always the result of a set of conscious decisions, it can have serious consequences.[28]

Women teachers, like all workers, may overtly resist intensification and the loss of their autonomy and skills. At other times, from the outside it may seem as if they are "passively" accepting a separation of conception from execution or the deskilling of their jobs. However, as we know from an immense amount of research, most individuals on their jobs will attempt to take even the most alienating experiences and turn them to their own advantage, if only to maintain control over their own labor to simply keep from being alienated and bored,[29] or as in this case to solve other equally real problems brought about by the conditions of fiscal scarcity, overwork, bureaucratic realities, and external constraints. Teachers are never dupes, never simply the passive puppets that structural models would have us believe. Their agency and their actions in concrete situations such as these may have contradictory results. They may have elements of "good sense" and "bad sense" in tension as they construct their responses to a crisis in the economy, in authority relations, and in education. Yet the fact that they do construct these responses once again shows the very possibility of difference. In a time when the right would like to commodify education[30] and to once again turn our schools into factories, that possibility is of no small importance. These constructions are not preordained. They can be reconstructed in ways that will allow us to join with teachers to challenge the redefinitions of skills and power that are currently going on. Too much is at stake if we don't.

III

Democratic Possibilities:
When Does Technology Empower?

CHAPTER 7

Control and Power in Educational Computing[1]

PETER H. KAHN, JR. and
BATYA FRIEDMAN

> The [high school] computer center is overseen by a student group, the Computer Users Society. Members have keys to the room, and may gain access at any time, day or night, weekends. One Sunday morning, Harvey [the high school teacher] recalls, he came in around 10 a.m. thinking he would get some work done while the place was quiet. He could not find a free terminal.
>
> —Dormer, 1981

> The Computer Center User Society . . . holds regular meetings to decide the policies and rules of the computer program. Managing the computer system are six students, called "superusers," who oversee the use of the computers. . . . [One student] explained that although superusers have access to everything, by the time a student gets to the point of being a superuser, immoral actions such as looking at grades are "the last thing we'd have to worry about. This place is so special . . . it would be such a downfall that no one would want to risk it."
>
> —Appel, 1985

These educational computing practices formed part of the computer education that Harvey (1980, 1983) initiated in an otherwise traditional high school. In this paper, we want to say more about the direction in which Harvey points. It is toward student participation, cooperation, and interest, and a school culture that is imbued with using computer technology to foster democratization.

More broadly, we seek to convey an account of educational computing based on the primacy of human agency. Toward this end, we distinguish between control and power. In our use of these terms, control occurs when people direct coercively another person, or direct the action or process of a

157

non-person (e.g., a machine). The key here is that within social relations control is usually unethical because it undermines others' autonomy. Power, in turn, occurs only in social relations. It can be coercive, and in such cases power refers to how people control others. But power can also refer to non-coercive relationships within which people influence, organize, and lead others. After developing this distinction, we take up several questions: How do we teach students that humans, and often the students themselves, control computer technology and are responsible for the consequences of computer-mediated action? How do we teach future computer scientists to design systems that foster such understandings? And how do we teach students that by controlling computer technology—and choosing wisely—people have power to effect meaningful and ethical change in educational settings and beyond?

Computers: Objects or Others?

Consider this brief event: A friend of ours sought to make an airline reservation and called the airline company to charge her ticket. In the process of writing the ticket, the reservationist requested a home phone number. Now, it happened that our friend was between academic jobs and in transit for the summer. Thus she did not have a home phone. Although the reservationist listened sympathetically to this explanation, he insisted that he be given a phone number: "Our computer program has to have a phone number or it won't work. I can't even get to the next screen. It's the computer's fault." How many times have we heard that? "It's the computer's fault." Well is it? Can computers be at fault?

Such questions arise because computer technology often appears volitional and intelligent. Computer systems, for example, can "track" credit histories and "decide" to reject loan applications. Computer-guided missiles, as noted by Dawkins (1976), often appear to "search actively" for their target, to "predict" and "anticipate" the target's evasive moves. Medical expert systems "diagnose" illness and "recommend" cures. In terms of educational software, intelligent tutors "decide" which problems a student will work on, "correct" students when they are wrong, and "judge" when a student is ready for more advanced problem sets. Tracking. Deciding. Searching. Anticipating. Recommending. Tutoring. Correcting. Judging. Such terms would seem to imply that we believe computers are not so different from humans and that they have, to varying degrees, intentional states such as thoughts, desires, consciousness, free will, and the capability to make intelligent decisions. How did we come to believe such things about computers?

One response is that we do not believe such things. Another response is that we believe such things because they are true. Both responses are worth our attention. In the first, it might be granted that in conversations people readily talk about "intelligent tutors" or "smart missiles." Or, like the airline reservationist noted earlier or a student who hands in a late term paper, one might say "it is the computer's fault." But, it could be argued, what appears as sincere instantiations of attributing agency to computational systems are nothing more than superficial verbal responses, and that people do not really conceive of computers as human or humanlike.

Research bears on this first response. Turkle (1984), for example, interviewed children about their experiences with an interactive computer game called Merlin that plays Tic-Tac-Toe. Her findings indicated that children attributed psychological characteristics to Merlin: that Merlin, for example, was capable of cheating. Similar findings appear with adults (cf. Rumelhart and Norman, 1981; Weizenbaum, 1976). Kiesler and Sproull, for example, have shown that when the interface presents the computer as a persona, users engage in cooperative behavior with the computer (Kiesler and Sproull, in press) and attribute some personality traits to the computer (Sproull, Subramani, Kiesler, Walker, and Waters, 1996). Along similar lines, Nass, Steuer, Tauber, and Reeder (1993) tested computer-literate college students using different types of computer-based tutoring and testing systems. Their findings showed that when a computer mimics even a minimal set of characteristics associated with humans (such as simple textual cues) that users attributed to the computer human-like qualities, such as friendliness. More recently, based on their research, Nass, Moon, Morkes, Kim, and Fogg (in press) have suggested that people respond positively to flattery from a computer, are attracted to dominant or submissive programmed characteristics embedded in the interface of a computer, and, most generally, treat computers as social actors.

Another study by Friedman and Millet (1995) employed social cognitive methods to assess individuals' reasoning about computer agency and computer capabilities, and individuals' judgments of moral responsibility in two situations that involved delegation of decision making to a complex computer system. One situation involved an automated computer system that evaluates the employability of job seekers and rejects a qualified worker. The second situation involved an automated computer system that administers medical radiation treatment and over-radiates a cancer patient. Computer science majors from a research university were interviewed. Results showed a complex pattern of results. On the one hand, most of the students attributed either decision making or intentions to computers, and over one-fifth of the students explicitly held computers morally responsible for error. On the other hand, most of the students judged computer decision making and computer intentions to be different from that of humans. Reasoning focused, for example, on rule-based systems (e.g., "[the computer] can decide in a sense that somebody has programmed rules, which it follows, and in that sense it chooses a course") and algorithmic processes (e.g., "[the computer] is deciding based on a very clear strict algorithm . . . it's a decision but not an open-ended one"). Moreover, virtually all (96 percent) of the students' reasons for blaming the computer referred to the computer's participation in the sequence of events that led to harm. In contrast, most (80 percent) of the students' reasons for blaming people (such as the system designers, human operator, or administrators) referred to failing to meet some commonly expected reasonable level of performance, including appeals to inadequate design of the computer system, inadequate testing or debugging of the program, inadequate monitoring, and personal carelessness. Thus, while this study does not support the stronger claims by Nass and his colleagues that people treat computers as social actors, it does suggest that in certain respects people attribute agency to computer technology, and that such attributions go well beyond superficial use of language.

If people attribute agency to a computer, it could be argued—and this is the second response—that this attribution occurs quite simply because computers have agency. Historically, the military has been committed to this view philosophically and financially. The military has sought to develop "smart" and "autonomous" computer-based weaponry and to use computers to train military personnel. In turn, the military has had an enormous impact on shaping the fields of computer science and educational computing. For example, according to Thomborson (cited in Noble, 1991, p. 13) 70 percent of all academic research in computer science has been funded by the Department of Defense. Similarly, according to Noble (1991), "military agencies have provided three-fourths of all funding for educational technology research over the last three decades, and within government agencies, the military spends seven dollars for every civilian dollar spent on educational technology research" (p. 2). Thus, most of the research in computer science and most of our nation's computer-based educational applications comes out of a tradition that believes that computer technology can mimic, if not duplicate, human agency. Is such a belief warranted?

Perhaps the most sustained and incisive critique of the idea that computers can be intelligent in the sense of having intentional states has been advanced by Searle (1980, 1984, 1990, 1992). While this is not the place to go in depth into Searle's thinking, it is worthwhile to review the skeleton of his well-known Chinese room argument. Through it, we stake out our philosophical position toward technology, which, in turn, provides a cornerstone for our educational practice.

Searle's thought experiment goes something like this: Imagine that you do not understand Chinese writing or speaking, and you are put in a room with a basketful of Chinese symbols. You are then given a rule book in English that tells you how to match up certain symbols with other symbols, based only on their visual configuration. For example, a double-bent squiggle might get matched with a half-bent squoggle. Now, imagine that a Chinese person from outside the room writes you a question to try to determine if you know Chinese. You receive the written question, which to you are only meaningless Chinese symbols, and according to the rules of your English rule book, you match up the symbols with other appropriate symbols, and then send out the response. With a good rule book, the Chinese person will not be able to tell the difference between your answers and the answers given by a Chinese-speaking person in that room. The outside questioner might ask with Chinese squiggles, "Would you like a Big Mac or a Whopper?" You might respond with Chinese squoggles, "A Whopper, for I find Big Macs just a tad too greasy." But now we ask the question, would you understand what you just said? Or, more generally, when you correctly manipulate the symbols, do you *understand* Chinese? Searle argues, absolutely not. After all, when you send out an answer, you do not know what you are sending out. All you are doing is matching symbols with other symbols based on the rule book. That is, there is nothing in the formal symbol manipulation (the syntax) that provides the understanding of Chinese (the semantics). So, too, with computers. Because computational systems are purely formal (syntax), and because purely formal systems have no means to generate semantics, Searle argues that computational systems do not have the properties that are central to human agency.

Searle's position has generated a great deal of debate, starting with twenty-six rebuttals in the journal where his initial article first appeared (see Searle, 1980). For example, one rebuttal (often referred to as "the systems reply") to Searle goes like this: "Searle has confused levels of mental organization. The rule-follower in the Chinese room represents a piece of the human brain, and the entire room represents the person. Thus, while it is true that the rule-follower in the Chinese room does not understand Chinese, the entire room does." In Searle's (1981) reply, he asks that we go ahead and assume that the person in the Chinese room internalizes all of the elements of the room: the rule book, the data banks of Chinese symbols, everything. The person can then do the calculations in a location outside the room. All the same, the person understands nothing of Chinese. Thus neither does the room, because there is nothing in the room (the system) that is not in the person.

In our view and that of others, Searle has defended himself well against his critics. This is not to say that humanlike agency might not someday be realized in material or structures other than biological brains. It is to say that computers as we can conceive of them today are not such materials or structures. Thus while humans may (sometimes with valid justification) delegate decision making to computer technology, fundamentally it is humans who control technology.

In the last handful of years, some members of the Artificial Intelligence (AI) community appear to have backed off from their strong philosophical claims (see, for example, the editorial by Chandrasekaran, 1992, editor-in-chief of the artificial intelligence journal of the IEEE). Their current position goes something like this: Regardless of whether or not computers actually have intelligence, computers act as if they do, and thus we can rightly design and interact with them as if they do. On the one hand these AI researchers give up a good deal of philosophical ground to those like Searle. On the other hand, they keep their research agenda fully in place—to build intelligent-like computer systems. But if computers continue to be designed as if they have agency, and if in their interactions with computers people act as if computers have agency, then it seems likely that people will think so as well. Thought and action cannot be so easily compartmentalized. Thus we have argued elsewhere (Friedman and Kahn, 1992) that increasingly sophisticated computer systems should be designed not to mimic human agency, but to support it. For example, computer interfaces should not be designed to intercede in the guise of another "agent" between human users and the computational system, but to "disappear" such that the user is freed to attend directly to, and take responsibility for, the tasks at hand (see, also, Shneiderman, 1987; Winograd and Flores, 1986). The same holds for the emerging work on software agents.

Here is where we have been heading. We suggest that children and adults in various ways mistakenly attribute agency to computer technology. And we say mistakenly because it is our claim that computers as we can conceive of them today in materials and structures do not have agency. Moreover, we suggest that people should control technology, take responsibility for the consequences of computer-mediated action, and minimize if not eliminate control within relations that involve power between people.

To develop these last points a little more fully, consider the following example. Drawing on Arnstine (1973), imagine the hijacker who points a gun at an airline pilot and says, "Fly me to Havana or I'll blow your brains out." The gun could be said to coerce the pilot. After all, without the gun the threat would have little force. However, contrary to some theorists who argue that objects can have a social life (Appadurai, 1988), we maintain that the gun is fundamentally an inanimate tool mediated by a person (see also Scheffler, 1991, chap. 8): in this case a tool used for the purpose to establish control over another person. In this explicit psychological sense, we agree with the statement, "guns don't kill people, people do." It is also the case, however, that once people build tools, the tools have built-in features such that people usually use the tools in certain ways, toward certain ends (cf. Bromley, 1992). Thus with a gun, or with a computer-driven weapon, people often exert power to control other people.

During the Persian Gulf War, United States Patriot missiles were used to detect and intercept Iraqi Scuds. However, the precision of a Patriot's calculations to predict the location of a Scud while in flight depended in complex ways on the continuous running time of the Patriot's computer system. The longer the system was running, the greater the imprecision. This systematic software error resulted in the death of at least 28 Americans in Dhahran (US General Accounting Office, 1992). In such situations, it is easy to say, "it's the computer's fault," not unlike what the airline receptionist said whom we mentioned earlier. We have argued that it is not. Rather, the responsibility for harm incurred through computer-mediated action lies ultimately with people. Depending on the specific situation, responsibility will perhaps rest with one or more of the following: the programmers who wrote the software, the administrators or other individuals who chose to implement the particular hardware or software, the designers or manufacturers of the hardware, or the operators of the computer technology.

Constructivist Education

In terms of educational computing, our distinction between control and power motivates several questions. How do we teach students that humans, and often the students themselves, control computer technology and are responsible for the consequences of computer-mediated action? How do we teach future computer scientists to design systems that foster such understandings? Finally, how do we teach students that by controlling computer technology, people have power to effect meaningful and ethical change in educational settings and beyond? Our answers build on a constructivist account of education. Thus, before highlighting specific computing activities, we should like to say a few words about this perspective by elaborating on four constructivist principles proposed and practiced by DeVries and her colleagues (DeVries, 1988; DeVries and Kohlberg, 1990; DeVries and Zan, 1994).

From Instruction to Construction

Many people believe that for students to learn, teachers must instruct, by which it is meant that learning depends on a teacher who correctly sequences curriculum content, drills students on correct performance, corrects mistakes, and then tests for achievement. Granted, one might note a few sidewise embraces of critical thinking and cognition. But if push comes to shove—if, for example, test scores go down—the call is clear. Back to basics. Instruction in the Three Rs. In contrast, in the move from instruction to construction, learning involves neither simply the replacement of one view (the incorrect one) with another (the presumed correct one) nor simply the stacking, like building blocks, of new knowledge on top of old knowledge, but rather transformations of knowledge. Transformations, in turn, occur not through the child's passivity, but through active, original thinking. As Baldwin (1897/1973) says, a child's knowledge "at each new plane is also a real invention. . . . He makes it; he gets it for himself by his own action; he achieves, invents it" (p. 106).

Think of it this way. On a daily level, children encounter problems of all sorts: logical, mathematical, physical, social, ethical. Problems require solutions. The disequilibrated state is not a comfortable one. Thus the child strives toward a more comprehensive, more adequate, means of resolving problems, of synthesizing disparate ideas, of making sense of the world. Constructivist education, therefore, centrally involves experimentation and problem solving, and student confusion and mistakes are not antithetical to learning, but a basis for it.

From Reinforcement to Interest

Traditional educators often seek to shape student behavior through four types of reinforcement procedures: positive reinforcement, punishment, response cost, negative reinforcement (Rohwer, Rohwer, and B-Howe, 1980). Each procedure builds on a conception that children learn through stimulus-response conditioning, and that for effective instruction the teacher needs to strengthen, weaken, extinguish, or maintain learned behaviors through such reinforcement procedures. In contrast, as we have argued, humans have not just syntax, which leads to a conception of the child as a computer, to be programmed, but semantics, meaning. It is not surprising, then, that children construct meaning more fully when engaged with problems and issues that they find meaningful, that captivate their interest. Thus, from a constructivist perspective, teachers find out what interests their students and build curriculum to support and extend those interests. They allow students to help shape the curriculum and the freedom to explore, to take risks, to make mistakes. Indeed, it can be argued that many of the behavior problems that traditional teachers try so hard to suppress arise precisely because students find the curriculum drudgery.

From Obedience to Autonomy

Construction and interest do not thrive in an environment in which the teacher is the authority demanding obedience. Moreover, obedience leads to conformity and to the acceptance of ideas without understanding. Thus, from a constructivist perspective, teachers should move away from demanding obedience and toward fostering the child's autonomy. Now, by autonomy we mean in part something like independence from others. For it is only through being an independent thinker and actor that a person can refrain from being unduly influenced by others (for example, by neo-Nazis, youth gangs, political movements, and advertising). Autonomy in this sense is necessary for an individual to control technology. But by autonomy we do not mean a divisive individualism, as constructivist autonomy is often said to be (Hogan, 1975; Shweder, 1986). Rather, within a constructivist framework (Baldwin, 1897/1973; Kohlberg, 1969, 1984), autonomy is highly social, developed through reciprocal interactions on a microgenetic level, and evidenced structurally in incorporating and coordinating considerations of self, others, and society. In other words, the social constrains or bounds the individual(ism), and vice-versa.

From Coercion to Cooperation

In some sense, the movement from coercion to cooperation reflects the flip side of obedience to autonomy, but more from the student's and not the teacher's standpoint. As does autonomy, cooperation entails incorporating and coordinating one's own feelings, values, and perspectives with those of others. Given that adults' relationships with children are laden (often necessarily so) with coercive interactions, peer relationships are centrally important. Through them, concepts of equality, justice, and democracy flourish (Piaget, 1932/1969), and academic learning is advanced (Vygotsky, 1978).

   These four constructivist educational principles comprise part of a larger social-cognitive research tradition (e.g., Arsenio and Lover, 1995; Damon, 1977; Friedman, 1997; Kahn, 1992; Kahn and Friedman, 1995; Kohlberg, 1969; Laupa, 1991; Nucci, 1996; Piaget, 1932/1969; Selman, 1980; Smetana, 1995; Turiel, 1997; Wainryb, 1995). These principles are also, in many respects, compatible with other educational theories, for example, those that are progressive (Dewey, 1916/1966) and experiential (Wigginton, 1986). We prefer, however, the constructivist label for two reasons. First, it highlights that no matter how social the discourse, elaborate the organizational structure, or co-constructive the reciprocal interaction, fundamentally it is a self (a morally responsible agent) who makes meaning in the world. Second, constructivism allows best for the modern as opposed to postmodern epistemology which guides our work and which provides a foundational basis for checking abuses of power (Kahn, 1991, 1993, 1995; Lourenco, 1996).

Constructivist Computing in the Classroom

Educational computing can be enhanced by software designs which shift more of the control over technology, and responsibility for learning, back on the student. Historically, Papert's development of the LOGO microworld is perhaps most well known along these lines. Through programming computers with turtle geometry, Papert (1980) showed how a child "both acquires a sense of mastery over a piece of the most modern and powerful technology and establishes an intimate contact with some of the deepest ideas from science, from mathematics, and from the art of intellectual model building" (p. 5). More recently, this orientation toward the technology and learning is embedded in computer construction kits. *Interactive Physics II* (Baszucki, 1992), for example, allows the user to access a large number of physical components (springs, ropes, blocks, and disks) and properties (forces and gravity) to model and investigate two-dimensional physical systems. Through such construction kits, the user engages actively in a design, receives immediate data by which to judge its success, and then is positioned to rework a better design, and thus continue the generative process.

Educational software can also be designed to allow students to explore hypothetical social situations (not just mathematical or physical) from multiple perspectives, and to follow different courses of action of each. For example, in the computer simulation *Our Town Meeting* (Snyder 1985a), students working in groups are assigned to one of three town agencies, each with its own agenda. Through the simulation, students find that cooperative strategies often provide the most effective means for resolving disputes and achieving agency-specific goals. Cooperation is also encouraged in another computer simulation, *The Other Side* (Snyder, 1985b), where students work in teams to build the economy of their own country while working toward building a bridge between their own and a rival country.

Such software moves educational computing in a good direction. However, we have seen many cases where "traditional" teachers use such software while remaining largely unaware of how they constrain the software's use. For example, Friedman (1988) conducted an ethnographic evaluation of a computer education program in an elementary school known for successful innovation. Friedman found that fourth and fifth graders were taught graphics programming largely by rote: "After two years of instruction, students still primarily drew pre-determined images on the computer screen using a single well-drilled algorithm" (p. 4). Teachers seldom asked or even allowed students to seek novel solutions or define their own problems, although the technology allowed for such possibilities.

One compelling way teachers can support such possibilities is to have students use computer technologies as tools to generate, share, and argue about ideas. Consider, for example, a student-run newspaper. Word processors and desktop publishing tools support students' writing. Spelling checkers help the presentation. Spreadsheets can help students to manage the financial aspects of running the newspaper, and databases to organize and access relevant information. Thus, students learn not only how to use a wide range of computer applications but that, as students, they control computer technology and are responsible for the consequences of their computer-mediated action: namely, for their published ideas.

Electronic mail and more generally accessing the World Wide Web has of course been providing many classes with an even wider community for discourse (cf. Cummins, 1988; Horowitz, 1984; Martinez, 1993). Not uncommonly, for example, classes conduct science experiments in consort with other classes across geographical locations, using electronic mail to share their data and interpretations. Other schools have combined efforts across geographical boundaries to write a joint newspaper. Educational networks like Apple Global Education support such computing practices, and more (see, e.g., Kearsley, Hunter, and Furlong, 1992, chapters 5 and 8). In ways like these, computer technology can be used to enhance communication and understanding between students who might differ on the basis of geography, culture, race, age, and economic standing.

Students can also be engaged with computing issues which emerge within organizations. Here, for example, is an idea for a sustained project with older students. Have students choose an organization—McDonald's, a bank, a manufacturing plant, the school attendance office, most any will do—and have them research how the computer technology was brought into the organization, how it supports the organization's goals, and how it shapes social interactions. Students can collect "data" through observations, surveys, and extended interviews. Their data can inform on such questions as: Who decided that computer technology would be good to have in the organization? Who decided on the specific hardware and software? To what extent did workers and consumers participate in this process? What do managers and workers think about the technology's current use? Were there any unanticipated consequences from using the technology?

Such projects were successfully conducted by undergraduate students at our own institution. One group of students, for example, in an administrative science course, elected to study computer use in a small accounting firm. The firm used a computerized tax preparation program chosen for its ease of use and compatibility with existing hardware. In addition to these features (and unnoticed by the firm members at the time of purchase), the software kept a running tally of the number of tax forms completed by each accountant. This information on each accountant was revealed at the end of the tax season. Office discord followed. In response, the firm made a collective decision to "hide" this unsolicited information in subsequent years. Through reflecting on findings like these, students can identify situations where workers feel either controlled or supported by technology, and can be better positioned to propose changes for the work place.

Who Controls the Computer?—Democratic Communities

Alexander Randall has told of his experience walking the streets of places like Warsaw, Moscow, and Kiev during their recent struggles for independence (Lewis, 1992). Randall talked with people in various organizations, with dissidents, and with mainstream journalists. He asked, "What is the next step to make sure that freedom of speech and free government survive?" Their answers surprised him. They all said they wanted desktop publishing equipment. It dawned on him. "What is freedom of the press if you don't have the press?" For such reasons, Randall founded the East-West Foundation. This nonprofit organization solicits used (and by many standards outdated) personal computers from Westerners and provides them free of charge to dissidents and journalists in the Eastern European countries. In Randall's words, "Our old XT's and AT's and Mac 512's are awesome tools to people who don't have them. . . . The fall of Communism did not axiomatically mean the rise of democracy. This is our people's response to insure that the forces trying to make democracy happen will ultimately succeed" (p. F12). In such ways, people can control computer technology to enhance political freedom.

If we accept, moreover, that children develop understandings about political freedom and of how to create societies in which such freedoms thrive, then it follows that such understandings and practice need to be made an integral part of children's education. Toward this end, we suggest that schools be organized to increase student self-governance (e.g., Kohlberg, 1980, 1984, 1985; Power, Higgins, and Kohlberg, 1989). In such schools, students determine many of the policies that regulate their own classroom and school activities, and thus gain experience with democratic and consensus decision-making processes. The teacher's primary role is to guide the process. Teachers may help students become aware of and understand issues when they arise,

and ensure that all students have an opportunity to voice their views in pol-
icy-setting meetings. Since teachers are themselves members of the self-governing community, they too may act as advocates, influencing the selection of
issues for which students set policy. Teachers may also need to limit the range
of acceptable agreements, particularly when majority agreements conflict
with minority rights and welfare, or when community decisions conflict with
legal requirements on the societal level.

Such "authoritarian" interventions in self-governing classrooms and
schools occur less frequently than perhaps would be expected. Recall, for
instance, the educational practices quoted at the outset of this paper that Harvey initiated in his high school computer center. Students held regular meetings to decide their policies and rules. By this means, students delegated
"superusers" who oversaw the use of the computer systems and had access to
most all of the files (including grades). One student "explained that although
superusers have access to everything, by the time a student gets to the point
of being a superuser, immoral actions such as looking at grades are 'the last
thing we'd have to worry about. This place is so special . . . it would be such
a downfall that no one would want to risk it'" (Appel, 1985). In this situation,
one would perhaps like to see more consideration for the privacy of others
(vis-a-vis grades), and the psychological harm that can occur when such privacy is violated. Yet what is admirable with Harvey's students is that they
bounded their own actions ethically by recognizing that harmful repercus-
sions would otherwise fall on their community as a whole.

Friedman (1986, 1991) provides further suggestions for how self-governance can be implemented with somewhat younger students. For example, in
one situation Friedman (1986) taught eight- to eleven-year-olds in a classroom
in which each student did not have his or her own computer. Thus, along with
most teachers nationwide, Friedman faced a common problem: how should
the computer resources be allocated? Instead of dictating a solution, Friedman
turned the "problem" itself into an educational experience. She divided the
students into small groups of four or five and asked them to come up with a
solution by consensus. In addition, she imposed the requirement that any solution could not prevent a student from completing class work. Initial proposals
ranged from flipping a coin, to relay races, to "those who want to share can
share," to "people who shared yesterday don't have to share today." The class
then discussed the proposals and voted to implement one. Not surprisingly,
students often implemented many imperfect or less than fair solutions. Thus
Friedman further guided the process. She asked that the class live with the
implemented solution for a week, at which time the policy would be assessed
and the process repeated. Accordingly, no policy was binding for an unbear-
able period of time. Moreover, students had rich opportunities to increase

their understandings of resource allocation and participatory democracy.

True, even in such "self-governing" classrooms, teachers have power. But here is a crucial point. Power can be used well—wisely, ethically, not to control students, and not to undermine their autonomy but to promote it. Moreover, as we noted earlier, by autonomy we do not mean a divisive individualism but a commitment to cooperative interactions that coordinate considerations of self, others, and society. Thus, for example, Friedman guided her students through a consensus-building process and allowed students the freedom to make mistakes. Similarly, Harvey allowed his students the freedom to choose which programming languages they wanted to learn and, indeed, the freedom to learn no programming language at all. Harvey (1980) writes that educational freedom means first of all that students can make significant choices, not trivial ones invented by a teacher. Self-governance allows for such significance and thus embraces an educational freedom that seems to us but part and parcel of political freedom.

Educating Computer Scientists

If it is important to teach students across ages and academic fields about the social implications of computer technology, then all the more so for computer science students. These are the students who in the coming years will design and build the computational systems that shape our computing environments. Teaching such students about the social responsibilities that come with their technical expertise has received increasing attention in the literature (Bynum, Maner, and Fodor, 1992; Denning, 1992; Friedman and Kahn, 1992; Johnson and Nissenbaum, 1995; Kling, 1996; Ermann, Williams, and Gutierrez, 1990; Friedman and Winograd, 1990; Gotterbarn, 1992; Johnson, 1985; Miller, 1988; Parker, Swope, and Baker, 1990; Perrolle, 1987; Winograd, 1992). It has also become part of the core curriculum recommended by leading computing organizations ("A Summary of the ACM/IEEE," 1991) and by which computer science departments are judged for national accreditation. Thus we wish to describe several means to integrate social concerns into students' computer design experiences, such that when students define and implement computer systems, standard issues include not only technical ones (such as "What data structure should I use?"), but social ones (such as "How does my system impact the intended users?").

Recent analyses of bias in computer system designs lead toward one such means. Friedman and Nissenbaum (1996) have identified three overarching categories of bias (systematic unfairness to individuals or groups): preexisting social bias, technical bias, and emergent social bias. Preexisting social bias has its roots in social institutions, practices, and attitudes. It occurs when computer systems embody biases that exist independently of, and usually prior to, the creation of the software. For instance, a legal "expert" system was written to offer advice to immigrants seeking citizenship in Britain. Some have argued (Berlins and Hodges, 1981), however, that the British immigration laws are themselves biased against certain nationalities and people of color. To the extent that they are, such biases also became embedded in the expert system. In contrast to preexisting social bias, technical bias occurs in the resolution of technical design problems that often arise due to limitations of the programming tools or algorithm. For instance, in the above legal expert system, the programming language, Prolog, sometimes went into infinite loops and thus failed to prove theorems that were logically implied by the axioms. Due to this technical limitation of the programming language, it follows that the system systematically would fail to identify individuals who were otherwise entitled to British citizenship. Finally, emergent social bias emerges in the context of the computer system's use, often when societal knowledge or cultural values change or the system is used with a different population. For instance, since the early 1970s, the computerized National Resident Medical Match Program has placed most medical students in their first jobs. In the system's original design, it was assumed that only one individual in a family would be looking for a residency, and the system thereby inadvertently discriminated against couples. At the time, such an assumption was perhaps not out of line since there were few women residents. But as women have increasingly made their way into the medical profession, marriages between residents are now not uncommon. Such bias against couples only emerged when the social conditions changed.

These three categories of bias can be used pedagogically within computer science courses. In a course on data structures, for example, students were asked to design and implement a computer dating program. The technical material focused on the use of records and linked lists. The issue of bias arose when students determined issues like who would be included in the database and how individuals in the database would be searched. Some students, for example, assumed only heterosexual users, and their programs were critiqued by other students on the basis that the program resulted in the unfair exclusion of homosexuals, due either to oversight or to the programmer's preexisting bias against homosexuals. Other programs searched for matches with a first-entered first-searched strategy, and thus unfairly favored those individuals who joined the database earlier over those who joined later. This instance of technical bias commonly arose because students used a linear linked list. To remove the bias, some students redesigned the program with a circular linked list. Our point here is that the social import of system design, and the designer's role and responsibility for the design, can emerge compellingly from students' own design experience.

Moreover, the social dimensions of computing become more sensible to students when they design computer software for use by real people in real settings. Such design makes salient the need to take seriously debugging, prototyping, field testing, interface issues, and user satisfaction. Based on our experience, students have successfully pursued a variety of design projects. For example, one student wrote a customized program for helping a baseball coach keep track of his team statistics. Another student built an interactive videodisk of selected artwork and performances for an art history teacher. Yet another student designed a program for the college's radio station that would identify the daily records played and the station's top ten hits. It is also often desirable for students to work on such projects collaboratively. In this context, which is akin to that of a business environment, students must decide what program modules to create, who will take major responsibility for each module, how to fit the modules together, and, once together, how to remove the errors. Thus, to be successful, students must be not only capable intellectually and able to assert themselves on intellectual ground, but able to discuss, cooperate, and build with others.

We are well aware that educational computing can be hindered by the coercive power wielded by organizations beyond the immediate scope of any single individual or school. When this occurs, other organizations need to respond; and though it is beyond our purposes here to say much about how this response can best be organized, we do suggest that effective response can build on our distinction between control and power. Here is an example. In choosing the standard by which to measure academic computing achievement among high school students, the Educational Testing Service (ETS) selected a single programming language, Pascal, for the Advanced Placement Exam in Computer Science. (Note: ETS says that it expects to change to C++ by 1998, or later.) There is undoubtedly an interesting story about why ETS chose specifically Pascal. But what we find especially remarkable is that ETS chose only one programming language. After all, in the field of computer science there is no standard programming language. For example, on the college level, computer science departments in their introductory courses often choose C, C++, Scheme, Modula-2, or Java instead of Pascal. In turn, in advanced high school computer study, teachers and students with interest in artificial intelligence would find most useful the languages of LOGO or LISP, while those interested in operating systems with access to UNIX would find most useful C. Thus why only Pascal on the Advanced Placement Exam? We suspect that part of the answer hinges on the increased costs that arise from creating and administering exams in multiple languages. But, whatever the reason, the end is the same. ETS uses its power to coerce high schools into teaching Pascal (and in the next decade C++), and they thereby unreasonably dictate what counts as advanced computing at the high school level.

How might the educational community address this problem? Minimally, those in secondary and higher education need to discuss these problems with ETS, such that a choice of programming languages is provided on the Advanced Placement Exam. But perhaps this process, even if it is successful, misses the larger point, for it still compels high schools to teach to standardized tests if their students are to be competitive in their college applications. Another solution is possible, which would also solve the problem that arises if ETS is unable or unwilling to add additional programming languages to the Advanced Placement Exam. Namely, in their admissions process, colleges and universities can go beyond standardized testing to assess the depth, scope, and integrity of student's high school computer science education. In this way, standards still matter, as they should. Excellence counts. Indeed, as exemplified in Harvey's computer center, excellence thrives because high school educators and students gain increased freedom to make significant choices to pursue advanced computer science as best suited to their interests, talents, and resources.

Conclusion

We have argued that students should learn that they themselves can control computer technology, and by choosing wisely they have the power not only to promote their academic learning but to effect meaningful and ethical change in and around their lives. Toward these goals, we offered a constructivist account of educational computing and a range of educational activities for both users and future system designers. We should be clear, however, that many of these activities encourage users to think about design considerations and designers to consider the social impact of their work. Our goals here fit within some of the broader conceptions in the field of human-computer interaction, which seeks not only to create better designs sensitive to the users' needs but to enfranchise and validate users in the design process (Bodker, 1991; Greenbaum and Kyng, 1991; Namioka and Schuler, 1990; Shneiderman and Rose, in press; Winograd and Flores, 1986). Through such considerations, power can be apportioned more equitably. Moreover, the idea of the "technocrat" as keeper and definer of the technology can give way to a more embracing conception of the designer and user as essentially linked to help create the infrastructure within which we live and work.

CHAPTER 8

Using Computers to Connect
Across Cultural Divides

BRIGID A. STARKEY

Introduction

This volume raises important questions about the pedagogical value of using computers in the classroom, as well as questions about the relationship of technology to social structure. There is currently a major push underway at the postsecondary level to integrate computers and other technology more into the daily curriculum. Yet experiences at the elementary and secondary levels indicate that computers, the main conduit of the technological revolution, have broadened the already wide gulf between classrooms that "have" and those that "have not." The International Communication and Negotiation Simulation (ICONS) Project at the University of Maryland has made efforts to counter this trend. Through a computer-assisted simulation model, it uses technology to connect students across intercultural divides with a program that facilitates participation from across the socioeconomic spectrum.

Cast as high-level international negotiators, participants use computer and communications capabilities to engage in discussions with peers at institutions around the United States and the world. Built upon POLIS,[1] one of the earliest distributed gaming exercises in the social sciences, ICONS has been working since the early 1980s to facilitate effective learning about the complex topic of international relations. This chapter presents the ICONS approach and discusses how the project has attempted to counter certain negative patterns often intensified in the technological classroom.

Project ICONS

The ICONS simulation is interactive, emulating the all-human tradition in gaming[2] more than the man-machine variety. Unlike many other exercises in which a computer interface is utilized, the technological component is intended to support a cooperative, active learning process, not to define the process itself. Using a project-generated scenario that outlines issues to be negotiated, students work on country-teams. Tasks include preparation to play roles, development of policies to bring to the negotiation table, and interpretation of the moves of partners and counterparts. The need to cooperate is embedded in the process, at both a conceptual and a practical level. Intergroup conflict over the interpretation of treaties is matched at the lower end by confrontations over such issues as a fair division of labor during the research process.

The simulation exercise is open-ended in that there is no predetermined course. Project administrators manage the many simultaneous exercises and provide scenarios. There is also a "simulation coordinator," whose job is to monitor the flow of events and act as a sort of chairperson for the talks. ICONS software handles messages in two modes. The first is akin to electronic mail. Daily "diplomatic cables" sent from team to team wait in recipients' queues to be picked up. But the core of the exercise is the real-time conferencing capability. This feature allows country-teams to sign on for multilateral summits. There have been instances when students from four different time zones have "congregated" on-line for such discussions.

The use of negotiation as the focus for these simulation exercises serves important pedagogical purposes. First, to study negotiation is to study process. Negotiation between parties requires reciprocity and, ultimately, the synthesis of ideas and positions. The participants determine the course of events, and they have the opportunity to see cause and effect. Second, the unnatural division of issue areas that is suggested by the division of, for example, geography, history, and environmental science into distinct subjects at the elementary and secondary levels and "majors" at the postsecondary level is countered as participants are introduced to linkages between issues.

Teachers and students have expressed overwhelming support for the ICONS experience over time. However, as with other learning models that require technological infrastructure, teacher creativity, and administrative support, there is a tendency for advantaged schools to be the quickest to engage in the experience and for advantaged students to be the ones to grab onto the opportunity without question. To use technology as a means and not an end in the educational process is a challenge. Issues of technology-appropriateness and access must be of central importance to ICONS and other initiatives that are pushing the further development of the "virtual" classroom.

The Risks of Teaching with Technology

Questions about how students learn effectively are a constant source of speculation in a variety of disciplines. Yet creativity and experimentation are largely lacking, particularly at the postsecondary level. Studies have long shown that students learn by doing.[3] Despite these findings, the traditional method of teaching is to lecture while students sit and listen. Advocates of computers stress their interactive nature, which they feel counters passivity. But critics point to the similarities between computer and television screens and stress that "cyberspace" has simply created a new brand of passivity.

To summarize a complex debate, technology can exacerbate some fundamental problems with the learning process. With instructor-student contact already low, particularly in many college settings, video lectures and instructional software can further isolate the student. While computer chat groups may provide "cyber" friends and the Internet can provide a channel of access to faraway worlds, the focus on technology can detract from day-to-day social interaction among students and between instructors and their pupils. The creation of distance learning communities is not a suitable substitute for cooperative learning within one's own classroom and community.

Creativity can also be stifled with everything from language editors to graphic design software taking the individuality out of work and inciting the creation of homogeneous end-products. If, as asserted, students learn best in problem-solving situations,[4] then learning should be an open-ended process. Technology can facilitate experimentation and creativity, but it can also make everything too easy and create a world in which the "right" answers are only a click away on the mouse.

Finally, and perhaps most troubling, technology is like fashion. The ability of the individual student to afford the latest hardware and software becomes yet another painful point of differentiation in our schools. Access, whether by the individual or the school district, has most to do with money and power. As has been expounded upon in earlier chapters, the gap between those who have the technology and those who do not takes on an even more dangerous turn when educational goals are tied to technology and the language of "progress" becomes computer terminology. In these situations, technology is allowed to become the end and not the means through which we try to relate to our students.

Countering the Risks

Goals must be definable independent of the tools used to reach them. Technology is a tool. For the ICONS Project, central goals have been the enhancement of cultural awareness and the promotion of a collaborative learning model. The intent is to use computers and communications capabilities to provide a venue for authentic and purposeful cross-cultural communication. This is the distance element of the ICONS model, and computers are central to its achievement. However, the use of distance learning is intended to enhance the building of a classroom community, not replace it. While the on-line nature of the negotiations focuses attention around the computer, the operation of country-teams is most dependent on traditional interpersonal communication and cooperation. An active, collaborative learning model is encouraged by the role-playing required in the simulation. Evaluations of the ICONS project have shown that the leap of imagination required of the role-playing student is facilitated by the anonymity, and indeed the mystery, afforded by the computer.

Like the structure of the exercise, the simulation software promotes collaboration. It is text-based, which promotes a focus on the co-construction of messages,[5] which is the central endeavor for team members. They communicate as a unit with the other players in the simulation.

Although any educational tool that requires its users to have certain hardware is, by nature, exclusionary, ICONS has tried to address this issue. All that is currently required of a group wishing to participate, as with the very first ICONS simulation, is a personal computer, printer, network access (or a modem), and communications software. Text-based communication, which requires less and less-expensive hardware and software remains the medium.[6] Participation in the early ICONS simulations required access to commercial networks, which then provided the link to the host computer at Maryland. ARPANET and Telenet (Sprintnet) were often the facilitators of the connection. Eventually, access provided by NSFNET and ultimately, Internet opened up availability of the exercise to a much broader audience.

Although Internet access is now a mainstay on many college campuses, the costs associated with participation for high schools and other institutions that do not have this access can still be great. In order to facilitate adaptation of the model to the secondary level, the project developed a regional center concept to work with community outreach. With the help of funding from the United States Institute of Peace, Centers were established in California, Connecticut, Florida, and Iowa.[7] These Centers, as well as the ICONS "headquarters," offer periodic teacher training sessions for potential participants. Through the regional centers, ICONS has been disseminated to students in areas as diverse as rural Iowa; Dade County, Florida; Queens, New York; and Los Angeles. Using the technological infrastructure and faculty resources of the universities helps put technology within reach for the surrounding communities.

Computer as Learning Enhancer

Many successful simulations are run without computers or other kinds of advanced technology, but conducting the ICONS negotiations on the computer rather than in a face-to-face mode serves several useful purposes. First, by removing visual images from the exercise, participants are forced to rely on their imaginations in conceptualizing the "other side." The written word gains in importance over visual and audio images. Emulating the importance of the diplomatic cable, messages sent from one team to another are analyzed word for word. There is no easy way to retract a misinterpreted statement. Moreover, there is a tendency for students to take the exercise more seriously when their negotiation counterparts are unknowns, rather than classmates. International participants have been recruited over time, lending an element of authenticity to the process. ICONS becomes a true cross-cultural experience when Japanese and American students debate international trade issues or a group of Israeli students portray Syria in a regional security dialogue.

Empirical evaluations of ICONS have pointed to substantial cognitive gains and high levels of involvement in the class activity for participants of all levels.[8] Three levels of communication enhanced by the electronic structure of the simulations have been identified as central to the learning process: (1) between-team interaction among peers representing different countries and sending messages via the computer network, (2) within-team interaction and co-construction of messages in oral discourse resulting in message entry, and (3) individual processing and cognitive restructuring.[9] Using data collected through field and video observation, ICONS Evaluator Judith Torney-Purta notes that "task-related" behavior, such as reading messages, processing the main points of those messages, and communicating those points to peers, accounts for the majority of activity during the actual simulation. She attributes the high involvement levels of students in the process to the following:

> First, the computer screen is an object of highly focused student attention because it is constantly changing and providing valuable information in a way the blackboard or textbook does not; this appears to enhance individuals' processing of information. . . . The process of co-construction and group revision of the message on the screen provided a potent stimulus for elaborating individuals' representations, and for students' discovering that what seemed obvious to one about a situation was not obvious to another. Often participants would see complications even in a simple proposal. The computer system provided information corresponding to examples in a science text to be dealt with at a deep or surface level.[10]

The simulation process keeps students involved in a cycle of thinking, revising, and explaining that carries over from the within-team dialogue to the between-team negotiations. "Getting it right" in this context involves presenting one's viewpoint clearly, listening to what others have to say, and synthesizing different viewpoints as part of the group process. A group of University of Maryland students portraying France in a 1993 simulation carried on the following peer dialogue as they co-constructed messages during an on-line conference:

A: We have to send the right message—what we mean.
B: An allotment of immigrants, that's what we can propose.
C: Can we use economic aid as an incentive?
A: Send it to the Ukraine.
B: To everyone. In response . . .
A: It is France's mission . . .
C: Moral responsibility as an individual country . . .
D: No, in the UN . . .
B: Individual countries should
A: . . . be monitoring individual immigration applications and circumstances.
D: I have a book with something about that, I'll bring it in on Monday.
C: The UN should
A: The UN should monitor
D: Monitor what?
A: Oversee not monitor
C: Why?
A: We have to respond strongly. It is the responsibility of the EC to enforce . . ."[11]

Success with ICONS, as with any active-learning strategy, is reliant on the facilitating instructor's ability to put the exercise in context for the students and to organize their participation. Hands-on training in negotiation should be the complement to a curriculum that focuses on various aspects of the international relations of states—from foreign policy decision making to the import of issues such as trade, development, conflict, human rights, and nuclear proliferation. At the high school level, administrative goodwill and collegiality are required to carve out enough time for student participation. The interactive and distance elements of the exercise necessitate team representation at online conferences that may occur during non-ICONS class periods. Ideally, the endeavor should be a cooperative one at the participant secondary institution, with cross-curriculum support for student involvement. This would apply not only to the blocks of time required for adequate involvement, but also to efforts to help students see the connections across disciplines.

The facilitator must secure the proper equipment (networked PC or PC-modem, with printer) and make sure that all participants practice how to access the simulation and learn how to send and receive messages. During the exercise, student deliberations should be mediated by thoughtful questioning. Reflections on "power distribution" in the international system can be stimulated by a question, such as, "what seems to be the more important bargaining lever in the negotiations, natural resource wealth or military power?" However, ultimately it is the ability of the teachers to relinquish some of the control they traditionally exercise over the classroom that will contribute most to the success of the experience. The students must devise a cooperative process for completion of tasks and must devise a method for reconciling divergent opinions. They will learn the most if they must do this themselves, with only guidance from their teacher.

Instructor reaction to this mode of learning has highlighted its ability to motivate students, expand their cultural horizons, enhance their self-esteem, and lift them to higher levels of cognitive thinking. A French teacher in the state of Washington, whose class portrayed Canada in a simulation, reflected, "ICONS makes them look at the world from a different perspective, which to me is the number one priority," and "they find out how telecommunications works, think on their feet, [and] learn how to reach a compromise."[12] A fellow teacher expressed similar sentiments, "This teaches them problem solving, decision making, critical and analytical skills, and how to think on their feet. . . . They also have to learn that this is negotiation—not debate. Both sides have to win."[13] Kathleen Rottier, a social studies teacher and curriculum development specialist in suburban Washington, D.C., wrote,

> I recall with amazement the telephone call I received from a group of my second-semester seniors on their spring break. They were actually preparing for the simulation by doing research at the Library of Congress, having driven about thirty miles from Brandywine, Maryland.[14]

Rottier also noted in her comments about the program that Project ICONS is designed in such a way that it enables every student to succeed, regardless of beginning skill level and interests. This has been borne out by the project's involvement in disadvantaged settings.

Reaching Out with Technology:
Using ICONS in Disadvantaged Settings

Concrete, hands-on activities can be much more engaging for students who for a variety of reasons are less engaged in the learning process than some of their peers. Studies have shown that a good number of these students do respond to more tangible exercises, despite being unable or unwilling to fit comfortably into the traditional curriculum.[15] Moreover, when the technology is accessible across income, gender, and ethnic divides, the computer can actually be an equalizer. A team comprised primarily of Haitian-Americans in Dade County, using the simulation not only for social studies purposes but for English as a Second Language instruction, is recognized as the country it portrays—Canada, Brazil, Mexico, or the United States—in just the same way as its simulation counterpart in Ontario or in the more affluent suburbs of Miami. In this setting, the knowledge these students possess about the language and culture of a region other than the United States can be used to advantage and to foster self-esteem.

Role playing and distance community building can make unique contributions to conflict resolution training as well, a curriculum component that is much in demand in both the United States and in many locations around the world. ICONS has been introduced into a number of secondary schools in Israel,[16] for example, which use the simulation to heighten cross-cultural awareness.

ICONS With "At-Risk" Students

Over time it has become clear that the creativity inspired by the ICONS simulations is readily transferable from the advantaged classroom to the disadvantaged one. ICONS programs in California, run by the California ICONS Regional Center at Immaculate Heart College Center and the Center for Research in International Studies at Stanford University, have made significant inroads into various "at-risk" communities. In the greater Los Angeles area, ICONS has been introduced into economically depressed settings and has been used with learning impaired students and students with limited English proficiency. Teachers in these settings have found that ICONS can empower students for whom the educational experience is often a very trying one. The simulation curriculum is student-centered and introduces students, many for the first time, to primary source materials. There are no textbooks that are readily adaptable to this learning model. The negotiation dialogues are the focal point of the process, and students prepare for them by thinking and talking about issues and relationships between ideas and action plans.

There are three main components to the empowerment achieved through the ICONS experience. The first is support for diversity. The anonymity afforded by the computer, as mentioned, is one aspect of this component. But of equal importance is the emphasis on teamwork and the creative leap supported by role playing. It can be a liberating experience for inner-city students to learn about the problems facing struggling nations and to grapple with these problems with the help of peers and teachers.[17] Comments made by teachers during debriefings suggest that simulation activities frequently engage students who had not previously been identified as academic "stars." Gender, ethnic, and class differences can be subsumed within the team and across teams, as countries struggle to achieve cooperative solutions to regional and global problems. Individual differences or class disparities, rooted in inner-city versus wealthy suburban schools, take a backseat to the power differentials between the countries the students are portraying.[18] Of course, students playing "weak" nations in the international system will experience frustrations related to that disadvantage, but they learn that even resource-poor or ethnically divided nations can exert leverage over other nations through clever bargaining strategies.

Second, as documented by Torney-Purta, participation in ICONS provides a context in which reading and writing skills can be improved. This can be an especially important outcome for students who are learning English as a second language. A California high school teacher, who uses the simulation in a "sheltered" English class comprised mainly of students of Asian background, reports that having his students play an Asian country builds self-esteem and increases confidence at the same time that they build English language skills. Putting language learning into the context of a "language experience" is sound practice. The need to communicate in a realistic setting stimulates new levels of effort by the students.[19] The need to communicate concisely and clearly brings language alive for the students, as they pool their respective vocabulary resources to come up with the "right" word, and discuss tone and emphasis to ensure that their point will be understood, but not so strong as to offend. A teacher from Moreno Valley, a rural area in San Bernadino County, used a glossary of simulation terms to build language skills. He reported that the messages received via the computer were the "focal stimulant" for his students, who worked very hard to answer with messages that were clear and sophisticated on behalf of the nation they were portraying, the Ukraine.[20]

ICONS and Conflict Resolution Training

The ICONS experience provides relevance in learning through its emphasis on the real world and on the development of problem-solving skills to handle the complex difficulties that face the nations of the world. International negotiation is about the avoidance of armed conflict and the escalation of disputes to the violent stage. When violence occurs, negotiation has failed. Learning about conflict resolution at the international level is an indirect but effective way for students to build their own dispute-resolution skills. Students learn about the role of perceptions, misunderstandings attributable to language and cultural differences, tendencies toward self-preservation, and even utility maximization. Indeed, one of the hardest aspects of the simulation process for the students to handle is the fact that at the end there is often no concrete outcome. At the conclusion of the exercise, as they engage in debriefing, students lament the absence of a definitive resolution to the many problems their nation faced. This disappointment fosters a realization that progress is slow and does not always involve an outcome that can be declared a "win."

There are lessons for individuals to be extrapolated from the relations between states. Power is not easily defined. Size is not the key determinant, nor is wealth always the answer. Narrow self-interest usually ends up backfiring, as do simplistic motivating factors such as revenge, irredentism, and self-aggrandizement.

In the few cases where ICONS has been used with the actual parties to a conflict, the ability to play "the other" has proven to be a particularly powerful tool. This was the case for a group of Israeli high school students who at first refused, but then acquiesced, to portray the bordering nation of Syria.[21] As they learned to define the seemingly neutral term 'neighbor,' they embarked on a journey of self-discovery. For even if two nations perceive each other as intense security threats, there are other areas in which bordering states must cooperate if they are to coexist and thrive. Focusing on shared natural resources and the safety of border populations can elucidate this point for students.

Israeli and Palestinian university students engaged in a three-phase approach when they were led on an experiment in conflict resolution using ICONS.[22] Encouraged to portray the other side, they were asked first to vent emotions and frustrations over the conflict, then to attempt to frame the problems underlying the frustrations, and finally to suggest possible steps toward a solution to various contentious issues. During debriefing, many of these students described the experience as cathartic, and there was general agreement that the process revealed to them a distinct "mirror imaging" within the conflict. For example, because they are aware of the importance and reverence with which the "other side" views the city of Jerusalem, both sides are afraid to compromise on its status. Whether working with parties to real-world international conflicts or using the examples of these conflicts with students who know little of the world outside their own communities, working on resolutions to international problems teaches dispute-resolution skills in an effective and exciting manner.

"People track" conflict-resolution techniques are empowering in that they counter the tendency for individuals, societies, and nations to look for solutions from dominant authority structures. Whether it is the boys in the street peacefully resolving a dispute before the police intervene, or Israeli students learning about Syria outside of their state-sanctioned curriculum, the results are similar: finding ways to resolve differences by focusing on shared interests.

Conclusion

Technology enhances the ICONS experience and allows it to be introduced in classrooms around the country and the world. Its text-based format discourages participants from engaging in a competitive race for bigger and better hardware and software. The team approach, embedded in the simulation and in negotiation as a process, encourages collaboration, cooperation, and critical thinking. Language is a means to better understanding, not an abstract end in itself.

While the project cannot claim to replace the need for creative, dedicated teachers to bring this active learning experience to their students, it has attempted to address issues of access and infrastructure through the development of the regional center concept. Community outreach through school-college collaboration is a cost-effective way to bring technological innovation to the secondary level during these times of scarce resources in education.

On the most obvious level, ICONS is designed to teach students about the world outside their own national borders. Debt and development issues come alive for students who must take such constraints into account when making decisions for the nation they are portraying. Over time we have learned that ICONS is fun, because students learn about the world by making decisions that feel important. We have also begun to learn that the problems of nations and methods of negotiation are translatable to individuals, families, and communities. One ICONS veteran was heard to remark during debriefing that the end was a letdown because "tomorrow, we'll go back to being just students again."[23]

CHAPTER 9

Learning to Exercise Power:
Computers and Community Development[1]

ANTONIA STONE

The Beginning

When, in 1980, I started talking to funding sources and policy makers about the need for equitable access to technology, about the potential of technology to widen the gulf between the "haves" and "have nots" of our society, about the importance of technology access and education for all segments of our population, I encountered varying degrees of wonderment and disbelief. I remember once saying to a Ford Foundation program officer, "Experience with technology is vital. People are not going to be able to get along without it." She pounced on my word, 'vital.' "Don't use the word 'vital,'" she said. "Food, housing, clothing, health—those are the vital things."

She was wrong. People can be provided with food, housing, clothing, and healthcare, and they can live. But they can't take charge of their lives, they can't get jobs (never mind good jobs), they can't participate actively in decision making at any societal level (even when those are decisions directly affecting them) unless they can acquire the know-how, the information, the skills, the education that is needed in their society.

Clearly, the kind of education and skills needed in our society today includes the ability to use technology—to *use* it as opposed to being manipulated by it or by those few who do have the knowledge to use it. Equally clear is that the opportunities to acquire this ability along with an understanding of the issues involved may be available only to a small portion of our population.

It was this concern that took me to the Ford Foundation in 1980. And it was with their help, and the help of many others, that I founded, that same year, Playing To Win, a nonprofit organization to address issues of equitable technology access and education. Playing To Win opened, in 1983, this country's first neighborhood technology learning center to be established in a low-income urban environment. Playing To Win's Harlem Community Computing

Center has been in continuous operation for over ten years serving 500–600 local residents of all ages weekly.

Many other organizations have followed suit, either incorporating technology access and education with existing services or establishing stand-alone centers. Some public libraries offer computing opportunities to their general public; a number of museums, youth organizations, after-school programs, youth conservation corps sites, churches, community colleges, family service organizations, community centers, day care facilities, adult literacy providers, and senior citizen programs are offering their members/clients hands-on computing activities.

What is a neighborhood technology learning center like? Is it like a school?

My sense is that a neighborhood technology center is very different from a school. Perhaps one way to understand what it is is to look at the ways in which it is different from a school.

People Vote With Their Feet

Unlike students in school, people must come to your center voluntarily. There is no legal mandate. This is important. If a program doesn't meet people's needs as they perceive them, they don't come back. You lose them, and they lose too.

In addition, because participation is voluntary, people don't have to seek you out. You have to seek them out, so recruitment and outreach are an important part of your work. And when you're reaching out in a neighborhood with a high rate of illiteracy or of non-English speaking people, you can't do it with flyers and letters. I always think of the sign I once saw in the NYC subways: *Learn to read*, it said, followed by a lot more in smaller print.

In getting the Harlem Community Computing Center going, we made similar mistakes, and many others as well. At first we thought that the lure of technology would be all that was needed to bring people in in droves. It was certainly true for a few, but for many more, the disbelief that they could make use of such a complex (as they thought) instrument, that they could succeed, either kept them away or resulted in their bringing their children and saying, "My kids, yes, they need it, but for me, no, I couldn't do it."

Today "Open Hours"—sessions when as many as fifty or sixty people drop-in to use, or to learn to use computers—are the mainstay of the Harlem Center schedule. One of the "hooks" teachers at the Harlem Center came up with is to make sure that everyone, regardless of age, leaves their first session at the center with a product—something they have produced using the computer—as evidence of their success. It could be a greeting card or a flyer made using a simple printing or publishing program; it could be an image they have scanned from a wallet photo; it could be a story, poem, or letter they have written, or a picture they've drawn; it could be their name printed in elaborate and oversized type and decorated with clip art.

An instance where this method worked almost too well was the case of a middle-aged woman who came in rather hesitantly one day. She wanted to know if there was something she could do with a computer. She had not the faintest notion what that something might be. A staff member suggested a greeting card. Would she need to read much, she asked, because, she admitted, she didn't read very well. The staff member introduced her to Print Shop. She asked for help at virtually every key stroke, but eventually produced her card. The next day, and the next, the woman returned to make another and another. After some months of this, and almost a hundred greeting cards later, one of the staff asked if she wouldn't like to try doing something else—learn another program perhaps. "Oh no," she said. "You don't know what this has done for me. I have lots of friends now. I send these cards to people, and they write back. Some even write letters. I'm learning to read so I can read those letters. I couldn't stop making the cards."

You might think that because attendance is not mandated, a neighborhood program like ours would have things easy. After all, the people who do come are there because they want to be there. It's true. But sometimes the people you most want to come don't, and then you have to figure out not only ways to attract them but ways to keep them coming.

Over the years of the center's operation, older teen-agers, particularly teen-aged males, have been difficult to recruit. A fair number would drop in, have an initial experience, and drop out again. We puzzled over this: the standard applications like word-processing or graphics didn't make it, even as an employment skill; the simulation games (like *Carmen Sandiego* or *SimCity*) apparently weren't exciting enough. We had a little luck with cartooning for a while, but when we wouldn't allow them to create porn, that too palled. Our greatest success to date has come with the advent of multimedia.

Two or three teens, brainstorming with one of our teachers about how to use some equipment recently donated to the Center, came up with the idea of creating a kind of electronic Harlem directory. It started with a subway map and some text about what to find in the area of each station (and what to avoid), along with some scanned pictures of the location. This idea caught on, and the initial group has now expanded well beyond our expectations. The project, too, has grown. Named by its creators *What's Homey about Harlem,* the directory has become much more than an annotated subway map. It now shows where each of them lives. It has pictures of their families and friends and of favored spots in their neighborhoods. Some have used a camcorder to do live interviews and have incorporated segments of their videos in the directory. Each person works on the elements they find most rewarding. All learn the processes of integrating their work into a single multimedia database. And best of all, they keep coming back and bringing others with them.

The "Curriculum" Is What Each Person Makes It

What's Homey About Harlem was largely the brainchild of the teens involved. And this is typical of our center. There are no grade levels, no mandated curriculum, and no tests or exams. Since our goal is to help people understand and master technology as a personal tool (rather than as a subject), it's important for each person to identify something that he or she would like to accomplish. After all, if you were trying to teach people to use a hammer, you wouldn't start with a lecture about peens and claws; you'd ask them to find something that needed to be held together with a nail.

Asking people to take control of their own learning right from the start can be off-putting to many who come bearing the baggage of traditional school environments. Even some who left school because it was boring or unrewarding feel somehow that there ought to be desks, lectures, textbooks, workbooks, and people to tell them what to do. To be immediately invited to sit down at a computer to accomplish something they want to accomplish seems more like playing than learning, and when it's fun and easy (and our teachers work very hard to make it both easy and fun), the process is doubly suspect.

Sometimes trying to identify what a person wants to accomplish can be extremely frustrating. I think of the experience of one of our volunteers. A young girl had arrived with a group of her peers—single expectant mothers from a residential prenatal care facility. She was sitting at a computer, her head resting on her hands, which in turn were resting on the keyboard. "Hey, there," our volunteer began. "Aren't you interested in doing what the others are doing?" (They were designing birth announcements.) No answer from the young woman. He tried again, "Well, how about writing something—a poem or a story?" Again, no response. "Maybe there's someone you'd like to write a letter to?" No response. "How about a hate letter?" Her head came up abruptly. "Hey, yeah!"

Occasionally, people not only know what they want to accomplish, but they have a preconception of how to accomplish it. I remember a teacher who came with a class of court-adjudicated boys. He wanted them to improve their math skills. Our teacher talked about the joys of spreadsheets. He was unimpressed. "Don't you have something that will teach them about decimals?" Our teacher reluctantly offered a program dealing with the placement of the decimal point in multiplication. "This is perfect," thought the boys' teacher, and set them to work. A couple of sessions later, he announced that he wouldn't be bringing the boys again. "They're bored with computers," he explained. Tentatively, our teacher again suggested spreadsheets, "Let me work a couple of classes with them, see what you think." Some months later, that teacher sent us a letter: "Watching my boys work with a spreadsheet totally changed the way I'd been thinking about teaching. I saw them doing stuff, making up their own problems, working with each other, and enjoying the whole process, and suddenly I thought, this is really what technology is for. It's going to take me a while to get as good at it as you folks are, but believe me, I'm going to do it. Thank you."

Not infrequently people are themselves unaware of their ambitions (or talents). One of the wonderful things about technology is that it can open doors to undreamed-of possibilities. A young woman dropped in from the neighborhood youth action agency, hoping to create a program for their annual year-end ceremony. She had entered all the text and was musing over a sample printout. "It looks so dull," she confessed. "What can I do to jazz it up?" "Try a fancy border" someone suggested, "or put a little diploma picture there." Accomplishing these tasks turned out to be only the beginning of a totally new career objective—in computer graphics. This young woman didn't know it, but she already had the flair and the taste; all that was needed to unearth them was the computer turn-on.

Teachers Have To Know Too Much, or Do They?

Remembering these stories (and many more that must be left untold) leads me to acknowledge what an extraordinary staff of teachers the Harlem Center has, and has had through the years. And this brings up yet another important difference between a neighborhood technology learning center and a school. There is no pool of experienced, credentialed professionals from which to acquire staff. Of course, if there were, it's not clear that that's where you would look, since the overriding qualification for a position at a place like the Harlem Center is not skill with applications of technology. Rather it is the ability to make people feel comfortable, to make them believe that they can be successful, to make them feel respected for what they themselves bring to the learning process.

Best of all, of course, is when teachers emerge from the participating community. Playing To Win is fortunate that a number of our teachers have come through our own program. People who have progressed from bewilderment to competence often make the best teachers. Perhaps because they still think of themselves as learners rather than as founts of knowledge, asking questions comes more easily than answering them. "What do *you* think you should do?" or "What have you tried so far?" or even "Remember the last time this happened? What did you do then?" puts the burden on the student but also increases the pride that comes with a successful solution: "Hey, wow, I did it!"

One of our teachers describes as her proudest moment a time when in the middle of a class she saw a kid across the room waving his hand in the air. As she was moving towards him, she heard his neighbor lean over and say, "What you want to ask her for? She don't know nothing. Ask me. I'll help!" Cultivating an environment of peer tutoring and self-reliance is not easy, yet it is crucial to the development of self-esteem and confidence in one's ability to learn.

Another difference between our center and a school is the ratio of employees to volunteers. At any given moment there can be zero to ten times as many volunteers as staff teachers working at the Center. Some come from the community—to help out at the front desk, to help oversee our after-school drop-in hours, to stuff envelopes, whatever needs to be done. It's wonderful for us—necessary, in fact—and it seems to give them a sense of ownership— a piece of the rock.

Another volunteer group has had to be actively recruited specifically to handle technological needs outside the domain of our expertise. We call them our volunteer professionals. Not too long ago, two or three center members indicated a desire to learn the programming language Pascal. No one on staff was up to the task, but one of our volunteer professionals stepped in. It was an odd group of learners—an eleven year old, an older teen, and a woman in her forties—that settled down with our professional programmer/volunteer to learn Pascal together, but it worked for them.

Some of our volunteers have a hard time adjusting to Playing To Win's hands-on philosophy. Showing people—doing it for them—seems to be a great temptation, and yet it is diametrically opposite to the way we believe people learn most easily, particularly when what they are learning is how to handle a powerful machine. One volunteer in particular, a fellow who used to conduct a desktop publishing workshop, found it virtually impossible to give up the keyboard to the participants. You'd walk through the center and there he'd be, glibly executing commands and describing the process to an increasingly disenchanted group of students. We used to joke about presenting him with a pair of toy handcuffs, but his workshop drop-out rate eventually made the winning argument.

Where the Money Comes From

I've said how extraordinary the staff at the Harlem Center is and has been. What is perhaps equally extraordinary is that some have stayed with us for years, one ever since the center opened in 1983. Staff turnover is a particularly disheartening problem, not just for Playing To Win's Harlem Center but for many of the other centers with which we have worked, and the reason, in the vast majority of cases, is money.

No sooner does a teacher emerge as talented and dependable than he or she is leaving for a better paid position. It's little wonder, since by virtue of working at the center people acquire skills that are not only marketable but in considerable demand. So you rejoice with them, compliment them on their success, and then groan at the necessity, once again, of locating or developing a teacher who will work for the pittance you are able to offer.

Finding money to support operating costs is an endemic problem of community-based organizations (and technology learning centers are no exception). Unlike the school system, community organizations have no pot of public money upon which to draw. Every penny for salaries, equipment, rent, supplies, security, and maintenance must be raised either through revenues or through grants and contributions. Inevitably this leads to tight budgets and low salaries.

'Revenue'—now there's an attractive word. But how do you derive revenue from an operation that is designed to serve people who don't have the money—for home computers or computer camps or workshops or training courses, and sometimes not even for food? When Playing To Win started the Harlem Center, we hoped to make it free to all. Well, that didn't work, but not because no money was coming in. It didn't work because the service wasn't valued. A group would sign up to come for a couple of hours on a Monday, say, and then with the sun shining would decide to go to the park instead, and we'd have an empty center.

Our Harlem Center Advisory Committee suggested a membership structure (by the way, we have found a local advisory committee to be essential for outreach, for keeping a finger on the pulse of the community, and for generating a sense of ownership in the neighborhood). While we bought into the idea and have continued it, the question of what to charge has never been settled to everyone's satisfaction. Currently, it costs $25 a year for the first adult in a family unit, $5 for each additional adult, and $2.50 for each child (we did have to set a limit on the number of individuals that could register as a family; it turned out there were nine spaces on the application blank to list names, so nine became the maximum number). Any member can use up to fifteen hours a week of computer time for no additional charge. It's got to be the best deal in the City of New York! But as revenue, it's hardly substantial, particularly when you consider that fees are waived for people to whom they constitute a hardship.

What's left when revenue fails? Grants and contributions. I'm sure that the loyal funders who believed in Playing To Win's mission and, more importantly perhaps, in our ability to do what we said we would do, and who have supported the organization consistently through the years would only agree with me when I say that start-up grants are not nearly so hard to obtain as ongoing support. One of the solutions that has worked to the benefit both of the center and of others has been what we loosely refer to as "project-based funding."

As you come to know funding organizations—corporations and private foundations—you realize that each has its own agenda for making a difference. In seeking project-based funding, your objective is to find an area of common agreement between the funder's agenda and your own. In the best of cases this entails reexamining the services you are already providing (for which you need support) and repackaging a subset of these—perhaps adding a product such as a manual, a newsletter, or a set of workshop outlines—as a project that falls under the funder's umbrella. There are pitfalls, such as biting off more than you can chew, but if carefully engineered, such projects can serve both you and the funder effectively.

A particularly successful example from Playing To Win's roster of project-based grants was one from NYNEX to support documentation and broader, nationally based testing of the Harlem Center's approach to using technology as an environment for literacy learning. The result was a much acclaimed book called *Keystrokes to Literacy* which brings in quarterly royalties (revenue!) to Playing To Win and at the same time satisfies the desire of the people at NYNEX to make a contribution to literacy learning across the country.

Another example was funding from the Greenwall Foundation to develop a family math and technology program in collaboration with the public schools. We called the project *MathTech* and, again, part of the mandate was to produce a manual documenting the activities we designed and used. We're hoping that, too, will be a royalty producer.

Other Differences and Similarities

There are probably at least a dozen other ways in which a neighborhood technology learning center is different from a school—ways that don't fit neatly under headings. Take, for example, the matter of telecommunications. When the Harlem Center was offered a chance to participate in a start-up network for New York City youth, we just said yes. And access to that small network has resulted in access to larger regional and national networks.

Or consider again the *What's Homey about Harlem* project. We didn't have to think about what discipline or what curriculum it would fit into. And this is a major blessing. If we can find a way to involve people, young and old, in learning, in doing something they consider valuable, we don't have to satisfy any higher authority.

Or think about schedule. The Harlem Center is open from 9 am to 9 pm Monday through Friday, and on Saturdays from 10 to 4. It's open on most school holidays, during vacations, and throughout the summer.

Actually when we think about it, we'd have to admit that we consider ourselves better off than the schools. Although we don't have the tax base support, and we certainly have problems galore, we also have freedom: freedom from precedent, from bureaucratic constraint, freedom to experiment, to find out what works and what doesn't, the freedom of time limited only by participants' interest rather than by the end of a school year, and the freedom to spend the money we have the way we want to spend it.

There is at least one important similarity with schools as well. The Harlem Center and others like it are places where people learn and where they discover the motivation to learn more.

The Larger Politics

A finding of the 1988 National Assessment of Educational Progress (NAEP) report on computer competence was that students who knew the most about computers learned most of what they knew *outside of school*. While this report was published five years ago, I believe the same would be found today. Why? Because people, students included, learn about technology by playing and experimenting with it, indulging in casual, informal exploration. And they learn how to use technology for the same reasons they learn anything else—because *they believe* they want or need to learn.

No place, I believe, can do the job better than a neighborhood technology learning center. Such a place can be open all year, even around the clock, and can offer a range of technologies to explore. Such a place can serve as a resource center, and as a way-station on the electronic highway. Such a place can welcome both those without their own personal resources and those who want to learn about new technologies they may not yet have access to. Such a place can be to information technology what the public library is to print materials.

A neighborhood technology learning center can do still more. It can serve as a laboratory for developing engaging ways to use technologies in more formal educational settings. It can model learning environments. It can be a proving ground for innovation in technology and in learning. Is Playing To Win's Harlem Center such a place? Partly. What about the other access programs I mentioned? The answer there, too, is partly. We are all trying.

What is needed is not only significantly more support, but more people to try. In this nation of over 260 million people, there may be 700 individual programs seeking to remediate difficulty of access to technology and technology education for underserved people. Even if these programs were to serve an average of 100 people each (and most serve far fewer), the effort thus far falls way short of providing equal opportunity.

Before the day when a neighborhood technology learning center is conveniently available to anyone who wants one, a number of important changes need to occur.

Recognition of the Need

The perception of technology education as something less than vital must change. Too many people would still today echo the sentiments of the Ford Foundation grants officer I encountered in 1980. Too many educated people today will still confess, with a smile that smacks more of pride than of apology, "You know I'm still a technology-illiterate."

- All teachers need to recognize the computer as more than a drill master or a curriculum delivery system. They need to understand its potential as a powerful tool they can use to achieve their goals, to understand ways in which technology can open doors to new learning and new, experientially-based learning environments. Teachers need to understand the necessity of enabling all students to harness the power of technology in service of their own objectives.
- All parents, community and union leaders, and concerned adults in all walks of life need to recognize that it is not only children but they themselves who must understand the uses of technology. The technologically dominated society is upon us. The jobs and tasks that require or are facilitated by technology already exist. Weighty and far-reaching decisions that will affect our lives and those of our children are being made today. If we are ignorant, we are powerless and will be bypassed.
- All business and industry leaders need to require that all their employees have some degree of technological skill, understanding, and resourcefulness. How else is American productivity to regain the competitive edge?
- All people in the technology industry itself must broaden their concept of "market" to include all segments of society. The pace of technological

development is accelerating: ubiquity of print took hundreds of years, and ubiquity of automotive transportation decades; ubiquity of television only years. Can we expect the ubiquity of computer-based technologies to depart from this established curve?

Each of us, in fact, needs to wake up to the fact that it is in our own self-interest for all people to become technologically knowledgeable. Only then will we be able to exert sufficient influence to create an avenue to universal empowerment.

Development of the Model

Although, as I remarked above, Playing To Win's Harlem Center and other similar programs have made a start toward the development of model neighborhood technology learning centers, there is much that could be done to improve and extend those models.

There is some diversity in existing models: library programs don't look like storefront programs, community center access is quite different from museum access, and so on. But most of these programs serve areas of dense population. What of sparsely settled areas? A model needs to be developed for people who are widely separated geographically.

A number of existing programs encompass some range of technologies, but nowhere near sufficient and nowhere near state-of-the-art. Many technology access programs start and continue to operate with already outdated hardware and software because it's what they can get. Furthermore, we can hardly expect today's state-of-the-art to be tomorrow's. Libraries that never got newly published books would soon lose their constituencies.

Already there are programs amalgamating computer and video technologies: public access television stations merging with community computing centers. Is this an appropriate direction, and if so, what future technology mergers can be expected?

And what of the scale of the effort? Most of the currently operating programs are too small to handle even the demand of their own communities. Most, too, have sprung from the grassroots of those communities. Most enjoy the concomitant freedom that such grassroots efforts permit. Smallness, community roots, and freedom are strengths. Many program administrators, however, are ignorant of the existence of others' efforts, and lack the capacity or desire to design or participate in a national effort. Will it be possible to preserve these strengths within the larger framework?

What will be the relationship between the schools and these neighborhood technology centers? Today, many community educators see the schools as failed institutions (they have certainly failed the people whom the community organization must serve). On the other hand, community education efforts get little respect or support from the school system. They are regarded as amateurs (which, often, they are). How can this situation be turned into a collaborative effort resting on mutual respect?

All these, and a myriad of other issues large and small, will need to be addressed by people with vision who are willing to explore new ideas, people without a stake in preserving failed models for centers of learning and education, and people with broad experience in community service.

Supporting the National Effort

It has always seemed to me that those who stand to benefit from a service should be the ones to support that service. This works when those who benefit can afford to support. I have two, possibly naive, suggestions:

1. A voluntary dollar added to every taxpayer's income tax, as is currently done for support of political candidates. Isn't national technological enfranchisement equally important?
2. A tithing of business and industry. Not the 10 percent rule developed by the churches; or even the mandated 5 percent of profits currently required of cable television operators to support local access programs; simply a small percent of the advertising/promotion budget. The cost of producing and airing a single television commercial might support one center for a whole year.

Perhaps the visionaries who are developing and extending the model will also envision new support mechanisms and revenue opportunities. The important thing is that if each and every one of us (or even a substantial majority) recognizes the need, and if there is a diverse set of practical and effective models, the support will be found.

Conclusion

The positive power of computer-based technologies lies in their ability to serve humankind and to enable people to do things better (more successfully, efficiently, pleasurably, and effectively) than they previously could by eliminating or lessening drudgery and enhancing creativity. Perhaps even more importantly, it lies in their ability to enable people to do things that they simply were not able to do (did not know they could do or did not have the capacity to accomplish even if they wanted to) without technology.

The inherent danger is, of course, the misuse of that power. And any concentration of power in the hands of the few or the ignorant increases the danger a hundred-fold.

The way to counterbalance this threat of technological misuse and potential elitism is through education. In the past, as other technologies have taken hold, we have looked to the school system to provide the necessary education. We had the luxury of time, and so did the schools. That avenue is no longer sufficient. Schools, encumbered by outmoded curriculum and pedagogy, harnessed to a set of academic disciplines, and enveloped in a vast bureaucracy, cannot be asked to do it all.

What is needed is a new paradigm for technology education that is more consistent with the learning necessary, more adaptable to circumstances, more amenable to change, and one that is available to all, regardless of age, gender, economic or social condition, or geographic location. Neighborhood technology learning centers offer such a model, not as a substitute for schools, but as part of a greater educational partnership designed to insure that *everyone* has equal opportunity for technological enfranchisement.

Notes

Introduction

1. An earlier version of portions of this essay appeared in Bromley 1997b.

2. For more on how technologies can have certain values built into them, see "Do Artifacts Have Politics?" in Winner 1986.

3. David Noble writes that technology is "hardened history, frozen fragments of human and social endeavor" (Noble 1984, p. xi). Or, as Bruno Latour says, "technology is society made durable" (Latour 1991).

4. For an effort to navigate the conceptual thicket entailed by trying to accord full consideration simultaneously to both aspects of this mutually constituting relationship, avoiding the dual temptations of technological determinism and technological neutralism, see Bromley 1997a.

5. For a critical analysis of this proposal and its social and ideological compromises, see Apple 1992.

6. Dickens could have done no better.

7. I thank Teresa McMahon for pointing out this connection.

8. The power relations built into many technologies, computers included, are often oriented along gender lines. Although I have elsewhere focused specifically on the gendered nature of technology (Bromley 1995), I have not emphasized that element of the analysis here, only because other contributors so ably address it. What I would otherwise have included in this section would overlap particularly with Zoë Sofia's chapter.

9. See Robins and Webster 1989, chapter 3, for an argument that the wealthiest potential customers—other corporations—set the agenda for what forms of information access become available.

10. see Hacker 1993 (especially pp. 11–19 and their copious footnotes) and Noble 1977 (especially chapters 8 and 9)

11. Douglas Noble has extensively studied the development of this concept and its infiltration of the classroom via "instructional systems" technologies based on the same philosophy and developed by the same people as military training systems; see his *Classroom Arsenal* (1991) and briefer "Mental Materiel" (1989).

12. Accounts of a range of such practically based resistances may be found in Apple and Beane 1995.

Chapter 1

1. Frank Webster and Kevin Robins, *Information Technology: A Luddite Analysis* (New Jersey: Ablex, 1986), esp. Chapter 2; Douglas Noble "Computer Literacy and Ideology," in *The Computer in Education: A Critical Perspective*, ed. Douglas Sloan (New York: Teacher's College Press, 1984).

2. Arthur Kroker, "Virtual Capitalism," in *Technoscience and Cyberculture*, ed. Stanley Aronowitz, Barbara Martinsons and Michael Menser (New York: Routledge, 1986), pp. 167–68.

3. Sherry Turkle, *The Second Self: Computers and the Human Spirit* (New York: Simon and Schuster, 1984), esp. Chapter 6. On the masculine eroticization of technology, see essays by Sally Hacker in *Pleasure, Power, and Technology: Some Tales of Gender, Engineering, and the Cooperative Workplace* (Boston: Unwin Hyman, 1989), esp. Chapters 1 and 3; and in *Doing It the Hard Way: Investigations of Gender and Technology*, ed. Dorothy Smith and Susan M. Turner (Boston: Unwin Hyman, 1990), esp. Chapter 9, "The Eye of the Beholder: An Essay on Technology and Eroticism."

4. Sherry Turkle, "Computational Reticence: Why Women Fear the Intimate Machine," in *Technology and Women's Voices: Keeping in Touch*, ed. Cheris Kramarae (New York: Routledge & Kegan Paul, 1988), pp. 41–61. On gender differences in attitudes and contextual orientation, see Valerie A. Clarke, "Girls and Computing: Dispelling Myths and Finding Directions," in *Computers in Education*, ed. A. McDougall and C. Dowling (North-Holland: Elsevier Science Publishers B.V., 1990), pp. 53–58; Valerie A. Clarke, "Sex Differences in Computer Participation: Extent, Reasons and Strategies," *Australian Journal of Education* 34, no. 1 (1990): 52–66; Morwenna Griffiths, "Strong Feelings About Computers," *Women's Studies International Forum* 11, no. 2 (1988): 145–54; Celia Hoyles, "Introduction and Review of the Literature," in *Girls and Computers: General Issues and Case Studies of Logo in the Mathematics Classroom*, ed. C. Hoyles (London: Institute of Education, 1988), pp. 1–12; and Pamela E. Kramer and Sheila Lehman, "Mismeasuring Women: A Critique of Research on Computer Ability and Avoidance," *Signs* 16, no. 1 (1990): 158–72.

5. D. W. Winnicott, "The Use of an Object and Relating through Identifications," in *Playing and Reality* (New York: Routledge, 1989 [London: Tavistock, 1971]), pp. 86–94.

6. Sherry Turkle, "Computational Reticence" (see n. 4).

7. Sherry Turkle and Seymour Papert, "Epistemological Pluralism: Styles and Voices Within the Computer Culture," *Signs* 16, no. 1 (1990): 128–57.

8. Sue Curry Jansen, "Gender and the Information Society: A Socially Structured Silence," *Journal of Communication* 39, no. 3 (1989): 196–215.

9. This chapter is a synthesis of ideas and writings about technology, gender, computer culture and the arts developed for mainly Australian audiences over several years of talks and publications (in the names Sofoulis and Sofia) and condensed here for northern readers. The material on women artists comes out of collaborative interview-based research conducted with artist Virginia Barratt for our prospective book *Double Agents*, on technology from the perspectives of women artists working in digital media (for which we gratefully acknowledge funding assistance and other support from the Australia Council, ANAT [Australian Network for Art and Technology], Murdoch University, and the University of Western Sydney, Nepean). Material in the present chapter is drawn from the following (especially 1994a, and 1995b, 1995c, 1993a, 1993b):

(Sofia) 1996a. "Contested Zones: Futurity and Technological Art." *Leonardo* 29(1): 59–66.

(Sofoulis) 1996b. "Interactivity, Intersubjectivity and the Artwork/Network." *Mesh* 10, women@art.technology.au supplement: 32–35. Also at *Mesh* web site, http://www.peg.apc.org/~experimenta.

(Sofia) 1995a. "Of Spanners and Cyborgs: De-homogenizing Feminist Thinking on Technology." In *Transitions: New Australian Feminisms*, ed. Barbara Caine and Rosemary Pringle, pp. 147–63. St. Leonards, NSW: Allen & Unwin.

(Sofoulis) 1995b. "Cyberfeminism: The World, The Flesh and the Woman-Machine Relationship." Keynote address to Australian Computers in Education Conference, Perth, July 1995. In *Learning without Limits: Proceedings of the Australian Computers in Education Conference 1995*, Vol. 1, ed. Ron Oliver and Martyn Wild, pp. 71–81. Perth: Educational Computing Association of Western Australia; another version appears as "Creative Ambivalence and 'Interactivity,'" *geekgirl* 3 (1995): 21.

(Sofoulis) 1995c. "Hackers versus Cyborgs: Jacking (and 'Jilling') into the Matrix." (Text of talk given at *Sex/Gender in Technoscience Worlds* Conference, University of Melbourne, July 1993). *Aedon-Melbourne University Literary Arts Review* 3, no. 1: 46–55.

(Sofoulis) 1994a. "Computers: The Mythic Dimensions." Keynote address to *APITITE* (Asia-Pacific conference on Information Technology in Training and Education), Brisbane, July 1994. Partial version in *APITITE 94 Proceedings*, Vol. 1, ed. Michael Ryan, pp. 29–34.

(Sofoulis) 1994b. "Slime in the Matrix: Post-Phallic Formations in Women's Art in New Media." In *Jane Gallop Seminar Papers*, ed. Jill Julius Matthews, pp. 83–106. Canberra: Humanities Research Centre, Australian National University.

(Sofia) 1993a. *Whose Second Self? Gender and (Ir)rationality in Computer Culture*. Geelong: Deakin University Press.

(Sofoulis) 1993b. "Gender and Technological Irrationality." In *A Gendered Culture: Educational Management in the Nineties*, ed. Diana Baker and Madeleine Fogarty, pp. 28–43. St. Albans: Victoria University of Technology Press.

(Sofia) 1992a. "Hegemonic Irrationalities and Psychoanalytic Cultural Critique." *Cultural Studies* 6(3): 376–94.

(Sofia) 1992b. "Virtual Corporeality: A Feminist Perspective." *Australian Feminist Studies* 15: 11–24.

10. J. David Bolter, "The Computer as a Defining Technology," in *Turing's Man* (Chapel Hill: University of North Carolina Press, 1984), pp. 4–14.

11. Valerie Walkerdine, *The Mastery of Reason: Cognitive Development and the Production of Rationality* (London: Routledge, 1988), esp. pp. 186–87; she takes up the notion of "Reason's dream" from mathematician Brian Rotman.

12. Donna Haraway, "Situated Knowledges: the Science Question in Feminism and the Privilege of Partial Perspective," in Haraway, *Simians, Cyborgs, and Women: The Reinvention of Nature* (New York: Routledge, 1991), p. 189.

13. Norman O. Brown, *Life Against Death: The Psychoanalytical Meaning of History* (Middletown CT: Wesleyan University Press, 1959), p. 236.

14. Martin Heidegger, *The Question Concerning Technology and Other Essays,* trans. W. Lovitt (New York: Harper Torchbooks, 1977), esp. pp. 21, 141.

15. Terry Winograd and Fernando Flores, *Understanding Computers and Cognition: A New Foundation for Design* (New Jersey: Ablex Publishing Corporation, 1986), esp. pp. 176–78.

16. Paul N. Edwards, "The Army and the Microworld: Computers and the Politics of Gender Identity," *Signs* 16, no. 1 (1990): 102–27.

17. On hackers, see Sherry Turkle, *The Second Self* (n. 3 above); Steven Levy, *Hackers, Heroes of the Computer Revolution* (New York: Anchor Doubleday, 1984); and Andrew Ross "Hacking Away at the Counterculture," in *Technoculture*, ed. Constance Penley and Andrew Ross (Minneapolis: University of Minnesota Press, 1991). For classic examples of cyberpunk see William Gibson's collection *Burning Chrome* (New York: Ace, 1987), his trilogy *Neuromancer* (New York: Ace, 1984), *Count Zero* (New York: Arbor House, 1986), and *Mona Lisa Overdrive* (Toronto: Bantam, 1988),

and Bruce Sterling's edited collection *Mirrorshades: The Cyberpunk Anthology* (New York: Arbor House, 1986). Standard references in the burgeoning literature on cyberstudies include Larry McCaffery, ed., *Storming the Reality Studio: A Casebook of Cyberpunk and Postmodern Science Fiction* (Durham, NC: Duke University Press, 1991); Michael Benedikt, ed., *Cyberspace: First Steps* (Cambridge, MA: MIT, 1992); Mark Dery, ed., *Flame Wars: The Discourse of Cyberculture*, special issue of *South Atlantic Quarterly* 92, no. 4 (1993). See also Mark Dery, *Escape Velocity: Cyberculture at the End of the Century* (London: Hodder & Stoughton, 1996); Scott Bukataman, *Terminal Identity: The Virtual Subject in Postmodern Science Fiction* (Durham, NC: Duke University Press, 1993); and recent collections, including Chris Hables Gray, ed., *The Cyborg Handbook* (New York: Routledge, 1995); Gabriel Brahm Jr. and Mark Driscoll, eds., *Prosthetic Territories: Politics and Hypertechnologies* (Boulder: Westview, 1995); Stanley Aronowitz, Barbara Martinsons and Michael Menser, eds., *Technoscience and Cyberculture* (New York: Routledge, 1996); Mike Featherstone and Roger Burrows, eds., *Cyberspace, Cyberbodies, Cyberpunk: Cultures of Technological Embodiment* (London: Sage, 1996). For feminist orientations to cyborgs and cyberculture see Donna Haraway, *Simians, Cyborgs, and Women* (n. 12, above), especially the essays "A Cyborg Manifesto," "Situated Knowledges," and "The Biopolitics of Postmodern Bodies"; as well as Claudia Springer, "The Pleasure of the Interface," *Screen* 32 no. 3 (1991): 303–23; Zoë Sofia, *Whose Second Self?* (1993a, n. 9 above); Sadie Plant, "Beyond the Screens: Film, Cyberpunk and Cyberfeminism," *Variant* 14 (1993), and "The Future Looms: Weaving Women and Cybernetics," *Cyberspace, Cyberbodies, Cyberpunk*, ed. Featherstone and Burrows; and Anne Balsamo, *Technologies of the Gendered Body: Reading Cyborg Women* (Durham, NC: Duke University Press, 1996).

18. Mike Synergy, interviewed in the film *Cyberpunk* by Peter von Brandenburg and Marianne Trench (distributed by Voyager Company, 1990).

19. See n. 4.

20. Carol Gilligan, *In a Different Voice*, (Cambridge, MA: Harvard University Press, 1982), esp. pp. 9–11; she cites Janet Lever, "Sex Differences in the Games Children Play," *Social Problems* 23 (1976): 478–87 and "Sex Differences in the Complexity of Children's Play and Games," *American Sociological Review* 43 (1978): 471–83, as well as Jean Piaget, *The Moral Judgment of the Child* (New York: The Free Press, 1965 [1932]). See also Walkerdine's *The Mastery of Reason* (n. 11 above).

21. Moira Corby interviewed by Virginia Barratt, 1994. See also "Elena Popa and Moira Corby interviewed by Rosie X," *geekgirl* 3 (1995): 18–95.

22. This point is made by Dale Spender in *Nattering on the Net* (Melbourne: Spinifex, 1995); see also Judith Smith and Ellen Balka, "Chatting on a Feminist Computer Network" in *Technology and Women's Voices: Keeping in Touch*, ed. Cheris Kramarae (New York: Routledge & Kegan Paul/Methuen, 1988); and on the feminization of the telephone, see Lana F. Rakow "Women and the Telephone: The Gendering of a

Communications Technology," in Kramarae, ed., and Ann Moyal, "The Feminine Culture of the Telephone: People, Patterns and Policy," *Prometheus* 7, no. 1 (1989): 5–31. For discussions and examples of contemporary feminist (and postfeminist) network culture, see "the world's first cyberfeminist magazine" *geekgirl* (at www.geekgirl.com.au); Carla Sinclair *Net Chick* (NY?: Henry Holt & Co., 1996; Net Chick Clubhouse at http://www.cyborganic.com/people/carla/); and Rye Senjen and Jane Guthrey, *The Internet for Women* (Melbourne: Spinifex Press, 1996).

23. Marge Piercy, *Body Of Glass* (London: Penguin, 1991; retitle of US, *He, She, It* [Fawcett, 1991]); for discussions of Piercy's visions of embodiment and cyberspace, see Kevin McCarron, "Corpses, Animals, Machines and Mannequins: The Body and Cyberpunk," in Featherstone and Burrows, eds. (n. 17 above), pp. 261–73, and essays by Vara Neverow, Peter Fitting, and June Deery in *Utopian Studies* 5, no. 2 (1994).

24. Pat Cadigan *Synners* (New York: Bantam, 1989). Anne Balsamo identifies four kinds of postmodern embodiment on the basis of distinctions between "presence" of marked and laboring present bodies of the women characters and the "absence" of the virtual and repressed male bodies in Cadigan's novel; see "Feminism for the Incurably Informed," in Balsamo, *Technologies of the Gendered Body* and *Flame Wars*, pp. 681–712 (n. 17 above).

25. Elizabeth Reba Weise in *Wired Women: Gender and New Realities in Cyberspace*, ed. Lynn Cherny and Elizabeth Reba Weise (Seattle: Seal Press, 1996), p. xv.

26. Haraway, "A Cyborg Manifesto" (n. 12 above), p. 175.

27. Haraway, ibid., p. 181.

28. Glenn Russell, "Aspects of Gender and Computing Participation," *Australian Educational Computing: Journal of the Australian Council for Computers in Education* 8, Special Conference Edition (July 1993): 225–29.

29. Russell, ibid., p. 225.

30. For critical introductions to these different approaches, see Griselda Pollock, "What's Wrong with 'Images of Women'?" in *Framing Feminism: Art and the Women's Movement 1970–1985*, ed. Rozsika Parker and Griselda Pollock (New York: Pandora, 1987), pp. 132–38; S. Danuta Walters, "From Images of Woman to Woman as Image," in her *Material Girls: Making Sense of Feminist Cultural Theory* (Berkeley & LA: University of California Press, 1995), pp. 29–49; and Catriona Moore's introduction and various essays (especially Helen Grace and Ann Stephen, "Where Do Positive Images Come From? And What Does a Woman Want?" and Elizabeth Grosz, "Feminist Theory and the Politics of Art") in *Dissonance: Feminism and the Arts 1970–90*, ed. Catriona Moore (St. Leonards, NSW: Allen & Unwin with Artspace, 1994).

31. See n. 17.

32. David Lavery, *Late for the Sky: The Mentality of the Space Age* (Carbondale: Southern Illinois University Press, 1992); see also Zoë Sofia, "Exterminating Fetuses: Abortion, Disarmament, and the Sexo-Semiotics of Extraterrestrialism," *Diacritics* 14, no. 2 (Summer, 1984): 47–59.

33. Londa Schiebinger, "Feminine Icons: The Face of Early Modern Science," *Critical Inquiry* 14 (Summer, 1988): 661–91.

34. Andreas Huyssen, "The Vamp and the Machine: Fritz Lang's *Metropolis*," in *After the Great Divide: Modernism, Mass Culture, Postmodernism* (Bloomington: Indiana University Press, 1986), pp. 65–81.

35. Sadie Plant, "Cybernetic Hookers," *ANAT News* [Australian Network for Art and Technology] (April/May 1994): 4–8; "The Future Looms: Weaving Women and Cybernetics," in Featherstone and Burrows (see n. 17), esp. pp. 58–64. For other discussions of the cyborg metaphor see Judith Halberstam, "Automating Gender: Postmodern Feminism in the Age of the Intelligent Machine," *Feminist Studies* 17, no. 3 (1991): 439–59; Claudia Springer's essays "The Pleasure of the Interface," *Screen* 32, no. 3 (Autumn 1991): 303–23; and "Sex, Memories and Angry Women," in *Flame Wars,* ed. M. Dery (see n. 17): 713–33; Alluquere Rosanne Stone, *The War of Desire and Technology at the Close of the Mechanical Age* (Cambridge, MA: MIT, 1995); for a critique of Haraway and the cyborg see Carol A. Stabile, "Calculating on a Frictionless Plane," in *Feminism and the Technological Fix* (Manchester: Manchester University Press, 1994), pp. 134–60.

36. Haraway, "A Cyborg Manifesto" (see n. 12 above). *Cyberfeminist Manifesto for the 21st Century* was originally presented in billboard form at the Tin Sheds Gallery, Sydney 1992, and has appeared in various other forms and exhibitions since then. For discussions of VNS Matrix and other Australian women technological artists, see Glenda Nalder, "Under the VR Spell? Subverting America's Masculinist Global Hologram," *Eyeline* 21 (Autumn 1993): 20–22; also Nicola Teffer, "Body with Organs," Margriet Bonnin, "Zero 1: Technology and Future Art," and Cath Kenneally, "All New Gen," all in *Natural/Unnatural* issue of *Photofile* 42 (June 1994); Jyanni Steffensen, "Gamegirls: Working with New Imaging Technologies," *Mesh: Journal of the Modern Image Makers Association* 3 (Autumn 1994): 8–11; Bernadette Flynn, "Woman/Machine Relationships: Investigating the Body within Cyberculture," *Body's Image* special issue of *Media Information Australia* 72 (May 1994): 11–19; Zoë Sofoulis, "Slime in the Matrix" (1994b, n. 9 above), and "VNS Matrix and Virginia Barratt Interviewed by Bernadette Flynn," in *Electronic Arts in Australia,* ed. Nicholas Zurbrugg, special issue of *Continuum: The Australian Journal of Media and Culture* 8, no. 1 (1994): 419–32.

37. Jean-François Lyotard, *The Postmodern Condition,* trans. G. Bennington & B. Massumi (Minneapolis: Minnesota University Press, 1984), esp. pp. 25–27.

38. Melanie Klein, "Early Stages of the Oedipus Conflict" [1928] in Klein, *Love, Guilt and Reparation and Other Works 1921–1945,* ed. R. E. Money-Kyrle (London: Hogarth Press and the Institute of Psychoanalysis, 1975).

39. Melanie Klein, "Love, Guilt and Reparation," in Klein (see n. 38), esp. pp. 333–38.

40. Melanie Klein, "Early Stages" (see n. 38), p. 191. See also Eva Kittay, "Womb Envy as an Explanatory Concept" in *Mothering*, ed. Joyce Treblicott (Totowa, NJ: Rowman & Allanheld, 1984), pp. 94–128.

41. For if an archetypal masculine fear is of phallic castration, the loss of an external organ, a corresponding feminine fear is of internal bodily destruction.

42. On different computer-related research styles, see Knut H. Sørensen, "Towards a Feminized Technology?: Gendered Values in the Construction of Technology," *Social Studies of Science* 22, no. 1 (1992): 5–31; for an account of comparable differences in approaches to scientific research, see Evelyn Fox Keller's *A Feeling For The Organism: The Life and Work of Barbara McClintock* (San Francisco: W. H. Freeman, 1983).

43. See Erich Neumann, *The Origins and History of Consciousness* (Princeton, NJ: Bollingen/Princeton University Press, 1970), esp. section on "The Hero Myth," pp. 131–91; and Joseph Campbell, *The Hero with a Thousand Faces*, 2nd ed. (Princeton, NJ: Princeton University Press, 1968).

44. Sherry Turkle, 1984 (see n. 3), esp. Chapter 6.

45. See, for example, Sara Kiesler, Lee Sproul, and Jacquelynne Eccles, "Pool Halls, Chips, and War Games: Women in the Culture of Computing," *Psychology of Women Quarterly* 9 (1985): 451–62; and Eugene F. Provenzo, Jr., *Video Kids: Making Sense of Nintendo* (Cambridge, MA: Harvard University Press, 1991).

46. Anton Ehrenzweig, "The Origin of the Scientific and Heroic Urge (the Guilt of Prometheus)," *International Journal of Psycho-Analysis* 30, no. 2 (1949): 108–23; reworked in the chapter "The Devoured and Burned God," in Ehrenzweig, *The Hidden Order of Art: A Study in the Psychology of Artistic Imagination* (London: Weidenfeld, 1993), pp. 228–56.

47. On male masochism and its representations see Gilles Deleuze, *Masochism: An Interpretation of Coldness and Cruelty* (New York: George Braziller, 1971); Steve Neale, "Masculinity as Spectacle," *Screen* 24, no. 6 (1983): 2–16; Gaylyn Studlar, "Masochism and the Perverse Pleasures of the Cinema," in *Movies and Methods*, Vol. 2, ed. Bill Nichols (Berkeley: Univ. of California Press, 1985), pp. 602–21; Kaja Silverman, "Masochism and Male Subjectivity," *Camera Obscura* 17 (May 1988): 30–67; Klaus Theweleit, *Male Fantasies*, Vol. 1 (London: Polity, 1987).

48. The phrase "change for the machines" is a leitmotif in Pat Cadigan's *Synners*, (see n. 24) where it refers both to coins to feed vending machines and to people's willingness to alter their bodies and minds for machines.

49. For an account of psychasthenia, see Roger Callois, "Mimicry and Legendary Psychasthenia," trans. John Shepley, *October* 31 (Winter 1984): 16–32; on contempo-

rary cultural manifestations of psychasthenia, see Celeste Olalquiaga, *Megalopolis: Contemporary Cultural Sensibilities*, (Minneapolis: University of Minnesota Press, 1992), esp. Chapter 1; on psychasthenia and computer culture see Elizabeth Grosz, "Space, Time and Bodies," in *Space, Time and Perversion* (St. Leonards, NSW: Allen and Unwin, 1995), pp. 83–102; Kevin Robins' essay "Cyberspace and the World We Live In," in Featherstone and Burrows, eds. (see n. 17, above), pp. 135–55, does not use the term but examines like phenomena.

50. "The Ultimate Game Buster," advertisement in *PC Format* 31 (April 1994), p. 136.

51. See, for example, Kobena Mercer and Isaac Julien, "Race, Sexual Politics and Black Masculinity: A Dossier" in *Male Order: Unwrapping Masculinity*, ed. Rowena Chapman and Jonathan Rutherford (London: Lawrence Wishart, 1988), esp. pp. 131–53.

52. "Review: Super Putty" *Hyper* 7 (July, 1994), p. 40.

53. Christine Tamblyn, *"She Loves It, She Loves It Not: Women and Technology,* an Interactive CD-ROM," *Leonardo* 28, no. 2 (1995), esp. pp. 101, 103; see also Grahame String Weinbren, "Mastery: Computer Games, Intuitive Interfaces, and Interactive Media," *Leonardo* 28, no. 5 (1995): 408. For a discussion of other points of women artists' dissension from high-tech hype, see Zoë Sofia, "Contested Zones" (1996a, n. 9 above).

54. Ken Wark, "The New Abstraction," *World Art* 3 (1995): 61; see also Mona Sarkis, "Interactivity Means Interpassivity," *Media Information Australia* 69 (August, 1993): 13–16.

55. Linda Dement, "Linda Dement Interviewed by Glenda Nalder," in *Electronic Arts in Australia*, ed. Nicholas Zurbrugg (see n. 36 above), pp. 166–77, esp. 171.

56. See Sofoulis 1996a, 1996b, 1995b (n. 9 above); Sofia, "Technoscientific Poesis: Joan Brassil, Joyce Hinterding, Sarah Waterson," *Electronic Arts in Australia*, ed. Nicholas Zurbrugg (n. 36 above), pp. 364–75; Sofoulis, "Artist's profile: Sarah Waterson," in *women@art.technology.au* supplement to *Mesh* 10 (1996): 50–51.

Chapter 3

1. An earlier version of this chapter appeared in the *Journal of Educational Computing Research*, Vol. 10, no. 3 (1994): 199–221.

2. "Educational computing" here refers to a diverse range of uses to which computers are put in educational contexts, with the intention of providing thereby significant opportunities for learning, such as after-school computer clubs, word-processing in a Grade 2 classroom, or email pen-pal correspondence between children in two different cities.

3. It has been argued at length in the literature on "computers and society" (see Boyd, 1988; Kling, 1983; Forester, 1989; Noble, 1991) that a range of discrete factors present in social contexts, including political affiliations, gender, and the like, "influence" both access to and uses of computers in schools and other institutional settings. These analyses typically provide a theoretically opaque and deterministic account of such "effects." Our use of narrative critique in this paper is premised on a post-structural argument (developed by Foucault, 1980; Walkerdine, 1988) that studying language-in-use, or "discursive practices," provides a methodology for exposing *how* it is that these contextual factors "take shape," and how it is that the identities of the participants in those settings, as well as social relations therein, are constituted.

4. For the sake of brevity, we can only, en passant, refer the reader to a long-standing literature on the forms and functions of narrative and storying (see, for example, Blanchard, 1980; Bruner, 1985; Chafe, 1990; Polkinghorne, 1988). A related and rapidly growing literature well worth consulting here explicitly relates research on stories to inquiries into teachers' knowledge and sense-making (see, for example, Carter, 1993; Clandinin and Connelly, 1992; Richert, 1990).

5. Here we are referring to Habermas's (1987) notion of "knowledge-constitutive interests," or the sociopolitical context out of which a particular "point of view" is formed and by which it is constrained.

6. Papert's (1980) autobiographical narrative entitled "The Gears of my Childhood" represents, in our view, a paradigmatic modernist/romantic tale.

Chapter 4

This chapter represents the contributions and ideas of many people. Most significant among them are Michael Apple, Hank Bromley, Lisa Byrd, Ann de Vaney, Dipti Desai, John Fiske, Jennifer Phelps, Kate Adams, Devon Rose, and David Shutkin.

The Spectrum HoloByte ad appeared in the July/August 1991 issue of *PC Home Journal*. The Video Toaster and DesignWare ads appeared in the August 1991 issue of *Amiga World*. The advertisement for Canvas 3 appeared in the September 1991 issue of *MacWorld*.

Permission to reprint the DesignWorks advertisement granted courtesy of Steve Cockwell, Lazarus Engineering Corp. Permission to reprint the Video Toaster advertisement courtesy of NewTek Inc. Permission to reprint the Canvas 3 advertisement granted courtesy of Deneba Software. Permission to reprint the Spectrum HoloByte advertisement granted courtesy of Spectrum HoloByte, Inc.

1. I would like to thank Hank Bromley for introducing me to this work.

2. The target of this violence is significantly different from that observed by John Fiske (1989) in his study of unemployed males in video arcades. There the targets were bosses. Here it is peers.

3. The film "War Games" most vividly brought these themes together—man and boy game players and mastery of the physical world exercised through computer interfaces.

4. At the time I wrote and originally presented this research, the connection between computers and pornography was seen as a relatively marginal issue. Recent concerns over the trade in pornography on the Internet, however, have made these connections a central feature in the public discourse on digital technologies.

5. I would like to thank Devon Rose for pointing this out to me.

Chapter 5

1. The authors wish to thank Lic. Rosalina Chacón and other staff members of Costa Rica's Fundación Omar Dengo, the students, teachers, and School directors who participated in this research, and the Lépiz Soto family who graciously hosted the first author. Appreciation is also extended to the College of Charleston for its financial support, and to Rosemary Brana-Shute and John Rashford of the College of Charleston and Jennifer Hardin of the University of South Florida for their valuable comments. All opinions expressed here are solely those of the authors.

2. English translations of all Spanish materials, including the interviews and conversations recorded in the lab and classrooms, are by the first author.

3. Pseudonyms are used for the schools, their teachers, and students.

4. In addition to introducing computers into primary schools, the Programa de Informática Educativa currently offers courses to the general public. Program personnel are also developing or plan to develop educational software, a network linking schools to information databases, and educational computing programs for secondary schools and universities (Fonseca, 1991, pp. 56–60).

5. There are minor differences between Fonseca's (1991, p. 55) and Harper's (1991, p. 43) figures. Also note that eighty laboratories were originally scheduled to be created during the third phase of this program's implementation. Only thirty are now planned.

6. Lic. Rosalina Chacón, FOD's Coordinator of Research, stated in a conversation with the first author that students are not encouraged to compete in the lab. A very competitive learning environment is thought to have somewhat undesirable outcomes in the lab. Students are encouraged to do their best but should work at their own pace.

7. Here Carlos Andrés used the English word "superman." Super heroes and cartoon characters such as Superman, the Incredible Hulk, the Smurfs, Snow White and the Seven Dwarfs, are familiar to many Costa Rican children who watch television or read comic books. It is also somewhat common for Costa Ricans to have English first names, such as Roy, Jimmy, Cindy, Mary Ann.

8. Costa Rica's Ministry of Education is currently considering proposals designed to increase the amount of time teachers spend with their students in the classroom (*La Nación*, 1992, p. 4A).

Chapter 6

1. See Michael W. Apple (1993), *Official Knowledge: Democratic Education in a Conservative Age*, New York: Routledge; and Michael W. Apple (1996), *Cultural Politics and Education*, New York: Teachers College Press.

2. Michael W. Apple (1995), *Education and Power*, second edition, New York: Routledge.

3. Stephen Ball (1988), "Staff Relations During the Teachers' Industrial Action: Context, Conflict and Proletarianization," *British Journal of Sociology of Education* 9 (number 3), p. 290.

4. The issue of the "proletarianization" of teachers is a complicated one. For further discussion, see Apple, *Education and Power*, and Apple (1988), *Teachers and Texts: A Political Economy of Class and Gender Relations in Education*, New York: Routledge. Some of the complexities are nicely articulated in Jenny Ozga and Martin Lawn (1988), "Schoolwork: Interpreting the Labour Process of Teaching," *British Journal of Sociology of Education* 9 (number 3), pp. 289–306. Much of the next section is based on Michael W. Apple and Kenneth Teitelbaum (1986), "Are Teachers Losing Control of Their Skills and Curriculum?" *Journal of Curriculum Studies* 18 (number 2), pp. 177–84.

5. Apple, *Education and Power* and Apple, *Teachers and Texts*.

6. As many of you may know, Tayloristic strategies have a long history of use in education. For further discussion, see Herbert Kliebard (1995), *The Struggle for the American Curriculum*, second edition, New York: Routledge; Michael W. Apple (1990), *Ideology and Curriculum*, second edition, New York: Routledge; and Apple, *Education and Power*.

7. Apple, *Education and Power*.

8. Apple, *Teachers and Texts*.

9. Ibid.

10. Lawrence Stedman and Marshall Smith (1983), "Recent Reform Proposals for American Education," *Contemporary Education Review* 2 (Fall), pp. 85–104; Apple, *Teachers and Texts*.

11. The negative impact of such testing and reductive objectives-based curriculum and evaluation strategies is a major problem. It is nicely documented in Andrew

Gitlin (1983), "School Structure and Teachers' Work," in Michael W. Apple and Lois Weis, eds. *Ideology and Practice in Schooling*, Philadelphia: Temple University Press, pp. 193–212. See also Linda McNeil (1986), *Contradictions of Control*, New York: Routledge.

12. Apple, *Teachers and Texts*.

13. Ibid. We are, of course, here making a "functional" argument, not necessarily an "intentional" one. Managers, policy experts, and others need not consciously plan to control specifically the work of women for it to have this effect.

14. Apple, *Education and Power*.

15. The economics and politics of textbook publishing are analyzed in much greater depth in Apple, *Teachers and Texts*, especially chapter 4. The history of some of the socioeconomic conditions that led to such adoption policies is investigated in Apple, *Official Knowledge*, especially chapters 3 and 4.

16. See, for example, Richard Edwards (1979), *Contested Terrain*, New York: Basic Books; and David Gordon, Richard Edwards, and Michael Reich (1982), *Segmented Work, Divided Workers*, New York: Cambridge University Press.

17. Ibid.; Apple, *Education and Power*.

18. A large portion of these data are reviewed in Apple, *Cultural Politics and Education*, pp. 68–90.

19. For a more detailed elaboration of the process and results of intensification, see Apple, *Teachers and Texts*, especially chapter 2.

20. Gitlin, "School Structure and Teachers' Work."

21. Ozga and Lawn, "Schoolwork," p. 333.

22. Whether such "literacy" is in fact necessary in the way its proponents propose, and the possible educational, social, and economic effects of such technology, are examined in greater depth in Apple, *Teachers and Texts* and Apple, *Cultural Politics and Education*.

23. Most of the material in this section is taken from Susan Jungck, "Doing Computer Literacy," unpublished Ph.D. Thesis, University of Wisconsin, Madison, 1985.

24. See Apple, *Teachers and Texts*, for further discussion of and references on this important point. Also of considerable interest is Andrew Gitlin and Frank Margonis, "The Political Aspect of Reform" (1995), *American Journal of Education* 103 (August), pp. 377–405.

25. This response, with all its contradictions, is similar historically to the calls by teachers in the later part of the nineteenth century for the provision of standard-

ized textbooks. Many teachers, especially young women, rightly felt exploited by low pay, poor working conditions, and an expanding curriculum for which they felt either ill prepared to teach or, more usually, had insufficient time to prepare quality lessons for. The standardized text was one way to solve parts of this dilemma, even though it may actually have undercut some of their emerging autonomy at the same time. Some elements of this story are told in Marta Danylewycz and Alison Prentice (1984), "Teachers, Gender, and Bureaucratizing School Systems in Nineteenth Century Montreal and Toronto," *History of Education Quarterly* 24 (Spring), pp. 75–100.

26. See, for example, Carol Gilligan (1982), *In a Different Voice*, Cambridge: Harvard University Press. For a general discussion of the issue of gender and experience, see R. W. Connell (1987), *Gender and Power*, Stanford: Stanford University Press; Leslie Roman, Linda Christian-Smith, and Elizabeth Ellsworth, eds. (1988), *Becoming Feminine*, Philadelphia: Falmer Press; and R. W. Connell (1995), *Masculinities*, Cambridge: Polity Press. We do *not* want to essentialize women, however; nor do we want to claim that all women are uniform. We instead are making a conjunctural argument that at this historical time, in this situation, such resources and strategies tend to come into play.

27. Sandra Acker (1988), "Teachers, Gender and Resistance," *British Journal of Sociology of Education* 9 (no. 3), p. 314. See also, Apple, *Teachers and Texts*; and the extensive review of the research on gender and teaching in Sandra Acker, "Gender and Teachers' Work," in Michael W. Apple, ed. (1995), *Review of Research in Education Volume 21*, Washington: American Educational Research Association, pp. 99–162.

28. Acker, "Teachers, Gender and Resistance," p. 307.

29. For a review of some of this literature, see Apple, *Education and Power*; and Alice Kessler-Harris (1982), *Out to Work*, New York: Oxford University Press.

30. Apple, *Official Knowledge*; and Apple, *Cultural Politics and Education*. For a more general theoretical discussion of the process of commodification and what conceptual resources might be necessary to understand it in all its complexity, see the dense but important book by Philip Wexler (1988), *Social Analysis and Education*, New York: Routledge.

Chapter 7

1. An earlier version of this paper was presented at the April 1993 annual meeting of the American Educational Research Association, Atlanta, Georgia. Authors' addresses: Peter H. Kahn, Jr., Department of Education and Human Development, Colby College, Waterville, ME 04901. Electronic mail: phkahn@colby.edu. Batya Friedman, Department of Mathematics and Computer Science, Colby College, Waterville, ME 04901. Electronic mail: b_friedm@colby.edu.

Chapter 8

1. The POLIS simulation was designed by Robert C. Noel of the University of California at Santa Barbara. He used ARPANET to link students at University of California campuses to one another in order to test the distance element of the exercise.

2. See Jonathan Wilkenfeld and Joyce Kaufman (1993), "Political Science: Network Simulation in International Politics," *Social Science Computer Review* 11:4 (Winter): 464–76, for a description of the roots and goals of simulation games in international relations.

3. See Thomas J. Shuell (1986), "Cognitive Conceptions of Learning," *Review of Educational Research* 56: 411–36, for support of this notion.

4. See Maryam Alavi (1994), "Computer-Mediated Collaborative Learning: An Empirical Evaluation," *Management Information Systems Quarterly* (June): 159–74.

5. Judith Torney-Purta (1995), "Conceptual Change Among Adolescents Using Computer Networks and Peer Collaboration in Studying International Relations," in *International Perspectives on the Design of Technology-Supported Learning Environments*, eds. Stella Vosniadou, Erik De Corte, Robert Glaser, and Heinz Mandl, Lawrence Erlbaum Associates.

6. As multimedia computer applications become more popular and more readily available, the project has begun to experiment with the possible incorporation of some of these elements into the simulation model.

7. ICONS Regional Centers are located at the University of Connecticut, Florida International University, The Heartland Area Education Agency in Des Moines, Iowa, and Immaculate Heart College Center in Los Angeles, California.

8. Torney-Purta, "Conceptual Change Among Adolescents," p. 215.

9. Torney-Purta, "Conceptual Change Among Adolescents," p. 206.

10. Judith Torney-Purta (1994), "Peer Interactions Among Adolescents Using Computer Networks in an International Role Playing Exercise," in *Technology-Based Learning Environments: Psychological and Educational Foundations*, eds. Stella Vosniadou, Erik De Corte, and Heinz Mandl, Heidelberg, Germany: Springer, p. 70.

11. Judith Torney-Purta (1993), "An Evaluation of the FIPSE ICONS Project." Unpublished Interim Evaluation Report (Spring), p. 6.

12. Susan Gordon (1995), "Tacoma's School for Diplomats," *The News Tribune* Tacoma, Washington (15 May), p. B1.

13. Ibid.

14. Kathleen L. Rottier (1995), "If Kids Ruled the World: ICONS," *Educational Leadership* 53: 51–54.

15. See David Kowalewski (1982), "International Simulation Satisfaction: A Quantitative Study," *International Studies Notes* 9: 12–17.

16. ICONS works with the Education Department of the Jewish Agency and the Migal Technology Center in Kiryat Shmona to bring ICONS to high school students in Israel. Eight Israeli secondary schools participated during the 1993–94 academic year. In addition, Hebrew and Bar Ilan Universities have participated in postsecondary exercises, and talks are underway with Bethlehem and Bir Zeit Universities, with predominantly Palestinian student bodies, to facilitate their participation in upcoming simulations.

17. Joyce P. Kaufman (1994), "Technology as 'Equalizer': Using Computer Technology to Empower Secondary and Post-Secondary Students," Presented at the 11th Annual International Conference on Technology and Education (ICTE), London, England.

18. Joyce P. Kaufman, "Technology as Equalizer," p. 2.

19. Merle Richards (1994), "Language Experience in Second-Language Teaching," *Mosaic* 1: 17–18.

20. Comments during instructor debriefings, conducted by Dr. Joyce Kaufman, Director, International Negotiation Project, Los Angeles, California.

21. ICONS staff members, in Israel to conduct a training workshop, were asked to meet with parents to discuss the educational value of having the students portray Syria. During the discussion, the group began to consider the meaning of such concepts as "enemy" and "neighbor." Eventually, there was general agreement that it would be very valuable to have the Israeli children portray their nation's enemy *and* neighbor, Syria.

22. Through a program entitled "Partners in Conflict," sponsored by the Center for International Development and Conflict Management on the University of Maryland campus, a group of Palestinian and Israeli university students traveled to College Park in 1993. Part of their experience involved an ICONS simulation which focused on the question of Jerusalem's future status.

23. Instructional Videotape: The ICONS Module for the Maryland Instructional Framework, Developed by the Maryland State Department of Education, 1993.

Chapter 9

1. The following contribution was written in 1992, when the author was still executive director of Playing To Win. While the details of the Harlem Center's practice have since evolved, the underlying issues addressed in the chapter remain pertinent.—Ed.

References

Introduction

Apple, Michael W. (1992). "Do the Standards Go Far Enough? Power, Policy, and Practice in Mathematics Education," *Journal of Research in Mathematics Education* 23:5 (November), pp. 412–31.

———. (1996). *Cultural Politics and Education*. New York: Teachers College Press.

Apple, Michael W. and James A. Beane, ed. (1995). *Democratic Schools*. Washington, DC: Association for Supervision and Curriculum Development.

Aufderheide, Pat (1994). "Media Beat" Column in *In These Times*, February 21, pp. 8–9.

Braverman, Harry (1974). *Labor and Monopoly Capital: The Degradation of Work in the Twentieth Century*. New York: Monthly Review Press.

Bromley, Hank (1995). "Engendering Technology: The Social Practice of Educational Computing," Ph.D. Dissertation, University of Wisconsin-Madison.

———. (1997a). "The Social Chicken and the Technological Egg: Educational Computing and the Technology/Society Divide," *Educational Theory* 47:1 (Winter), pp. 51–65.

———. (1997b). "Thinking about Computers and Schools: A Skeptical View," in Philip E. Agre and Douglas Schuler, ed., *Reinventing Technology, Rediscovering Community: Critical Explorations of Computing as a Social Practice*. Norwood, NJ: Ablex.

Burris, Beverly H. (1989). "Technocratic Organization and Gender," *Women's Studies International Forum* 12:4, pp. 447–62.

Business Week (1994). Special report on "The Learning Revolution," February 28 issue, pp. 80–88.

Celis, William (1993). "Corporate Rescuer is Selected To Head Schools in California," *The New York Times*, November 19 (national edition), pp. A1, A12.

Cohen, David K. (1987). "Educational Technology, Policy, and Practice," *Educational Evaluation and Policy Analysis* 9:2 (Summer), pp. 153–70.

Collins, Randall (1979). *The Credential Society: An Historical Sociology of Education and Stratification*. Orlando: Academic Press.

Cuban, Larry (1986). *Teachers and Machines: The Classroom Use of Technology Since 1920*. New York: Teachers College Press.

Edwards, Paul N. (1989). "The Closed World: Systems Discourse, Military Policy and Post-World War II US Historical Consciousness," in Les Levidow and Kevin Robins, ed., *Cyborg Worlds: The Military Information Society*. London: Free Association Books.

———. (1996). *The Closed World: Computers and the Politics of Discourse in Cold War America*. Cambridge, MA: MIT Press.

Edwards, Richard (1979). *Contested Terrain: The Transformation of the Workplace in the Twentieth Century*. New York: Basic Books.

Firkin, Judith, Maryellen Davidson and Lesley Johnson (1985). *Computer Culture in the Classroom*. Melbourne: Victorian Institute of Secondary Education.

Goldhaber, Michael (1986). *Reinventing Technology: Policies for Democratic Values*. New York: Routledge & Kegan Paul.

Hacker, Barton C. (1993). "Engineering a New Order: Military Institutions, Technical Education, and the Rise of the Industrial State." *Technology and Culture* 34:1 (January), pp. 1–27.

Hanson, Dirk (1982). *The New Alchemists: Silicon Valley and the Microelectronics Revolution*. Boston: Little Brown.

Hodas, Steven (1993). "Technology Refusal and the Organizational Culture of Schools," *Education Policy Analysis Archives* 1:10 (September 14). [EPAA is a peer-reviewed journal distributed electronically. Copies of articles are available at http://olam.ed.asu.edu/epaa/]

Horwitz, Tony (1994). "Young Professors Find Life in Academia Isn't What It Used to Be," *The Wall Street Journal*, February 15, pp. A1, A8.

Latour, Bruno (1991). "Technology is Society Made Durable," in John Law, ed., *A Sociology of Monsters: Essays on Power, Technology and Domination*. New York: Routledge.

Levidow, Les and Kevin Robins (1989). "Towards a Military Information Society?" in Les Levidow and Kevin Robins, ed., *Cyborg Worlds: The Military Information Society*. London: Free Association Books.

Mosco, Vincent (1988). "Introduction: Information in the Pay-per Society," in Vincent Mosco and Janet Wasko, ed., *The Political Economy of Information*. Madison: University of Wisconsin Press.

New York Times (1994). March 12 (national edition), chart on p. A7.

Noble, David F. (1977). *America By Design: Science, Technology, and the Rise of Corporate Capitalism*. New York: Knopf.

———. (1984). *Forces of Production: A Social History of Industrial Automation*. New York: Alfred A. Knopf.

Noble, Douglas D. (1989). "Mental Materiel: The Militarization of Learning and Intelligence in US Education," in Les Levidow and Kevin Robins, ed., *Cyborg Worlds: The Military Information Society*. London: Free Association Books.

———. (1991). *The Classroom Arsenal: Military Research, Information Technology, and Public Education*. London: Falmer.

Ragsdale, Ronald G. (1988). *Permissible Computing in Education: Values, Assumptions, and Needs*. New York: Praeger.

Robins, Kevin and Frank Webster (1989). *The Technical Fix: Education, Computers and Industry*. New York: St. Martin's Press.

Roszak, Theodore (1986). *The Cult of Information: The Folklore of Computers and the True Art of Thinking*. New York: Pantheon.

Smith, Dorothy E. (1993). "The 'Out-of-Body' Experience," lecture given at the Havens Center, University of Wisconsin-Madison, October 13.

Suppes, Patrick (1980). "The Teacher and Computer-Assisted Instruction," in Robert Taylor, ed., *The Computer in the School: Tutor, Tool, Tutee*. New York: Teachers College Press (originally published in *NEA Journal*, February 1967).

Thomborson, Clark (1987). "Role of Military Funding in Academic Computer Science," in David Bellin and Gary Chapman, ed., *Computers in Battle—Will They Work?* Boston: Harcourt Brace Jovanovich.

Tucker, Marc S. (1985). "Computers in the Schools: What Revolution?" *Journal of Communication* 35:4 (Autumn), pp. 12–23.

Webster, Frank and Kevin Robins (1986). *Information Technology: A Luddite Analysis*. Norwood, NJ: Ablex.

Winner, Langdon (1986). *The Whale and the Reactor: A Search for Limits in an Age of High Technology*. Chicago: University of Chicago Press.

Chapter 2

Benjamin, W. (1977). *The origin of German tragic drama.* John Osborne, tr. London: New Left Books.

Bowers, C. A. (1988). *The cultural dimensions of educational computing: Understanding the non-neutrality of technology.* New York: Teachers College Press.

Cole, M. (1993). *A cultural-historical goal for developmental research: Create sustainable model systems of diversity.* Paper delivered to a meeting of the Society for Research in Child Development, New Orleans, LA, March 28, 1993.

Csikszentmihalyi, M. and I. S. Csikszentmihalyi, eds. (1988). *Optimal experience: Psychological studies of flow in consciousness.* New York: Cambridge Universities Press.

Csikszentmihalyi, M. (1990). *Flow: The psychology of optimal experience.* New York: Harper & Row.

Edwards, Paul N. (1996). *The closed world: Computers and the politics of discourse in Cold War America.* Cambridge, MA: MIT Press.

Eraut, M., ed. (1991). *Education and the information society: a challenge for European policy.* London: Cassell, 1991.

Forrest, J. (1988). *Lord I'm coming home: Everyday aesthetics in tidewater North Carolina.* Ithaca, NY: Cornell University Press.

Harris, D. (1994). "The aesthetic of the computer." *Salmagundi,* Winter, n101–102, pp. 173–81.

Laboratory of Comparative Human Cognition (LCHC). (1989). "Kids and computers: A positive vision of the future." *Harvard Educational Review, 59*: 73–86.

Nicolopolou, A. and M. Cole. (1993). "The Fifth Dimension, its play world, and its instructional contexts: The generation and transmission of shared knowledge in the culture of collaborative learning." In N. Minnick and E. Forman, eds. *The Institutional and Social Context of Mind: New Directions in Vygotskian Theory and Research.* New York: Oxford University Press.

Noble, D. D. (1989*).* "Mental materiel. The militarization of learning and intelligence in US education." In L. Levidow and K. Robins, eds. *Cyborg Worlds: The Military Information Society.* London: Free Association Books.

———. (1991). *The classroom arsenal: Military research, information technology, and public education.* New York : Falmer Press.

Postman, N. and C. Weingartner. (1969, 1971). *Teaching as a Subversive Activity.* New York: Delta.

Schofield, Janet Ward, Rebecca Eurich-Fulcer, and Cheri L. Britt. (1994). "Teachers, Computer Tutors, and Teaching: The Artificially Intelligent Tutor as an Agent for Classroom Change." *American Educational Research Journal 31*(3): 579–607.

Vasquez, O. (1996). *A Look at Language as a Resource: Lessons from La Clase Mágica.* University of California, San Diego. Electronic edition of paper downloaded from: http://communication.ucsd.edu/LCHC/LCM/OlgasPapers/lookat.html.

Weizenbaum, J. (1976). *Computer power and human reason: From judgment to calculation.* San Francisco: W. H. Freeman.

Williams, Michael R., ed. (1996). *IEEE Annals of the History of Computing 18*(1) Special issue on the ENIAC computer.

Winegrad, D. (1996). "Celebrating the birth of modern computing: The fiftieth anniversary of a discovery at the Moore School of Engineering of the University of Pennsylvania." *IEEE Annals of the History of Computing 18*(1): 5–7.

Chapter 3

Apple, M., and S. Jungck. (1998). "'You don't have to be a teacher to teach this unit': Teaching, technology, and control in the classroom." In H. Bromley and M. Apple, eds. *Education/technology/power: Educational computing as a social practice.* Albany, NY: SUNY Press.

Aronowitz, S., and H. Giroux. (1991). *Postmodern education.* Minneapolis: University of Minnesota Press.

Barthes, R. (1977). *Roland Barthes by Roland Barthes.* Richard Howard, trans. New York: Hill & Wang.

Baudrillard, J. (1983). *Simulations.* Paul Foss, Paul Patton, and Philip Beitchman, trans. New York: Semiotext(e).

Belenky, A., B. Clinchy, N. Goldberger, and J. Tarule. (1986). *Women's ways of knowing.* New York: Basic Books, Inc.

Blanchard, M. (1980). *Description: Sign, self, desire.* The Hague: Mouton Publishers.

Bordo, S. (1990). "Feminism, postmodernism, and gender-scepticism." In L. Nicholson, ed., *Feminism/postmodernism.* New York: Routledge.

Bourdieu, P., and J. C. Passeron. (1977). *Reproduction in education, society, and culture.* Beverly Hills, CA: Sage Publications.

Bowers, C. (1988). *The cultural dimensions of educational computing.* New York: Teacher's College Press.

Bowles, S., and H. Gintis. (1976). *Schooling in capitalist America.* New York: Basic Books, Inc.

Boyd, G. (1988). "The impact of society on educational technology." *British Journal of Educational Technology*, 19: 114–22.

British Columbia Ministry of Education. (1990). *Supporting learning: Understanding and assessing the progress of children in the Primary program.* Victoria: Ministry of Education.

Broughton, J. M. (1984). "The surrender of control: Computer literacy as political socialization of the child." In D. Sloan, ed., *The computer in education: A critical perspective.* New York: Teacher's College Press.

Brown, J. S. (1985). "Process versus product: A perspective on tools for communal and informal electronic learning." *Journal of Educational Computing Research*, 1(2): 179–201.

Bruner, J. (1985). "Narrative and paradigmatic modes of thought." In E. Eisner, ed., *Learning and teaching the ways of knowing.* Chicago: University of Chicago Press.

Bryson, M. (1993). *New technologies/New Practices?: Teachers, machines, and the cultures of primary schooling.* Vancouver: University of British Columbia.

Bryson, M., and S. de Castell. (1995). "So we've got a chip on our shoulder?: Sexing the texts of educational technology." In J. Gaskell and J. Willinsky, eds., *Gender in/forms curriculum.* New York: Teachers College Press.

———. (1993). "En/Gendering equity." *Educational Theory*, 43: 341–55.

Carter, K. (1993). "The place of story in the study of teaching and teacher education." *Educational Researcher*, 22: 5–12.

Chafe, W. (1990). "Some things that narrative tells us about the mind." In B. Britton and A. Pellegrini, eds., *Narrative thought and narrative language.* Hillsdale, NJ: Erlbaum.

Clandinin, J., and M. Connelly. (1992). "Teacher as curriculum maker." In P. Jackson, ed., *Handbook of research on curriculum.* New York: Macmillan.

Cohen, D. (1987). "Educational technology, policy, and practice." *Educational Evaluation and Policy Analysis*, 9(2): 153–70.

Cuban, L. (1986). *Teachers and machines.* New York: Teachers College Press.

Damarin, S. (1993). "School and situated knowledge: Travel or tourism." *Educational Technology*, 33: 27–32.

De Lacy, J. (1989). "The sexy computer." In T. Forester, ed., *Computers in the human context*. Cambridge, MA: MIT Press.

Derrida, J. (1978). *Writing and difference*. Alan Bass, trans. Chicago: University of Chicago Press.

Ellsworth, E. (1989). "Why doesn't this feel empowering? Working through the repressive myths of critical pedagogy." *Harvard Educational Review*, 59(3): 297–324.

Emihovich, C., and G. Miller. (1988). "Effects of LOGO and CAI on black first graders' achievement, reflectivity, and self-esteem." *The Elementary School Journal*, 88(5): 473–87.

Felperin, H. (1985). *Beyond deconstruction: The uses and abuses of literary theory*. Oxford: Clarendon Press.

Forester, T., ed. (1989). *Computers in the human context*. Cambridge, MA: MIT Press.

Foucault, M. (1978). *The history of sexuality Volume 1: An introduction*. Robert Hurley, trans. New York: Random House.

———. (1980). *Power/knowledge*. New York: Pantheon Books.

———. (1983). "On the genealogy of ethics: An overview of work in progress." In H. Dreyfus and P. Rabinow, eds., *Michel Foucault: Beyond structuralism and hermeneutics*. Chicago: University of Chicago Press.

Fraser, N. (1989). *Unruly practices: Power, discourse and gender in contemporary social theory*. Minneapolis: University of Minnesota Press.

Freire, P. (1971). *Pedagogy of the oppressed*. New York: Harper and Row.

Giroux, H. (1981). *Ideology, culture and the process of schooling*. Philadelphia: Temple University Press.

Goodson, I., and M. Mangan. (1991). *Qualitative educational research studies: Methodologies in transition (Vol. 1). RUCCUS Occasional Papers*. London, Ont: Faculty of Education, University of Western Ontario.

Gore, J. (1993). *The struggle for pedagogies: Critical and feminist discourses as regimes of truth*. New York: Routledge.

Graff, H. J. (1988). "Whither the history of literacy? The future of the past." *Communication*, 11: 5–22.

Griffin, S., and M. Cole. (1987). "New technologies, basic skills, and the underside of education: What's to be done?" In J. Langer, ed., *Language, literacy and culture*. Norwood, NJ: Ablex.

Habermas, J. (1988). *Lectures on the philosophical discourse of modernity.* Cambridge, MA: MIT Press.

Haraway, D. (1989). *Primate visions.* New York: Routledge.

―――. (1990). "A manifesto for cyborgs: Science, technology, and socialist feminism in the 1980s." In L. Nicholson, ed., *Feminism/postmodernism.* New York: Routledge.

Heath, S. (1986). *Ways with words.* Cambridge, MA: Harvard University Press.

Hutcheon, L. (1989). *The politics of postmodernism.* New York: Routledge.

Joram, E., E. Woodruff, M. Bryson, and P. Lindsay. (1992). "The effects of revising with a word processor on writing composition." *Research in the Teaching of English,* 26: 167–92.

Kling, R. (1983). "Value conflicts in computing developments." *Telecommunications Policy,* 7: 12–34.

Lather, P. (1990a). "Staying dumb? Student resistance to liberatory curriculum." Paper presented at a meeting of AERA (American Educational Research Association), Boston.

―――. (1990b). "Postmodernism and the human sciences." *The Humanistic Psychologist, 18*(1): 64–84.

―――. (1991). *Getting smart.* New York: Routledge.

Lawson, H. (1989). "Stories about stories." In H. Lawson and L. Appignanesi, eds., *Dismantling truth: Reality in the post-modern world.* New York: St. Martin's Press.

Leach, M., and B. Davies. (1990). "Crossing the boundaries: Educational thought and gender equity." *Educational Theory,* 40: 321–32.

LCHC (Laboratory of Comparative Human Cognition). (1989). "Kids and computers: A positive vision of the future." *Harvard Educational Review,* 59(1): 73–86.

Luke, C., and J. Gore. (1992). *Feminisms and critical pedagogy.* New York: Routledge.

Marvin, C. (1988). *When old technologies were new.* New York: Oxford University Press.

McCorduck, P. (1985). *The universal machine: Confessions of a technological optimist.* New York: McGraw-Hill.

Means, B., and M. Knapp. (1990). *Models for teaching advanced skills to educationally disadvantaged children.* Unpublished paper. Menlo Park, CA: SRI International.

Motherwell, L. (1988). *Gender and style differences in a LOGO-based environment.* Unpublished doctoral dissertation. Boston: Massachusetts Institute of Technology.

Noble, D. (1991). *The classroom arsenal: Military research, information technology and public education.* London: Falmer Press.

Norris, C. (1985). *The contest of faculties: Philosophy and theory after deconstruction.* New York: Methuen.

Ogbu, J. (1983). "Literacy and schooling in subordinate cultures: The case of black Americans." In D. Resnick, ed., *Literacy in historical perspective.* Washington, DC: Library of Congress.

Papert, S. (1980). *Mindstorms.* New York: Basic Books.

———. (1984). "New theories for new learnings." *School Psychology Review*, 13(4): 422–28.

Persell, C. H., and P. Cookson. (1987). "Microcomputers and elite boarding schools: Educational innovation and social reproduction." *Sociology of Education*, 60: 123–34.

Polkinghorne, D. (1988). *Narrative knowing and the human sciences.* Albany: SUNY Press.

Propp, V. (1958). *Morphology of the folktale.* Bloomington, IN: Indiana University Press.

Ragsdale, R. (1988). *Permissible computing in education: Values, assumptions and needs.* New York: Praeger.

Richert, A. (1990). "Using teacher cases for reflection and enhanced understanding." In A. Lieberman and L. Miller, eds., *Teachers: Their world and their work.* New York: Teachers College Press.

Rorty, R. (1989). *Contingency, irony, and solidarity.* Cambridge: Cambridge University Press.

Shute, V., R. Glaser, and P. Resnick. (1986). *Discovering and learning to discover: An intelligent microworld for economics.* Paper presented at a meeting of AERA, San Francisco.

Stock, B. (1983). *The implications of literacy.* Princeton: Princeton University Press.

Suleiman, S. (1990). *Subversive intent: Gender, politics, and the avant-garde.* Cambridge, MA: Harvard University Press.

Sutton, R. (1991). "Equity and computers in the schools: A decade of research." *Review of Educational Research,* 61: 475–503.

Thompson, M. (1979). *Rubbish theory: The creation and destruction of value.* Oxford: Oxford University Press.

Turing, A. M. (1964). "Computing machinery and intelligence." In A. R. Anderson, ed., *Minds and machines.* Englewood Cliffs, NJ: Prentice Hall, Inc.

Turkle, S., and S. Papert. (1990). "Epistemological pluralism: Styles and voices within the computer culture." *Signs: Journal of Women in Culture and Society,* 16: 128–57.

Ulmer, G. (1983). "The object of post-criticism." In Hal Fosks, ed., *The anti-aesthetic: Essays on postmodern culture.* Seattle: The Bay Press.

Van Maanen, J. (1988). *Tales of the field: On writing ethnography.* Chicago: University of Chicago Press.

Walkerdine, V. (1988). *Mastery of reason.* New York: Routledge.

———. (1989). *Difference, cognition and mathematics education.* Unpublished paper. Birmingham Polytechnic, England.

Weiler, K. (1988). *Women teaching for change.* New York: Bergin Garvey Publishers.

White, H. (1973). *Metahistory.* Baltimore: The Johns Hopkins University Press.

Chapter 4

Baudrillard, J. (1983). *Simulations.* Paul Foss, Paul Patton, and Philip Beitchman, trans. New York: Semiotext(e).

Berger, J. (1972). *Ways of Seeing.* New York: Penguin Books.

Bernstein, B. (1977). *Class, Codes and Control Volume 3: Towards a Theory of Educational Transmission.* London: Routledge & Kegan Paul.

Butler, J. (1990). *Gender Trouble: Feminism and the Subversion of Identity.* New York: Routledge.

Connell, R. W. (1987). *Gender and Power.* Stanford: Stanford University Press.

de Certeau, M. (1984). *The Practice of Everyday Life.* Steven Rendall, trans. Berkeley: University of California Press.

de Lauretis, T. (1987). *Technologies of Gender: Essays on Theory, Film and Fiction.* Bloomington: Indiana University Press.

Doane, M. A. (1990). "Technophilia: Technology, Representation and the Feminine." In M. Jacobus, E. F. Keller, and S. Shuttleworth, eds., *Body/Politics: Women and the discourses of science,* pp. 163–76. New York: Routledge.

Dyer, R. (1988). "White." *Screen, 29*(4): 44–62.

Fiske, J. (1989a). *Reading the Popular.* Boston: Unwin Hyman.

——. (1989b). *Understanding Popular Culture.* Boston: Unwin Hyman.

Hebdige, D. (1988). *Hiding in the Light.* New York: Routledge.

Kleppner, O. (1986). *Otto Kleppner's Advertising Procedure* (9th ed.). Englewood Cliffs: Verrill.

Machung, A. (1988). "'Who needs a personality to talk to a machine?': Communication in the automated office." In C. Kramarae, ed., *Technology and Women's Voices: Keeping in Touch.* New York: Routledge & Kegan Paul.

Nelson, R. P. (1985). *The Design of Advertising.* Dubuque: W. C. Brown Publishers.

Nichols, B. (1988). "The Work of Culture in the Age of Cybernetic Systems." *Screen, 29*(1): 22–46.

Noble, D. F. (1984). *Forces of Production: A Social History of Industrial Automation.* New York: Oxford University Press.

Turkle, S. (1988). "Computational Reticence: Why Women Fear the Intimate Machine." In C. Kramarae, ed., *Technology and Women's Voices: Keeping in Touch.* New York: Routledge & Kegan Paul.

Zuboff, S. (1984). *In the Age of the Smart Machine: The Future of Work and Power.* New York: Basic Books, Inc.

Chapter 5

Abler, R. M., and W. Sedlacek. (1987). "Computer Orientation by Holland Type and Text." *The Career Development Quarterly, 36*: 163–69.

Abramovay, M., I. M. Ramírez Quirós, and M. Damasco Figueredo. (1991). *Detrás de Bastidores: Un Estudio de los mensajes producidos por organizaciones gubernamentales y no-gubernamentales trabajando con la mujer.* San José, Costa Rica: Centro Interamericano de Documentación e Información Agrícola.

Aguilar, F., A. Alvarado, A. C. Calderón, I. Fallas, S. Hernández, R. Pereira, M. G. Ramírez, and A. Vargas. (1989). *Ideas para la integración curricular.* Internal document of the FOD, San Jose, Costa Rica.

Apple, M. W. (1986). *Teachers and Texts: A Political Economy of Class and Gender Relations in Education.* New York: Routledge.

Asociación Demográfica Costarricense. (1984). *Census.* San Jose, Costa Rica.

Badagliacco, J. M. (1990). "Gender and Race Differences in Computing Attitudes and Experience." *Social Science Computer Review*, *8*(1): 42–63.

Badilla-Saxe, E. (1991). "Starting with Scribbles." *Logo Exchange*, *10*(2): 37–42.

Bem, S. L. and E. Lenney. (1976). "Sex-Typing and the Avoidance of Cross-Sex Behavior." *Journal of Personality and Social Psychology*, *33*: 48–54.

Bem, S. L., W. Martyna, and C. Watson. (1976). "Sex Typing and Androgyny: Further Explorations of the Expressive Domain." *Journal of Personality and Social Psychology*, *34*(5): 1016–23.

Bernhard, J. K. (1992). "Gender-Related Attitudes and the Development of Computer Skills: A Preschool Intervention." *The Alberta Journal of Educational Research*, *38*(3): 177–88.

Beynon, J. (1991). "'Just a Few Machines Bleeping Away in the Corner': A Review of Naturalistic Studies of Computers into Education in the UK." In R. L. Blomeyer, Jr., and C. D. Martin, eds., *Case Studies in Computer Aided Learning*, pp. 277–93. London: The Falmer Press.

Biesanz, R., K. Z. Biesanz, and M. H. Biesanz. (1988). *The Costa Ricans*. Prospect Heights, IL: Waveland Press.

Bowers, C. A. (1988). *The Cultural Dimensions of Educational Computing: Understanding the Non-Neutrality of Technology*. New York: Teachers College Press.

Brady, H., and T. Slesnick. (1985). "Girls don't like Fluffware either." *Classroom Computer Learning*, April–May, pp. 23–26.

Busch, T. (1995). "Gender Differences in Self-Efficacy and Attitudes toward Computers." *Journal of Educational Computing Research*, *12*(2): 147–58.

Campbell, N. J. (1988). "Correlates of Computer Anxiety of Adolescent Students." *Journal of Adolescent Research*, *3*(1): 107–17.

———. (1990). "High School Students' Computer Attitudes and Attributions: Gender and Ethnic Group Differences." *Journal of Adolescent Research*, *5*(4): 485–99.

Campbell, P. B. (1986). "What's a Nice Girl Like You Doing in a Math Class?" *Phi Delta Kappan*, *67*(7): 516–20.

Casasola, R., N. E. Morera, and P. Obando. (1983). "Consideraciones en torno a la incorporación de la mujer al proceso productivo: Area metropolitana." *Revista de Ciencias Sociales*, *25*: 27–46.

Chacón, R. (1989). *Sugerencias de contenidos de los planes de estudios para la integración curricular*. Internal document of the FOD, San Jose, Costa Rica.

Chambers, S. M., and V. A. Clarke. (1987). "Is Inequity Cumulative? The Relationship Between Disadvantaged Group Membership and Students' Computing Experience, Knowledge, Attitudes and Intentions." *Journal of Educational Computing Research*, *3*(4): 495–517.

Chavarría González, S. (1985). "Mujeres y matemática." *Revista de Educación de la Universidad de Costa Rica*, *9*: 89–93.

Chen, M. (1986). "Gender and Computers: The Beneficial Effects of Experience on Attitudes." *Journal of Educational Computing Research*, *2*(3): 265–82.

Chen Quesada, E. (1992). *Analisis Comparativo del Sistema de Computo en las Escuelas Primarias de Costa Rica y Albuquerque, Nuevo Mexico*. Albuquerque, New Mexico: University of New Mexico, M. A. Thesis.

Chipman, S. F., L. R. Brush, and D. M. Wilson. (1985). *Women and Mathematics: Balancing the Equation*. Hillsdale, NJ: Erlbaum.

Clarke, V. A., and S. M. Chambers. (1989). "Gender-Based Factors in Computing Enrollments and Achievement: Evidence from a Study of Tertiary Students." *Journal of Educational Computing Research*, *5*(4): 409–29.

Colbourn, C. J., and P. H. Light. (1987). "Social Interaction and Learning using Micro-PROLOG." *Journal of Computer Assisted Learning*, *3*(3): 130–40.

Colley, A. M., M. T. Gale, and T. A. Harris. (1994). "Effects of Gender Role Identity and Experience on Computer Attitude Components." *Journal of Educational Computing Research*, *10*(2): 129–37.

Collis, B. A. (1985). "Sex Differences in Secondary School Students' Attitudes Toward Computers." *The Computing Teacher*, *12*(8): 33–34.

Collis, B. A., and R. L. Williams. (1987). "Cross-Cultural Comparison of Gender Differences in Adolescents' Attitudes Toward Computers and Selected School Subjects." *Journal of Educational Research*, *81*(1): 17–27.

Deaux, K., and B. Major. (1987). "Putting Gender into Context: An Interactive Model of Gender-Related Behavior." *Psychological Review*, *94*(3): 369–89.

Demetrulias, D. M., and N. R. Rosenthal. (1985). "Discrimination Against Females and Minorities in Microcomputer Advertising." *Computers and the Social Sciences*, *1*: 91–95.

DeRemer, M. (1989). "The Computer Gender Gap in Elementary School." *Computers in the Schools*, *6*(3–4): 39–49.

Dyck, J. L., and J. A. Smither. (1994). "Age Differences in Computer Anxiety: The Role of Computer Experience, Gender and Education." *Journal of Educational Computing Research*, *10*(3): 239–48.

Dyer, J. (1988). "Computer Dreams Come True." *The Tico Times*. February 19. San Jose, Costa Rica.

Esquivel, J. M., and M. Brenes. (1988). *Gender Differences in Achievement in Costa Rican Students: Science, Mathematics and Spanish.* Paper presented at the National Association for Research in Science Teaching, April 10–13. Lake Ozarks, MO.

Feinman, S. (1974). "Approval of Cross-Sex Role Behavior." *Psychological Reports,* 35: 643–48.

——. (1981). "Why is Cross-sex Role Behavior More Approved for Girls than for Boys?: A Status Characteristic Approach." *Sex Roles,* 7(3): 289–300.

Fennema, E. (1980). "Teachers and Sex Bias in Mathematics." *Mathematics Teacher,* 73: 169–73.

Fish, M. C., A. L. Gross, and J. S. Sanders. (1986). "The Effect of Equity Strategies on Girls' Computer Usage in School." *Computers in Human Behavior,* 2(2): 127–34.

Fonseca, C. (1991). *Computadoras en la escuela pública costarricense: La puesta en marcha de una decisión.* San José, Costa Rica: Fundación Omar Dengo.

Francis, L. J. (1994). "The Relationship between Computer Related Attitudes and Gender Stereotyping of Computer Use." *Computers and Education,* 22(4): 283–89.

González Suárez, M. (1977). "La mujer en Costa Rica, división del trabajo, salarios y distribución de puestos directivos." *Revista de Ciencias Sociales,* 14: 31–42.

——. (1988a). "Barriers to Female Achievement: Gender Stereotypes in Costa Rican Textbooks." *Women's Studies International Forum,* 11(6): 599–609.

——. (1988b). "Modelos femeninos y masculinos en textos escolares." *Revista de Ciencias Sociales,* 39, 13–27.

Guntermann, E., and M. Tovar. (1987). "Collaborative Problem-Solving with LOGO: Effects of Group Size and Group Composition." *Journal of Educational Computing Research,* 3(3): 313–34.

Gutiérrez, I. (1994). "Importancia de la Perspectiva de Género para la Sensibilización en la Educación." In *Seminario Taller Nacional de Reflexión sobre Política en Informática Educativa.* San José, Costa Rica: Editorial Universidad Estatal a Distancia.

Guzmán, S. L. (1983). "Las nuevas formas de penetración capitalista en la industria costarricense y su impacto en la mano de obra femenina." *Revista de Ciencias Sociales,* 25: 9–26.

Harper, D. (1991). "Reports from Costa Rica, Venezuela, Brazil, and Israel." *Logo Exchange,* 10(2): 43–44.

Hativa, N., A. Lesgold, and S. Swisa. (1993). "Competition in Individualized CAI." *Instructional Science,* 21: 365–400.

Hattie, J., and D. Fitzgerald. (1987). "Sex Differences in Attitudes, Achievement and Use of Computers." *Australian Journal of Education, 31*(1): 3–26.

Hawkins, J. (1985). "Computers and Girls: Rethinking the Issues." *Sex Roles, 13*(3–4): 165–79.

Hawkins, J., K. Sheingold, M. Gearhart, and C. Berger. (1982). "Microcomputers in Schools: Impact on the Social Life of Elementary Classrooms." *Journal of Applied Developmental Psychology, 3*: 361–73.

Hernández, O. (1990–1991). "Análisis del abstencionismo en las elecciones presidenciales de Costa Rica en el período 1953–1986." *Anuario de Estudios Centroamericanos, 16*(2), *17*(1): 117–38.

Hess, R. D., and I. T. Miura. (1985). "Gender Differences in Enrollment in Computer Camps and Classes." *Sex Roles, 13*(3/4): 193–203.

Hodes, C. L. (1995). *Gender Representations in Mathematics Software.* Eric Document No. 380 277.

Hoyles, C., and R. Sutherland. (1989). *Logo Mathematics in the Classroom.* New York: Routledge.

Huber, B. R., and R. Scaglion. (1995). "Gender Differences in Computer Education: A Costa Rican Case Study." *Journal of Educational Computing Research, 13*(3): 271–304.

Huberman, M. (1987). "How Well Does Educational Research Really Travel?" *Educational Researcher, 16*: 5–13.

Huff, C., and J. Cooper. (1987). "Sex Bias in Educational Software: The Effect of Designers' Stereotypes on the Software They Design." *Journal of Applied Social Psychology, 17*(6): 519–32.

Hyde, J. S., E. Fennema, M. Ryan, L. A. Frost, and C. Hopp. (1990). "Gender Differences in Mathematics Attitudes and Affect: A Meta-Analysis." *Psychology of Women Quarterly, 14*: 299–324.

Igbaria, M., and A. Chakrabarti. (1990). "Computer Anxiety and Attitudes toward Microcomputer Use." *Behavior and Information Technology, 9*(3): 229–41.

Institute of International Education. (1986). *Regional Education Profile: Central America.* New York: United States Information Agency.

Johnson, R. T., D. W. Johnson, and M. B. Stanne. (1985). "Effects of Cooperative, Competitive, and Individualistic Goal Structures on Computer-Assisted Instruction." *Journal of Educational Psychology, 77*(6): 668–77.

Kay, R. H. (1989). "Gender Differences in Computer Attitudes, Literacy, Locus of Control and Commitment." *Journal of Research on Computing in Education, 21*: 307–16.

Kiesler, S., L. Sproull, and J. S. Eccles. (1985). "Pool Halls, Chips, and War Games: Women in the Culture of Computing." *Psychology of Women Quarterly*, *9*(4): 451–62.

Kinnear, A. (1995). "Introduction of Microcomputers: A Case Study of Patterns of Use and Children's Perceptions." *Journal of Educational Computing Research*, *13*(1): 27–40.

Koohang, A. A. (1989). "A Study of Attitudes Toward Computers: Anxiety, Confidence, Liking, and Perception of Usefulness." *Journal of Research on Computing in Education*, *22*(2): 137–50.

Krendl, K. A., M. C. Broihier, and C. Fleetwood. (1989). "Children and Computers: Do Sex-Related Differences Persist?" *Journal of Communication*, *39*(3): 85–93.

La Nación. (1992a). *Programa de cómputo*. 6 July. 8A.

———. (1992b). *Ampliarían curso lectivo*. 17 July. 4A.

———. (1992c). *Instituto Nacional de Aprendizaje comunica la lista de personas admitidas en el Centro Nacional de Informática*. 24 July. 34A-35A.

Leinhardt, G., A. M. Seewald, and M. Engel. (1979). "Learning What's Taught: Sex Differences in Instruction." *Journal of Educational Psychology*, *71*(4): 432–39.

Levin, T., and C. Gordon. (1989). "Effect of Gender and Computer Experience on Attitudes Toward Computers." *Journal of Educational Computing Research*, *5*(1): 69–88.

Liu, M., W. M. Reed, and P. D. Phillips. (1992). "Teacher Education Students and Computers: Gender, Major, Prior Computer Experience, Occurrence, and Anxiety." *Journal of Research on Computing in Education*, *24*(4): 457–67.

Loyd, B. H., and C. P. Gressard. (1984). "Reliability and Factorial Validity of Computer Attitude Scales." *Educational and Psychological Measurement*, *44*: 501–05.

Loyd, B. H., D. E. Loyd, and C. P. Gressard. (1987). "Gender and Computer Experience as Factors in the Computer Attitudes of Middle School Students." *Journal of Early Adolescence*, *7*(1): 13–19.

Marín, G., and B. V. Marín. (1991). *Research with Hispanic Populations*. Applied Social Science Methods Series, Vol. 23. Newbury Park: Sage.

Martin, C. L. (1990). "Attitudes and Expectations about Children with Nontraditional and Traditional Gender Roles." *Sex Roles*, *22*(3/4): 151–65.

Mawby, R., C. A. Clement, R. D. Pea, and J. Hawkins. (1984). *Structured Interviews on Children's Conceptions of Computers (Technical Report No. 19)*. New York: Bank Street College of Education.

Mehan, H. (1989). "Microcomputers in Classrooms: Educational Technology or Social Practice?" *Anthropology and Education Quarterly*, *20*: 4–22.

Méndez Barrantes, Z. (1985). "La participación político-económica de la mujer en Costa Rica." *Mujer*, 2: 39–46.

———. (1988). "Socialización y estereotipos sexuales en Costa Rica." *Revista de Ciencias Sociales*, *39*: 29–45.

Mendiola, H. (1988). "Expansión de la educación superior costarricense en los 1970s: Impacto en la estratificación social y en el mercado de trabajo." *Revista de Ciencias Sociales*, *42*: 81–98.

Miura, I. T. (1987) "The Relationship of Computer Self-Efficacy Expectations to Computer Interest and Course Enrollment in College." *Sex Roles*, *16*(5–6): 303–11.

Montoya Gomez, A. (1990). "El eterno feminino." *Mundo de la Computación, 4*(22): 22.

Motherwell, L. (1988). *Gender and Style Differences in a LOGO-based Environment*. Doctoral dissertation, Massachusetts Institute of Technology.

Oficina de Registro, Universidad de Costa Rica. (1991). *Estadística de graduación: I y II ciclos de 1991* (Internal document). San José, Costa Rica.

Okebukola, P. A. (1993). "The Gender Factor in Computer Anxiety and Interest among some Australian High School Students." *Educational Research*, *35*(2): 181–89.

Pacheco, F. A. (1986). *Panorama de la educación costarricense en el primer año de labores*. San Jose, Costa Rica: Ministry of Education.

Papert, S. (1987). "Computer Criticism vs. Technocentric Thinking." *Educational Researcher*, *16*(1): 22–30.

Quirós, T., and B. Larrain. (1977). "La imagen de mujer que proyectan los medios de comunicación en Costa Rica." *Revista de Ciencias Sociales*, *14*: 5–13.

Robertson, S. I., J. Calder, P. Fung, A. Jones, and T. O'Shea. (1995). "Computer Attitudes in an English Secondary School." *Computers and Education*, *24*(2): 73–81.

Robinson-Staveley, K., and J. Cooper. (1990). "Mere Presence, Gender, and Reactions to Computers: Studying Human-Computer Interaction in the Social Context." *Journal of Experimental Social Psychology*, *26*: 168–83.

Romero R. M., P. Osorio, E. L. Piza, G. V. Crespo, C. V. León, and S. A. Montero. (1986). *La mujer en Costa Rica y su participación del país, II parte. (Serie Investigaciones, Number 7)*. San José, Costa Rica: Instituto de Investigaciones Sociales, Universidad de Costa Rica.

Sacks, C. H., Y. Bellisimo, and J. Mergendoller. (1993–94). "Attitudes Toward Computers and Computer Use: The Issue of Gender." *Journal of Research on Computing in Education*, *26*(2): 256–69.

Sadker, M., and D. Sadker. (1985). "Sexism in the Schoolroom of the '80s." *Psychology Today*, *19*: 54–57.

Sanders, J. S. (1984). "The Computer: Male, Female, or Androgynous." *The Computing Teacher*, *11*: 32–34.

Sanders, J. S., and A. Stone. (1986). *The Neuter Computer: Computers for Girls and Boys*. New York: Neal-Schuman Publishers, Inc.

Schofield, J. W. (1995). *Computers and Classroom Culture*. Cambridge: Cambridge University Press.

Schumacher, P., J. Morahan-Martin, and A. Olinsky. (1993). "Computer Experiences, Attitudes, Computer and mathematical Anxiety, and Grades of MBA Students." *Collegiate Microcomputer*, *11*(3): 183–93.

Shashaani, L. (1994). "Socioeconomic Status, Parents' Sex-Role Stereotypes, and the Gender Gap in Computing." *Journal of Research on Computing in Education*, *26*(4): 433–51.

———. (1995). "Gender Differences in Mathematics Experience and Attitude and Their Relation to Computer Attitude." *Educational Technology*, *35*(3): 32–38.

Siann, G., H. Macleod, P. Glissov, and A. Durndell. (1990). "The Effect of Computer Use on Gender Differences in Attitudes to Computers." *Computers and Education*, *14*(2): 183–91.

Smith, S. D. (1986). "Relationships of Computer Attitudes to Sex, Grade-level, and Teacher Influence." *Education*, *106*(3): 338–44.

———. (1987). "Computer Attitudes of Teachers and Students in Relationship to Gender and Grade Level." *Journal of Educational Computing Research*, *3*(4): 479–94.

Sutton, R. E. (1991). "Equity and Computers in the Schools: A Decade of Research." *Review of Educational Research*, *61*(4): 475–503.

Temple, L., and H. M. Lips. (1989). "Gender Differences and Similarities in Attitudes Toward Computers." *Computers in Human Behavior*, *5*(4): 215–26.

The Tico Times. (1989). $77.9 *Billion Budget Rushed Through Congress*. 8 December.

Trejos, A., ed. (1991). *Geografía ilustrada: Costa Rica*. San José, Costa Rica: Trejos Editores.

Turkle, S. (1984). *The Second Self: Computers and the Human Spirit*. New York: Simon & Schuster.

Turkle, S., and S. Papert. (1990). "Epistemological Pluralism: Styles and Voices Within the Computer Culture." *Signs: Journal of Women in Culture and Society*, *16*(1): 128–57.

Wahab, Z. (1983). *Education in Costa Rica: An Overview*. Paper presented at the Annual Conference of the Western Region of the Comparative and International Education Society and the Far Western Philosophy of Education Society, Los Angeles, CA.

Ware, M. C., and M. F. Stuck. (1985). "Sex-Role Messages vis-à-vis Microcomputer Use: A Look at the Pictures." *Sex Roles*, *13*(3–4): 205–14.

Wilder, G., D. Mackie, and J. Cooper. (1985). "Gender and Computers: Two Surveys of Computer-Related Attitudes." *Sex Roles*, *13*(3–4): 215–28.

Williams, J. E., and D. L. Best. (1982). *Measuring Sex Stereotypes: A Thirty Nation Study*. London: Sage.

Williams, S. W., and S. M. Rosenwasser. (1987–89). "Computer Interest Differences in Preschool Children According to Sex and Psychological Sex-Typing." *Psychology and Human Development*, *2*(2): 55–60.

Woodrow, J. E. (1994). "The Development of Computer-Related Attitudes of Secondary Students." *Journal of Educational Computing Research*, *11*(4): 307–38.

Chapter 7

"A Summary of the ACM/IEEE-CS Joint Curriculum Task force Report: Computing Curricula 1991." (1991). *Communications of the ACM*, *34*(6): 69–84.

Appadurai, A., ed. (1988). *The social life of things*. New York: Cambridge University Press.

Appel, C. (1985). "L-S 'superusers' run the computer room." *The Sudbury Town Crier*, May 16, pp. 3, 43.

Arnstine, D. (1973). "The use of coercion in changing the schools." *Educational Theory*, *23*: 277–87.

Arsenio, W., and A. Lover. (1995). "Children's conceptions of sociomoral affect: Happy victimizers, mixed emotions, and other expectancies." In M. Killen and D. Hart, eds., *Morality in everyday life: Developmental perspectives*, pp. 87–128. New York: Cambridge University Press.

Baldwin, J. M. (1973). *Social and ethical interpretations in mental development*. New York: Arno. (Original work published 1897)

Baszucki. (1992). *Interactive physics II*. [Computer program]. San Francisco: Knowledge Revolution.

Berlins, M., and L. Hodges. (1981). "Nationality Bill sets out three new citizenship categories." *The London Times*, January 15, pp. 1, 15.

Bodker, S. (1991). *Through the interface: A human activity approach to user interface design*. Hillsdale, NJ: Lawrence Erlbaum Associates.

Bromley, H. (1992). "Culture, power, and educational computing." In C. Bigum and B. Green, eds., *Understanding the new information technologies in education*. Deakin University, Australia.

Bynum, T. W., W. Maner, and J. L. Fodor. (1992). *Teaching computer ethics*. New Haven, CT: Research Center on Computing and Society.

Chandrasekaran, B. (1992). "What's in a logo?" *IEEE Expert*, 7(5): 2.

Cummins, J. (1988). "From the inner city to the global village: The microcomputer as a catalyst for collaborative learning and cultural interchange." *Language, Culture, and Curriculum*, 1(1): 1–13.

Damon, W. (1977). *The social world of the child*. San Francisco: Jossey-Bass.

Dawkins, R. (1976). *The selfish gene*. New York: Oxford University Press.

Denning, P. J. (1992). "Educating a new engineer." *Communications of the ACM*, 35(12): 83–97.

DeVries, R. (1988). *Constructivist education*. Paper presented to the Association for Constructivist Teaching, West Point Academy.

DeVries, R., and L. Kohlberg. (1990). *Constructivist early education: Overview and comparison with other programs*. Washington, DC: National Association for the Education of Young Children.

DeVries, R., and B. Zan. (1994). *Moral classrooms, moral children: Creating a constructivist atmosphere in early education*. New York: Teachers College.

Dewey, J. (1966). *Democracy and education*. New York: Macmillan. (Original work published 1916)

Dormer, J. (1981). "Computer center is a novel program." *Concord Journal*, June 18, p. 19.

Ermann, M. D., M. B. Williams, and C. Gutierrez, eds. (1990). *Computers, ethics, and society*. New York: Oxford University Press.

Friedman, B. (1986). "If I only had one more computer. . . . Facing the sticky issues of resource allocation." *Classroom Computer Learning*, October, pp. 44–45.

————. (1988). *Problems and solutions: A case study of an exceptional elementary school and its developing computer education program.* Paper presented at the annual meeting of the International Association of Computing Education, New Orleans.

————. (1991). "Social and moral development through computer use: A constructivist approach." *Journal of Research on Computing in Education, 23*: 560–67.

————. (1997). "Social judgments and technological innovation: Adolescents' understanding of property, privacy, and electronic information." *Computers in Human Behavior, 13*: 327–52.

Friedman, B., and P. H. Kahn, Jr. (1992). "Human agency and responsible computing: Implications for computer system design." *Journal of Systems Software, 17*: 7–14.

Friedman, B., and L. Millet. (1995). "'It's the computer's fault'—Reasoning about computers as moral agents." *Proceedings of the Chi' 95 Conference*, pp. 226–27. New York: Association for Computing Machinery.

Friedman, B., and H. Nissenbaum. (1996). "Bias in computer systems." *ACM Transactions on Information Systems, 14*: 330–47.

Friedman, B., and T. Winograd, eds. (1990). *Computing and social responsibility: A collection of course syllabi.* Palo Alto, CA: Computer Professionals for Social Responsibility.

Gotterbarn, D. (1992). "The use and abuse of computer ethics." *Journal of Systems Software, 17*: 75–80.

Greenbaum, J., and M. Kyng, eds. (1991). *Design at work: Cooperative design of computer systems.* Hillsdale, NJ: Lawrence Erlbaum Associates.

Harvey, B. (1980). *Using computers for educational freedom.* Paper presented at the Second annual Computer Conference, Lesley College, Boston.

————. (1983). *The Lincoln-Sudbury Regional High School computer department: History, goals, strategies, and problems.* Unpublished manuscript.

Hogan, R. (1975). "Theoretical egocentricism and the problem of compliance." *American Psychologist, 30*: 533–39.

Horowitz, P. (1984). "Telecommunications: An electronic, interstate school newspaper." *Electronic Learning*, p. 48.

Johnson, D. G. (1985). *Computer ethics.* Englewood Cliffs, NJ: Prentice-Hall.

Johnson, D. G., and H. Nissenbaum, eds. (1995). *Computers, ethics, & social values.* Englewood Cliffs, NJ: Prentice Hall.

Kahn, P. H., Jr. (1991). "Bounding the controversies: Foundational issues in the study of moral development." *Human Development, 34*: 325–40.

———. (1992). "Children's obligatory and discretionary moral judgments." *Child Development, 63*: 416–30.

———. (1993). *A culturally sensitive analysis of culture in the context of context: When is enough enough?* Paper presented at the biennial meeting of the Society for Research in Child Development, New Orleans. (ERIC Document Reproduction No. ED 365 616)

———. (1995). Commentary on D. Moshman's "The construction of moral rationality." *Human Development, 38*, 282–88.

Kahn, P. H., Jr., and B. Friedman. (1995). "Environmental views and values of children in an inner-city Black community." *Child Development, 66*: 1403–17.

Kearsley, G., B. Hunter, and M. Furlong. (1992). *We teach with technology: New visions for education.* Wilsonville, OR: Franklin, Beedle & Associates.

Kiesler, S. and L. Sproull. (in press). "Addendum to 'When the Interface is a Face,' or what is 'social' about a computer?" In B. Friedman, ed., *Human values and the design of computer technology.* Stanford: Center for the Study of Language and Information, Stanford University.

Kling, R., ed. (1996). *Computerization and controversy: Value conflicts and social choices* (2nd ed.). San Diego, CA: Academic Press.

Kohlberg, L. (1969). "Stage and sequence: The cognitive-developmental approach to socialization." In D. A. Goslin, ed., *Handbook of socialization theory and research*, pp. 347–480. New York: Rand McNally.

———. (1980). "High school democracy and educating for a just society." In R. L. Mosher, ed., *Moral education: A first generation of research*, pp. 20–57. New York: Praeger.

———. (1984). *Essays on moral development: The psychology of moral development.* Vol. 2. San Francisco: Harper & Row.

———. (1985). "The just community approach to moral education in theory and practice." In M. W. Berkowitz and F. Oser, eds., *Moral education: Theory and application*, pp. 27–87. Hillsdale, NJ: Lawrence Erlbaum.

Laupa, M. (1991). "Children's reasoning about three authority attributes: Adult status, knowledge, and social position." *Developmental Psychology, 27*: 321–29.

Lewis, P. H. (1992). "Nurturing democracy through used computers." *The New York Times*, November 8, p. F12.

Lourenco, O. (1996). "Reflections on narrative approaches to moral development." *Human Development, 39*: 83–99.

Martinez, M. (1993). *Developments in moral education across the curriculum.* Paper presented at the April meeting of the American Educational Research Association, Atlanta.

Miller, K. (1988). "Integrating computer ethics into the computer science curriculum." *Computer Science Education, 1*: 37–52.

Namioka, A., and D. Schuler, eds. (1990). *Proceedings of the 1990 Participatory Design Conference.* Palo Alto, CA: Computer Professionals for Social Responsibility.

Nass, C., Y. Moon, J. Morkes, E. Kim, and B. J. Fogg. (in press). "Computers are social actors: A review of current research." In B. Friedman, ed., *Human values and the design of computer technology.* Stanford: Center for the Study of Language and Information, Stanford University.

Nass, C., J. Steuer, E. Tauber, and H. Reeder. (1993). "Anthropomorphism, Agency, and Ethopoeia: Computers as social actors." In S. Ashlund, K. Mullet, A. Henderson, E. Hollnagel, and T. White, eds., *InterCHI '93 adjunct proceedings*, pp. 111–12. Amsterdam, The Netherlands.

Noble, D. D. (1991). *The classroom arsenal: Military research, information technology and public education.* London: Falmer Press.

Nucci, L. (1996). "Morality and the personal sphere of actions." In E. S. Reed, E. Turiel, and T. Brown, eds., *Values and knowledge*, pp. 41–60. Mahwah, NJ: Lawrence Erlbaum.

Papert, S. (1980). *Mindstorms: Children, computers, and powerful ideas.* New York: Basic Books.

Parker, D. B., S. Swope, and B. N. Baker. (1990). *Ethical conflicts in information and computer science, technology, and business.* Wellesley, MA: QED Informations Sciences.

Perrolle, J. A. (1987). *Computers and social change: Information, property, and power.* Belmont, CA: Wadsworth.

Piaget, J. (1969). *The moral judgment of the child.* Glencoe, IL: Free Press. (Original work published 1932)

Power, C., A. Higgins, and L. Kohlberg. (1989). "The habit of the common life: Building character through democratic community schools." In L. Nucci, ed., *Moral development and character education: A dialogue*, pp. 125–43. Berkeley: McCutchan.

Rohwer, W. D., Jr., C. P. Rohwer, and J. R. B-Howe. (1980). *Educational psychology: Teaching for student diversity.* New York: Holt, Rinehart, & Winston.

Rumelhart, D. E., and D. A. Norman. (1981). "Analogical processes in learning." In J. R. Anderson, ed., *Cognitive skills and their acquisition*. Hillsdale, NJ: Lawrence Erlbaum.

Scheffler, I. (1991). *In praise of cognitive emotions and other essays in the philosophy of education*. New York: Routledge.

Searle, J. R. (1981). "Minds, brains, and programs." In D. R. Hofstadter and D. C. Dennett, eds., *The mind's I*, pp. 353–82. New York: Basic Books.

———. (1984). *Minds, brains and science*. Cambridge: Harvard University Press.

———. (1990). "Is the brain's mind a computer program?" *Scientific American, 262*: 26–31.

———. (1992). *The rediscovery of the mind*. Cambridge: MIT Press.

Selman, R. L. (1980). *The growth of interpersonal understanding*. New York: Academic Press.

Shneiderman, B. (1987). *Designing the user interface: Strategies for effective human-computer interaction*. Reading, MA: Addison-Wesley.

Shneiderman, B., and A. Rose. (in press). "Social impact statements: Engaging public participation in information technology design." In B. Friedman, ed., *Human values and the design of computer technology*. Stanford: Center for the Study of Language and Information, Stanford University.

Shweder, R. A. (1986). "Divergent rationalities." In D. W. Fiske and R. A. Shweder, eds., *Metatheory in social science: pluralisms and subjectivities*, pp. 163–96. Chicago: University of Chicago Press.

Smetana, J. (1982). *Concepts of self and morality: Women's reasoning about abortion*. New York: Praeger.

Snyder, T. (1985a). *Our town meeting*. [Computer program]. Cambridge, MA: Tom Snyder Productions.

———. (1985b). *The other side*. [Computer program]. Cambridge, MA: Tom Snyder Productions.

Sproull, L., M. Subramani, S. Kiesler, J. H. Walker, and K. Waters. (1996). "When the interface is a face." *Human-Computer Interaction, 11*: 97–124.

Turiel, E. (1997). "The development of morality." In W. Damon, ed., *Handbook of child psychology*, 5th Ed., Vol 3: N. Eisenberg, ed., *Social, emotional, and personality development*. New York: Wiley.

Turkle, S. (1984). *The second self: Computers and the human spirit*. New York: Simon & Schuster.

US General Accounting Office. (1992). Patriot missile defense: Software problem led to system failure at Dhahran, Saudi Arabia (GAO/IMTEC-92–26). Washington, D.C.

Vygotsky, L. S. (1978). *Mind in society.* Cambridge: Harvard University Press.

Wainryb, C. (1995). "Reasoning about social conflicts in different cultures: Druze and Jewish children in Israel." *Child Development, 66*: 390–401.

Weizenbaum, J. (1976). *Computer power and human reason.* New York: Freeman and Co.

Wigginton, E. (1986). *Sometimes a shining moment: The Foxfire experience.* Garden City, NY: Anchor Books.

Winograd, T. (1992). "Computers, ethics, and social responsibility." *The CPSR Newsletter, 10*(3): pp. 17–27.

Winograd, T., and F. Flores. (1986). *Understanding computers and cognition: A new foundation for design.* Reading, MA: Addison-Wesley.

Contributors

MICHAEL W. APPLE is John Bascom Professor of Curriculum and Instruction and Educational Policy Studies at the University of Wisconsin, Madison. He has written extensively on the relationship between education and power. Among his many books are *Ideology and Curriculum, Education and Power, Teachers and Texts, Official Knowledge,* and *Democratic Schools.* His most recent volume is *Cultural Politics and Education.*

HANK BROMLEY is Assistant Professor in Sociology of Education, and Associate Director of the Center for Educational Resources and Technologies, at the State University of New York at Buffalo. His interests lie in the areas of education and social change, the politics of technology, and feminist theory. In an earlier incarnation, he studied computers at MIT, joined an artificial intelligence research group at AT&T Bell Laboratories, and wrote *Lisp Lore: A Guide to Programming the Lisp Machine.* He has recently published in *Educational Theory* and *Teaching Education* (with Alison Carr), and contributed a definition of "Identity Politics" to the *Dictionary of Multicultural Education,* edited by Carl Grant and Gloria Ladson-Billings. With David Shutkin, he is currently coediting a special issue of *Educational Policy* on "Social Power and Practices of Science and Technology within Education."

MARY BRYSON harbors deep-seated fantasies about becoming a Lesbian Avenger. Mary teaches (against all odds) at the Faculty of Education, University of British Columbia. Her current research involves interventions whose goal is to queer girls' and women's relations to new technologies.

SUZANNE DE CASTELL is Professor of Curriculum and Instruction in the Faculty of Education at Simon Fraser University. She holds a doctorate from the University of London, and has published numerous articles on educational history, philosophy, and theory, literacy studies, and technology/gender studies. Studying the epistemological implications of technologies of representation is her long-standing interest. Coedited books include *Literacy, Society and Schooling* (1980, with Allan Luke and Kieran Egan), *Language, Author-*

ity and Criticism (1986, with Allan and Carmen Luke) and *Radical In<ter>ventions* (1997, with Mary Bryson). Video work includes "Deviance by Design" and "Just the Way You Are."

BATYA FRIEDMAN is Associate Professor of Computer Science at Colby College. She received both her B.A. and Ph.D. from the University of California, Berkeley. Her areas of specialization are human-computer interaction and the human relationship to technology. She has written numerous research articles in addition to designing educational software and consulting on human values in system design. Currently she is editing a book titled *Human Values and the Design of Computer Technology* to be published in 1997 by the Center for the Study of Language and Information, Stanford University.

BRAD R. HUBER is an Associate Professor of Anthropology in the Department of Sociology and Anthropology, University of Charleston, South Carolina, Charleston, SC 29424. His research interests and publications are in the areas of educational computing, gender, and medical anthropology. He has undertaken research in Costa Rica, Mexico, and the United States.

SUSAN JUNGCK is a professor of education at National-Louis University. She has worked with researchers both in the United States and elsewhere on problems of critical ethnographic research. She has written on education and technology and on methodological and political issues in qualitative research.

PETER H. KAHN, JR., received his Ph.D. from the University of California, Berkeley in 1988. He has taught at the University of California, Davis and the University of Houston, and is now on the faculty at Colby College and codirector (with Batya Friedman) of the Mina Institute, an organization which seeks to promote, from an ethical perspective, the human and humane relationship with nature and technology. Peter's publications have focused on children's moral development, the development of children's environmental moral reasoning and values, environmental education, and technology and ethics. He is currently working on a book, to be published by The MIT Press, titled: *The Human Relationship with Nature: Development and Culture.*

JANET WARD SCHOFIELD is a Professor in the Department of Psychology and a Senior Scientist in the Learning Research and Development Center at the University of Pittsburgh. She received a B.A. magna cum laude in 1968 from Radcliffe College and her Ph.D. from Harvard University in 1972. Her recent book, *Computers and Classroom Culture*, published by Cambridge University Press, investigates how the social organization of schools and classrooms influences the use of computers and how, in turn, computer use affects the functioning of classrooms.

ANTHONY P. SCOTT is a consultant in computing and electronic publishing in Columbus, Ohio. He has been a researcher and teacher of communication, art education, and information technology in the British grade school system and the American university system. He is an Associate of the Center for Advanced Studies of Telecommunication at the Ohio State University. His research interests include the philosophical implications of technology for art, education, and publishing.

ZOË SOFIA (who also publishes as Zoë Sofoulis) developed her interest in what she calls "the sexo-semiotics of technology" at Murdoch University and completed her doctorate on metaphors of discovery and enlightenment in *Frankenstein* at the History of Consciousness program (University of California, Santa Cruz) with Donna Haraway. She has lectured in Women's Studies and Communication Studies at Murdoch University (Western Australia) and is now Senior Lecturer in feminist studies and cultural studies at the University of Western Sydney. Her publications include *Whose Second Self? Gender and (Ir)rationality in Computer Culture* (Deakin University, 1993), various papers on feminism, technology, art, and computer culture, and a book in progress (with Virginia Barratt) about relations to technology expressed by women artists in digital media. Current research draws on intersubjectivist psychoanalysis for understanding human-technology interactivity and "smart spaces" (responsive and intelligent environments).

BRIGID A. STARKEY is the Associate Director of the International Communication and Negotiation Simulation (ICONS) Project at the University of Maryland, College Park. In this capacity, she works on the development of active-learning curriculum for the secondary and post-secondary classrooms and teaches students about international negotiation. Dr. Starkey has published works on the ICONS computer-assisted negotiation model in *Educator's Tech Exchange* and *International Studies Notes* and has conducted research on conflict and cooperation in the Persian Gulf subregion of the Middle East. She is currently working on a multiyear project for the Fund for the Improvement of Postsecondary Education of the United States Department of Education, designed to bring the ICONS approach to students at minority-serving colleges and universities.

ANTONIA STONE is a pioneer in the area of technology access for underserved people. In 1980 she founded Playing To Win, Inc., and in 1983 established its Harlem Community Computing Center in the basement of a public housing project in East Harlem, the first publicly available technology access in a low-income inner city area. The Center is alive and well today, serving upwards of 500 area residents each week. More recently, Ms. Stone has established the

Community Technology Centers' Network (CTCNet), which, with funding from the National Science Foundation, brings together agencies and programs that share a commitment to providing technology tools for those who otherwise would have no access. The Network includes upwards of 75 affiliated technology providers nationwide, in Europe, and in Central America. In 1994, Ms. Stone was awarded the Norbert Wiener Award by Computer Professionals for Social Responsibility (CPSR), and in 1996 was presented an award for "lifetime achievement" by the Harvard University chapter of Women in Technology (WIT).

MATTHEW WEINSTEIN is Director of Secondary Education at Macalester College. His main research concerns the relationship of science to science education, and science education to U.S. culture. His book on tourism and science education, *Robot World: Education, Popular Culture, and Science*, will be published by Peter Lang in 1998.

Author Index

For indexed items located in the endnotes, the number in parentheses provides the page number in the main text where the endnote occurs.

Subject Index

For indexed items located in the endnotes, the number in parentheses provides the page number in the main text where the endnote occurs.

SUNY SERIES
FRONTIERS IN EDUCATION

Philip G. Altbach, editor

List of Titles

Class, Race, and Gender in American Education—Lois Weis (ed.)

Excellence and Equality: A Qualitatively Different Perspective on Gifted and Talented Education—David M. Fetterman

Change and Effectiveness in Schools: A Cultural Perspective—Gretchen B. Rossman, H. Dickson Corbett, and William A. Firestone

The Curriculum: Problems, Politics, and Possibilities—Landon E. Beyer and Michael W. Apple (eds.)

The Character of American Higher Education and Intercollegiate Sport—Donald Chu

Crisis in Teaching: Perspectives on Current Reforms—Lois Weis, Philip G. Altbach, Gail P. Kelly, Hugh G. Petrie, and Sheila Slaughter (eds.)

The High Status Track: Studies of Elite Schools and Stratification—Paul William Kingston and Lionel S. Lewis (eds.)

The Economics of American Universities: Management, Operations, and Fiscal Environment—Stephen A. Hoenack and Eileen L. Collins (eds.)

The Higher Learning and High Technology: Dynamics of Higher Education and Policy Formation—Sheila Slaughter

Dropouts from Schools: Issues, Dilemmas and Solutions—Lois Weis, Eleanor Farrar, and Hugh G. Petrie (eds.)

Religious Fundamentalism and American Education: The Battle for the Public Schools—Eugene F. Provenzo, Jr.

Going to School: The African-American Experience—Kofi Lomotey (ed.)

Curriculum Differentiation: Interpretive Studies in U.S. Secondary Schools—Reba Page and Linda Valli (eds.)

The Racial Crisis in American Higher Education—Philip G. Altbach and Kofi Lomotey (eds.)

The Great Transformation in Higher Education, 1960–1980—Clark Kerr

College in Black and White: African-American Students in Predominantly White and in Historically Black Public Universities—Walter R. Allen, Edgar G. Epps, and Nesha Z. Haniff (eds.)

Textbooks in American Society: Politics, Policy, and Pedagogy—Philip G. Altbach, Gail P. Kelly, Hugh G. Petrie, and Lois Weis (eds.)

Critical Perspectives on Early Childhood Education—Lois Weis, Philip G. Altbach, Gail P. Kelly, and Hugh G. Petrie (eds.)

Black Resistance in High School: Forging a Separatist Culture—R. Patrick Solomon

Emergent Issues in Education: Comparative Perspectives—Robert F. Arnove, Philip G. Altbach, and Gail P. Kelly (eds.)

Creating Community on College Campuses—Irving J. Spitzberg and Virginia V. Thorndike

Teacher Education Policy: Narratives, Stories, and Cases—Hendrick D. Gideonse (ed.)

Beyond Silenced Voices: Class, Race, and Gender in United States Schools—Lois Weis and Michelle Fine (eds.)

Troubled Times for American Higher Education: The 1990s and Beyond—Clark Kerr (ed.)

Higher Education Cannot Escape History: Issues for the Twenty-first Century—Clark Kerr (ed.)

The Cold War and Academic Governance: The Lattimore Case at Johns Hopkins—Lionel S. Lewis (ed.)

Multiculturalism and Education: Diversity and Its Impact on Schools and Society—Thomas J. LaBelle and Christopher R. Ward (eds.)

The Contradictory College: The Conflicting Origins, Impacts, and Futures of the Community College—Kevin J. Dougherty (ed.)

Race and Educational Reform in the American Metropolis: A Study of School Decentralization—Dan A. Lewis (ed.)

Professionalization, Partnership, and Power: Building Professional Development Schools—Hugh Petrie (ed.)

Ethnic Studies and Multiculturalism—Thomas J. LaBelle and Christopher R. Ward

Promotion and Tenure: Community and Socialization in Academe—William G. Tierney and Estela Mara Bensimon (eds.)

Sailing Against the Wind: African Americans and Women in U.S. Education—Kofi Lomotey (ed.)

The Challenge of Eastern Asian Education: Implications for America—William K. Cummings and Philip G. Altbach (eds.)

Conversations with Educational Leaders—Anne Turnbaugh Lockwood

Managed Professionals—Gary Rhoades

The Curriculum, Second Edition—Landon E. Beyer